THE
MIDAS
COMPLEX

HOW MONEY DRIVES US CRAZY AND WHAT WE CAN DO ABOUT IT

OTHER BOOKS BY AARON KIPNIS

Angry Young Men: How Parents, Teachers, and Counselors Can Help "Bad Boys" Become Good Men.

Knights without Armor: A Guide to the Inner Lives of Men.

Gender War, Gender Peace: The Quest for Love and Justice between Women and Men. (with Elizabeth Herron)

What Women and Men Really Want: Creating Deeper Understanding and Love in Our Relationships. (with Elizabeth Herron)

PRAISE FOR PREVIOUS BOOKS
KNIGHTS WITHOUT ARMOR

Dr. Kipnis' talks at Harvard were wonderful. He opened up many minds about the struggles that men endure in this culture and went a long way toward overcoming the blaming and divisions that have characterized the women's and men's movements.
—John E. Mack, Pulitzer Prize–winning professor of psychiatry, Harvard Medical School

A powerful volume and helpful guide.
—*Publishers Weekly*

Thoughtful and provocative.
—*San Francisco Chronicle*

Kipnis has written the testament for the emerging men's movement.
—*San Jose Mercury News*

Kipnis' elegant portraits of men offer poignant support for his claims.
—*Los Angeles Times*

A fresh vision and new understanding of men that points the way for a new male psychology and spirituality.
—From the foreword by Robert A. Johnson, author of *He, She, We...*

What Women and Men Really Want

A must read for anyone wanting deeper insight about how to improve relationships between men and women. An immensely useful, timely and important contribution.
—John Gray, author of *Men Are from Mars, Women Are from Venus*

Raises serious issues in an amusing, provocative, and accessible way.
—*Kirkus Reviews*

Goes beyond the problem to a possible solution: a ground breaking model for gender peace that might make it possible for men and women to quit blaming each other and start to truly get along.
—*Utne Reader*

In its celebration of what's good about gender differences, this book deals a well-deserved blow to the battle between the sexes.
—Susan Estrich, law professor, University of Southern California, and news commentator

Provocative, exciting and immensely useful! With grace and the force of truth, it propels our culture into the healing phase of gender relationships.
—Michael Gurian, author of *The Wonder of Boys* and *A Fine Young Man*

Moves into uncharted territory with grace and determination, and they wind up—both men and women—in a better place.
—Asa Baber, *Playboy* columnist and author of *Naked at Gender Gap*

Just as The Feminine Mystique *heralded the women's movement and* Iron John *catalyzed the men's movement,* What Women and Men Really Want *signals a third movement toward gender reconciliation.*
—Mark Gerzon, author of *A Choice of Heroes* and *A House Divided*

Moves with a narrative thrust that kept me interested...enthralled in fact, while incidentally offering—not Teaching—insights into male-female relationships that are profound.
—Bob Chartoff, Academy Award–winning producer, *The Right Stuff, Rocky, Raging Bull*

In this pioneering book, women and men reach out across the gender gap to find surprising insights and to teach us all how to touch one another more deeply.
—Connie Zweig, author of *Romancing the Shadow* and *The Holy Longing*

A masterful book about relationships. It is the best kind of adventure story, a passionate journey into the heart of the deepest mysteries and bonds, which connect men and women.
—Gay and Kathlyn Hendricks, authors of *Conscious Loving* and *Living at the Speed of Life*

This book offers us a way out of the divisive and stagnant gender talk of the moment. With its sensitivity to poetics and to honest emotion, it presents the current and eternal confusion of the sexes not merely as a problem, but as a mystery.
—Thomas Moore, author of *The Care of the Soul.*

Angry Young Men

Kipnis has seen deeply not only into the souls of troubled boys and adolescents but also into those aspects of the spirit of our culture and our epoch that have turned an unprecedentedly large proportion of our boys and young men into perpetrators and victims of violence. Aaron Kipnis writes with eloquence and passion, and his book is a model of how an author can accomplish the difficult and delicate task of showing the relationship between his own life history and the larger history of which he writes. Just as Freud used examples of his own dreams as a way to illustrate universal themes, so Kipnis uses his own life history to illuminate the universal relevance of his insights. As a result, his book is both enlightening and moving. Angry Young Men *is a wonderful book and a major accomplishment. I hope it will find its way into as many hands as possible.*
—James Gilligan, M.D., Harvard Medical School; author of *Violence: Our National Epidemic*

With unique passion and insight, Aaron Kipnis shatters the myths about troubled young men in our society. A compassionate look that compels each one of us into action.
—Michael Gurian, author of *The Wonder of Boys* and *A Fine Young Man*

With stories of the triumph of human courage against insurmountable odds, Aaron Kipnis clearly demonstrates that redemption, human dignity, and transformation are possible among the most troubled of our youth.
—Dr. Robert E. Roberts, executive director, Project Return, Tulane University Medical Center

Written with unflinching and often shocking candor, "Angry Young Men" is a heart-pounding reading experience. It tells in harrowing detail exactly how violent criminals are created by poverty, fractured families, prison-like schools, and a criminal justice system that creates more crime than it prevents. Complementing the author's personal experiences, "Angry Young Men" offers an especially thorough and persuasive agenda for changing the way our society's institutions encourage violent crime. The book is undoubtedly the indispensable document on the subject deserving very careful attention and respect.
—Jules Siegel, *San Francisco Chronicle*

Everybody committed to increasing our public safety will benefit from the effective strategies for healing 'bad boys,' thereby enabling them to become productive adults rather than career criminals.
—Senator John Vasconcellos, chair of the California Senate Public Safety Committee

One of the most important books written in the last decade.
—Robert Bly, author of *Iron John* and *The Sibling Society*

THE
MIDAS
COMPLEX

HOW MONEY DRIVES US CRAZY AND WHAT WE CAN DO ABOUT IT

AARON R. KIPNIS, PH.D.

ISBN: 0974509116
ISBN 13: 9780974509112

Library of Congress Control Number: 2013949614
Indigo Phoenix Books, Los Angeles, CA.

For Karen,
who taught me the meaning of real wealth

ACKNOWLEDGEMENTS

My deepest gratitude goes to my wife, Karen Olender Kipnis, who constantly created a loving and supportive atmosphere in which I could focus on this work. Karen, along with my two step-children, Jesse and Adele, were very patient and supportive during my times removed from family life, and continually reminded me of the priceless value of loving relationships when we were together. My father, Kip, taught me a great deal about the dark side of Money. He passed away while I was at work on this book and left me several stories that he had previously admonished me to never tell while he was alive. Bob Chartoff lent me wider perspective, potent insight, and, as so many times in the past, was continually supportive of my creative efforts. Dr. Connie Zweig has been a great cheerleader, editor, and the most solid of friends. Dr. Dan Hocoy helped me keep the faith during the times I felt this topic was just too large to wrestle to the ground. My old friend Peter, who carelessly lost half my life savings in bad investments, forced me to try to write and teach my way out of the losses. Without his influence I may not have kept at this difficult undertaking so long at this time of life.

My employer, Dr. Steven Aizenstat, founder and president of Pacifica Graduate Institute, was both personally and professionally supportive of this effort. The three-month-long paid sabbatical he gave me helped enormously in the final stages of this work. Moreover, the institute, in collaboration with my departmental chairs, Wendy DeVee and Willow Young, along with other colleagues and staff, gave me an open forum over the last decade in which to teach courses on the psychology of Money. These graduate seminars were an invaluable context in which to dynamically explore the ideas in this book with a wide range of very bright graduate students. My mentor at Pacifica, Dr. Mary Watkins, informed me about the emerging principles of liberation psychology, which helped shape my thoughts about how we might break the spell of the Midas Complex.

The few thousand students who took my courses or attended my public workshops on this topic all contributed valuable discussions, stories, and personal perspectives. Much of what people shared in these contexts was deeply personal. I have carefully changed facts as needed in any stories to assure that all privacies remain intact, unless otherwise instructed. While this book draws from many different research sources, the researchers connected with Alternet.com wrote or republished numerous hard-hitting, well-documented articles and studies about the Great Recession. They were invaluable to portions of this book. The writings of historian Howard Zinn, along with the psychologists mentioned in the introduction, taught me more about how to write and think more inclusively about cultural history. They also lent me the courage to speak in counterpoint to the dominant paradigms of my own era.

Sister Mary Lobo of Nari Jagran Manch in Bihar, India, provided me profound teachings on practical approaches to the eradication of the most severe forms of poverty. I will never again spend a dollar without remembering that amount was the entire—daily—family budget for many of the households I visited in rural central India.

I value all the rascals, con men, thieves, pirates, and clowns who, at the end of the first decade of the twenty-first century, brought America and most of the rest of the world to their financial knees. With out having witnessed the vast incompetence and rampant greed of so many at the head of our financial institutions, I may have lacked sufficient outrage to keep the writing engines at full bore. The psychological traumas that the Great Recession inflicted on our population will keep my trainees, colleagues, and me in work for decades to come.

TABLE OF CONTENTS

MIDAS' DAUGHTER TURNED TO GOLD

Epigraph

Then the god gave Midas control over the choice of a gift, which was pleasing, but futile, since he was doomed to make poor use of his reward. "Make it so that whatever I touch with my body, turns to yellow gold," he said. Bacchus accepted his choice, and gave him the harmful gift, sad that he had not asked for anything better.... His own mind could scarcely contain his expectations, dreaming of all things golden. As he was exulting, his servants set a table before him, heaped with cooked food, and loaves were not lacking. Then, indeed, if he touched the bread with his hand, it hardened. If he tried, with eager bites, to tear the food, the food was covered with a yellow surface. He mixed pure water with wine, but molten gold could be seen trickling through his lips. Dismayed by this strange misfortune, rich and unhappy, he tries to flee his riches, and hates what he wished for a moment ago. No abundance can relieve his famine: his throat is parched with burning thirst, and, justly, he is tortured by the hateful gold....

—Ovid, "Midas and the Golden Touch," in *Metamorphosis*

THE
MIDAS
COMPLEX

HOW MONEY DRIVES US CRAZY AND WHAT WE CAN DO ABOUT IT

A Note on Terminology

Throughout this book, I have capitalized the word *Money* as a more formal noun to give it the prominence it deserves. Money has a force and character that make it almost a personage—and in many cases that character takes on mythic proportions making it more like a god than an ordinary human being. Serious consequences can befall those of us who fail to treat the Gods with respect.

INTRODUCTION

Money. It's funny stuff. Cold, hard, and inert, yet it impacts our lives in dynamic and vital ways. Many risk life and limb for it. People work at jobs they hate, marry or divorce for it. Some people will even kill for Money. Others kill themselves over it. Most of us employ less drastic means in our relationships to this so-called medium of exchange. Even so, Money changes us like few other things. To some degree, most of our life plans include considerations about Money. It is one of the most powerful forces in the human world, yet most of us know little about its psychological nature.

Money is a subject often more taboo than discussions about sex, death, religion or political affiliation. As Bob Dylan once sang, "Money doesn't talk, it swears." I have found most people more willing to discuss their darkest sexual fantasies than their net worth. As a psychologist, I see the myriad Money complexes of my clients in many aspects of the therapeutic work we do together. Yet psychology as a field has been no better than other forums in hosting insightful dialogues on this topic. My graduate courses on the psychology of Money are some of the only such courses in the United States. Conflicts around Money are the number one reason that couples divorce, yet outside these courses, few family therapists receive even a single seminar about Money's influence on interpersonal relationships and individual psychology.

Even though financial concerns are a key reason for many self-destructive acts as well as the etiology for a great deal of violence toward others, mental health workers receive virtually no training in how to talk about or understand Money. Money is as notably absent from psychological literature as a missing front tooth. It is as if Money does not even exist as a factor in human development, mental health, or psychopathology. That tells me that Money, as a psychological force, is largely hidden in the shadow of our collective psyches. This book breaks the ubiquitous taboo about discussing the inner life of Money. It will aid readers in better understanding their own complexes and psychological relationships to Money, help them to better understand how Money drives our contemporary culture, and offer some pathways toward change that could be helpful.

There are thousands of books about how to make Money. However, the global market meltdowns of 2007–12 proved most Harvard University MBA experts wrong. Even the key leaders of the national economy were caught by surprise. Many lost millions, even billions. So what did they know? In any case, this book is not about how to obtain more Money; even though it may help readers increase their wealth, that is not its primary aim. There are also many books about how to cultivate some sort of magical attitude in order to coax more Money into our lives. Honestly, I think most of those only attract Money into their authors' bank accounts. In any case, this is not one of those books, either. The principles in this book can teach the reader how to become more prosperous, however, primarily because *prosperity is a state of mind*. And anyone can change his or her mind.

Money was a main topic of discussion at many of the social and professional events I attended during the so-called Great Recession. If people did not have stock portfolios or retirement accounts that had lost value, they were concerned about equity in their homes that had evaporated. Many of those who did not own stock or homes were equally worried about their jobs. Others were just trying to find work as some portions of my private practice became more about vocational coaching than psychotherapy. People tried to be brave. Wry commentary and jokes abounded. But in the background, there was a more somber note in the air, as if a skull was grinning at the banquet.

Even as some markets began to recover, many remained wary of investing and unsure about their financial futures. In my practice, Money concerns have increasingly shown up as primary challenges to businesses, marriages, family members' mental health, and individual well-being. Clearly, Money anxiety abounds today and many feel a sense of defeat in that even their most careful financial planning has been to no avail. Few understand what is happening to our economy or what both their personal and our collective financial futures hold in store. The search for helpful answers and ways to ameliorate the real stress, fear, and feelings of dislocation many people are experiencing today have led to this book.

This book does not simply focus on a meta-analysis on the dysfunctions of the American economic system. It is most concerned with the psychological shocks of that system to the mental health of individuals, families, and communities as a whole, regardless of where they are on the socioeconomic scale. Studies emerging every day point to the erosion of mental health in large segments of the American populace as directly attributable to the economic uncertainties and dramatic economic disparities of our time. Depression, anxiety, substance abuse, domestic violence, divorce, and suicide rates all rose through the years of the Great Recession and subsequent downturn. About one in six suicides are related to some sort of financial trauma. Money is a profoundly psychological substance.

MY PERSONAL CALL TO THE TOPIC

In my childhood, my parents and other caretakers exposed me to a wide range of pathological Money-driven behaviors and beliefs. I have lived at almost every point of the economic spectrum, from extreme poverty and homelessness in my youth to some of the more privileged enclaves in the world. I practiced for many years in Santa Barbara, California. Today my practice is in Santa Monica. Many of my clients have incomes and net worths that place them in the upper 1 percent of US wealth holders. I have also worked intimately with some of the poorest families on the planet, in central India and elsewhere. I have learned from this broad spectrum of experience that Money woes impact people at every level of society regardless of the amount they earn or possess. The psychology of Money courses

I have presented to thousands of therapists in training and in many public workshops have made it clear that, regardless of how much or how little Money an individual or a family owns, it is possible to have a more fulfilling relationship with it.

For over a century, psychologists have commented about the psychological conditions of the cultures their patients inhabit. Sigmund Freud and Carl Jung wrote extensively about the psychological conditions in European culture that led to World War II. Thomas Moore, James Hillman, Thomas Szaz, Robert J. Lifton, R. D. Lang, Viktor Frankl, Ervin Staub, and many others have made important contributions to our understanding of ways in which societies can generate a psychopathogenic (crazy-making) influence in the lives of their citizens. Therefore, it does not seem entirely out of my purview as a psychologist to write a book concerning a phenomenon like Money. At the outset, my intent was to focus solely on the psychology of Money. As the events of the Great Recession unfolded before me, however, the visible corruption in so many of our economic institutions gripped me. What evolved into this book now includes more social and cultural psychology than I previously conceived. It now looks both within and without us at our psychologically complex relationships to Money—our Midas Complex.

This book attempts to better understand and thus improve the quality of our relationships with Money as it comes and goes though our lives. Its primary aim is to help individuals, couples, families, and organizations overcome the myriad miseries and madness that Money can bring. Through making sense out of what is often a disturbing and sometimes a demoralizing phenomenon, we may gain skills for sustaining a saner relationship with Money. As a psychotherapist I naturally believe that *mental health is the ultimate wealth*.

This book may help readers learn how to identify and understand their own Money complexes—largely hidden, unconscious scripts—and develop strategies to both overcome and prevent the psychological challenges that Money or its absence can bring to life. The book demonstrates concrete ways to recover from dysfunctional attitudes and behaviors and to cultivate a more satisfying relationship with Money. One of the through lines for this book is a belief that in many cases we do not actually need more Money; what we need is more understanding about how to appreciate and use what we do have in different ways. In some cases, people can even become happier and more fulfilled by intentionally having fewer things than they have now.

A REFERENCE NOTE

Twenty years before this publication, my first book's publisher, Jeremy Tarcher, said, "Aaron, I have published hundreds of books in my time and yours has more facts and references per page than any other I have seen." As a young academic, I was a bit proud of that. I felt it showed I had done my homework well, carefully documented all the work, and qualified many of my controversial assertions with supporting studies that "proved" my point of view. Having translated my dissertation on the deep psychology of men and their gender-specific needs in psychotherapy into a popular book, I wanted my arguments to be strong. Coming out of the university system, I felt that layers of citation were one of the ways to do that. I did not realize at the time, however, that Jeremy was not really complimenting me. Nor did I understand how much extra it had cost him to publish all those pages of references.

With the advent of the Internet and powerful search engines, almost any fact or resource can now be found instantly, merely through typing in a few significant words. Since my first books, the Internet has made fact-checking a simple task for almost anyone. Moreover, the latest version of the research, updated as appropriate with additional relevant adjunctive citations, appear with just a click. In that we no longer require elaborate full references to find studies buried in library stacks, I have not provided them or littered the text with subnotes or hypertext. With electronic versions of the book available for search inside the text, finding anything within is also virtually instantaneous. Research, which used to take hours, now happens in seconds. In this book, therefore, I have chosen not to continually break the narrative with citations, to consume significant pages of paper with a reference section, or to create an index. Although I documented my past books in this fashion, I have decided to depart from that tradition here.

I have, as is proper, given credit in the text to any writer who contributed ideas or research to the book. If the citation for a governmental statistic, table, or other fact is absent, the interested reader can easily look up the most current information on that topic. By the time any book is published, most statistics are already out of date. This may irk some of my more scholarly friends and particularly my graduate students, from whom I must still require exhaustive citation. If so, I extend genuine apologies. As an ecologically minded person who is troubled about the number of trees converted into my books, I find the savings of so many pages worthwhile. We will see if this marks a new juncture in nonfiction writing or merely brings me censure and forces me back into the laborious tasks of indexing and referencing again.

Aaron Kipnis, PhD
Topanga, California
April 2013.

CHAPTER 1

WHAT IS MONEY?
A PSYCHOLOGICAL HISTORY

Money is something you got to make in case you don't die.
—Max Asnas

Midas Myth #1: *Money has always been a fundamental part of life.*
Reality: *Money is a recent occurrence in human culture.*

Many of us learn about King Midas and the golden touch as children. It is part of a canon of cautionary tales that attempt to convey essential life wisdom to children through storytelling. According to the ancient Greek myth, Midas was a very wealthy king who longed for even more. A god, who was grateful for a kindness Midas provided his servant, reluctantly granted him the magical power to change anything he touched into gold. His extraordinary gift soon became King Midas's curse. Why a curse? Because his gift turned *everything* into gold, including his food, his drink, the fragrant roses in his garden, and even his beautiful daughter.

1

The loss of his beloved child was the final transformation that shocked Midas into realizing that his gift was seriously tainted. His golden touch steadily transformed him from a wealthy king into a thirsty, starving, lonely man surrounded by glittering riches he could not enjoy as each living and vital thing he loved was hardened into gold. King Midas then awakened to the real meaning of wealth, rid himself of the golden touch through repentance, and restored his innate capacity to enjoy the simple pleasures of life.

THE MIDAS COMPLEX

Many of us today, who find suffering and limitation in our lives resulting from pursuit of Money beyond its capacity to provide basic needs, can be said to be suffering from a Midas Complex. This is a condition in which no amount of material acquisition brings personal fulfillment and where our pursuit of wealth paradoxically increases our suffering instead of bringing the liberation we ultimately seek. The psychology of liberation is distinct from most contemporary psychology that largely seeks to help its clients adapt to existing social norms. Liberation psychology looks for the etiology of mental illness in the symptoms of the dominant culture while also trying to correct cognitive disturbances within the mind of the individual.

The Midas Complex is a culture-wide phenomenon that divides psyche into fragments, families into factions, citizens into classes, and nations into hierarchies of power and submission. On a global scale, the pursuit of Money has been a prime contributor to the degradation of our real wealth: the quality of our water, the productivity of the land, the purity of the air we breathe, and even the stability of our global climate. Just as the mythological Midas almost starved because his food, wine, and water all turned to gold, many wealthy people today starve spiritually and psychologically while chasing Money. As more gold accumulates in the hands of fewer people, hundreds of millions of poor people are literally starving while the natural environment suffers from wealth extraction rates far beyond its capacity to renew. The human race today faces serious challenges to its survival unless we can change our attitudes about where our true riches lay and how to best preserve them.

The Midas Complex is a force seemingly as fundamental to the human psyche as the will to survive. Were there a Midas coin, it would have Eros emblazoned on one side and Thanatos on the other—the two great forces of the psyche described by Sigmund Freud almost a century ago in his book *Beyond the Pleasure Principle*. The Midas Complex paradoxically embodies both the will toward life and fascination with death. Money is one of the more powerful and transformational substances known to humankind, equal in intensity to powerful drugs, spiritual conversions, erotic passions, and traumatic reorganizations of the self.

The attempt to understand the deep symbolism and complex meanings of Money is a bit like trying to pull a fishhook out of a can of fishhooks. Each hook is intertwined with another and then another and another until the attempt to extract one hook drags the entire contents of the can along with it. This is one of the reasons, in my opinion, why there is so little useful psychological discussion about the meaning of Money and its impacts and affects on the human psyche. Money is so complex and its meanings so vast that attempts toward intelligent discussion and reflection tend to quickly collapse. As a way to begin, a brief examination of the history of Money may help us gain greater understanding about its true nature and just how it came to be such a potent force in our lives today.

THE HISTORY OF MONEY

For several hundred thousand years, human society evolved dynamically without the invention or intervention of Money. Fire making, hunting and gathering, tool-shaping, clothing fabrication, weaving, shelter building, medicine, art, the wheel, writing, pottery, the bow, sailing ships, social politics, religion, irrigation and agriculture, metallurgy, astronomy, calendars, animal domestication, villages, cities and states, monumental architecture, politics, and organized warfare all evolved before Money came into use. Money is a relative newcomer on the human landscape. Unlike the preceding partial list of human inventions, many of which repeatedly evolved independently in numerous locals, Money has few points of origination.

Fire making was discovered thousands of times, but Money has only a couple dozen traceable roots in human history. Since its invention, however, Money has raged virulently through human society. Like a virus from outer space, Money proved to be a particularly contagious and perilous concept for which most societies lacked any immunity. Every time a Money-using culture encountered a trade-based society, Money won, virtually destroying all previous traditions of trade and other systems for attributing value.

Soon, virtually every culture in the world became strongly defined by its currency and monetary system. Over the last few thousand years Money has becomes a potent force in shaping human culture. In many ways, it has replaced or become a substitute for kinship systems in which reciprocity and altruism linked members and helped assure our species' survival for hundreds of thousands of years. The invention of Money allowed dramatic stratification of roles and hierarchies of power to occur for the first time in human history. As such, it has had a powerful effect on human psychology. It has changed the way we view one another and ourselves. Money has increasingly defined our roles and even our personal sense of worth in many cases.

Throughout history, in hunting and gathering societies, individuals owned no more than they could carry from one place to another. What wealth existed was in the form of tools, foodstuffs, and other supplies, which the kinship group or the tribe generally shared among its members. Trade was a primary way in which tribal groups gathered more of the supplies they needed or shared other supplies, which they had in abundance. The rituals around trade also facilitated intermarriage, social alliances, cultural activities, and more. Trade was slow, and required that people spend time getting to know their trading partners. In many third world markets today, we can witness the same sorts of activities. There social commerce often seems equally important as whatever monetary exchanges are occurring.

Merchants and buyers share gossip and news in the course of bargaining for tomatoes or a fine weaving.

Money precipitated a move from relatively egalitarian, tribal cultures to class-based societies in which wealth could become concentrated into the hands of a few who could aggregate power over the many. Examinations around the world of the artifacts found in Neolithic and early agricultural sites reveal no indication of Money in early human history. In 2009, archeologists found a beautiful, hand-carved ivory goddess figurine in Germany's Hohle Fels cave. Archaeologists believe it is the oldest known sculpture of the human form. It is unique. There are a few other stone and clay goddess figures, like the famous Venus of Wollendorf, which adorns almost every Jungian psychology conference catalog and many books about the ancient Great Mother goddess. To the best of our knowledge, no one in the ancient world ever duplicated these artifacts.

Even though the few figurines that have survived the ravages of millennia appear to have been highly prized—even sacred—objects, there is no evidence in the archeological record of some factory or workshop that mass-produced identical objects for trade or barter. Likewise, archeologists do not find vast stores of basic materials for making tools. There are no large piles of flint, no stacks of dried hides, no baskets of arrowheads, no hoards of gold or silver, no coins. Surplus was found in the natural abundance of world, not horded in the cave. People tended to gather what they needed in whatever new places they found themselves. That is why anthropologists call them *hunting and gathering societies* instead of *accumulating and hording societies*.

In the 1970s, I often assisted my professor, Robert Greenway at Sonoma State University, in taking undergraduate students into the wilderness. We would go out for ten days or two weeks and survive as best we could with minimal gear and food, or sometimes none at all. During one of those trips, we met a very old, Yurok Indian in Northern California. He told us, "When I was a boy, our back lot was the supermarket. Game was plentiful then. When we needed some meat for dinner, I could sit on our porch with my rifle and pretty soon, something good for the fire would wander through. These days, you have to track all day to find game, but back then [in the early twentieth century] the woods provided just about everything we needed."

Pretechnological people did not accumulate or store mass quantities of goods. They apparently regarded anything more than they could carry on their backs as excess and a burden, not a surplus to which they could attribute value. There are some indications that there was limited trade and exchange with other groups in prehistory, but there does not appear to have been some symbolic, abstract measure of wealth that people could exchange for biological necessities of life. For hundreds of thousands of years human beings got along reasonably well without Money. It finally emerged on the scene in the millennium before Christ. Not too long thereafter, along with Money came the myth of Midas and the Midas Complex itself.

THE INVENTION OF CAPITAL

Money first appears in the form of domesticated animals. Before then, like Sam the Yurok, people hunted and gathered for what they needed. With the invention of agriculture and the domestication of animals, wealth emerged as a new concept in human culture. For the first time in human history, food could be stored—a lot of it. At the same time that surplus could be created and maintained, writing emerged, primarily as a means to keep track of this new form of wealth. Much of the ancient writings that have survived—etched into clay tablets from Mesopotamia, chiseled into stone, or inked onto papyrus scrolls from Egypt—are about this new phenomenon: Money. They note how many bushels of grain various people brought to the treasury or how many head of goats they gave to a priestess or king.

Cattle, in particular, are the oldest form of Money. In most parts of the world the domestication of animals predated the cultivation of grains. As late as the 1950s, in Africa, many people still used cattle as Money. They were so prized as a store of wealth that severe overgrazing continued to cause environmental problems in Africa into the 1980s. In fact our word *capital* comes from the Latin *capitale*, which means "cattle." Similarly, *per capita* designates "each head of cattle." Wild bulls are often featured in the art works on European Neolithic cave walls. They were highly valued for their stores of wealth throughout the ancient world. The Norse rune *Fehey* means cattle. It is also the root of our word *fee*, something germane to my own profession. Beyond their substantial concentrations of protein, cattle and their precursors, the Aurous bulls, which were so celebrated on the walls of Neolithic caves, also provided bone for tools and ornaments; hide for clothing, shoes, and shelters; and fat for lamps. Cattle were virtual supermarkets on the hoof. They were portable, with standardizable units of value, to a degree. Even though an unscrupulous trader might fill them up with water to make them weigh more at market, one really could not counterfeit them. They were either living, real cows or not.

As agriculture gained hold, storage of grains created another form of wealth—certificates. Banking first emerged in Mesopotamia during the third to second millennium before the Common Era. Temples and palaces provided safe storage for grains and other valuables. State leaders and merchants could issue some sort of certification that they securely held wealth there. The code of Hammurabi (1792–50 BCE) contained numerous laws about the proper use of Money and financial accords.

It is noteworthy that all the great stone constructions of that era happened without the use of Money. In slave cultures, or where large segments of the population were motivated by spiritual commitments or cultural loyalties, leaders did not have to float municipal bonds and pay workers to erect huge monuments or build cities. However, for other forms of commerce, moving around herds of animals or transporting wagonloads of grain was slow and cumbersome. As trade expanded in the ancient world so did the desire for new ways to account for and exchange wealth. Somewhere around 2150 BCE in Cappadocia, in what is now Turkey, the rulers guaranteed the weight and the purity of silver ingots through stamping them with their seal. This created the first real, widely accepted, concrete form of Money as we understand it today.

THE EVOLUTION OF CURRENCY

Like the ancient gods and goddesses depicted in the ruins of ancient temples and statues of antiquity, Money's physical manifestation has taken myriad forms: from biological necessities like herd animals, grains, and legumes to decorative items like beads, feathers, and shells. Money was often some sort of useful commodity like animal pelts and skins, which people could make into clothing, bags, shoes, and even shelters. Tools and precursors to tools such as flint, obsidian, and other useful stones were widely valued trade goods for thousands of years. There are the odd items like huge, round, quarried stones of the Yap islanders or woodpecker scalps, cowrie shells, porpoise teeth, or giraffe tails for various tribal groups. In fact, the Chinese character for Money evolved from the pictograph of a cowrie shell, which the Chinese used for Money in ancient times, as did Africans into the middle of the twentieth century.

Ancient Greeks and contemporary Africans use iron spits or elongated nails as Money. In Africa you can still find such "coins" that appear with a point, a twist, a flattened part, and an edge, all showing they are good metal that artisans can fabricate. Rare items of natural beauty such as gems have been widely used as stores of wealth along with metals such as gold, silver, and bronze, which people made into bullion and, eventually, coins. The Aztecs and Mayas kept gold dust in quills and used cocoa beans as currency. Metal tools and weapons have and still do represent great value. In 1619, the citizens of Virginia started using tobacco as currency, and this continued for another two centuries, eventually creating notes that replaced the trade in actual tobacco leaves—tobacco-backed Money.

About a thousand years after the Cappadocians created standardized bricks of silver bullion, so-called "tool" currencies began to appear in China. These bronze "coins" were miniatures of steel tools—like knives and spades—that had universal values. They had little holes in the end, so traders could string them on a cord. They thus facilitated the trade of hundreds or thousands of such tools or a trade equal to the value of the tools. Eventually, just the holes remained: round coins with a hole in the middle called "cash"—which China kept minting for over a thousand years, until 1912. Even piles of coins get cumbersome for large exchanges, so in the century before Christ, the Chinese emperor created a white deer-skin with his seal on it that equaled 40,000 "cash." This later evolved into the paper Money that stunned Marco Polo during his visit in the Middle Ages, and which he brought back to Europe along with gunpowder, silk, and spaghetti.

Ironically, it was not some great creative inspiration that called this major transition forth. In the early eighth century, Emperor Hien Tsung issued paper Money primarily because of a significant shortage of copper, which was the main element for the fabrication of Chinese coins. By the dawn of the first millennium, there was so much Chinese paper Money in circulation that inflation became rampant. Cycles of inflation followed by periods of monetary reform persisted for around five hundred years until, in the fourteenth century CE, before most nations in the world even began using it, the Chinese finally abandoned paper Money as an unreliable form of currency.

In Europe, the progenitors of modern Money began to emerge in the sixth century BCE. Silver and gold mixed coins appeared in Lydia, where Croesus was king; hence the enduring phrase, "Rich as Croesus." Some think Croesus was actually the model from which the myth of King Midas evolved. Within a hundred years, precious metal Money spread to Greece and Persia. Athens created a pure silver coin with the image of an owl stamped on it as the animal sprit of the goddess Athena. Athenian *owls* soon became widely recognized for their purity and consistency thus becoming a universal currency of the time. Like the Athenian's Money, most other currency from that time featured an image of a god, goddess, or revered element of the natural world. In Ephesus, minters stamped the coins with a bee, the symbol of Artemis, who was their patron goddess. Money was sacred. It was minted in the temples. Money was connected to and intertwined with spiritual life as well as the world of commerce. Moreover, people mined precious metals from the earth, furthering the sense of Money as a gift of nature and the gods and goddesses of the earth.

BIBLICAL TIMES

Regardless of whether or not we believe Jesus was the son of God, as a historical person he was at the least a radical philosopher and social transformation agent. He both upset and inspired a multitude of people. He also created lasting influences on our Western philosophy of Money, which earns him a section here. In Jerusalem, in 30 CE, Jesus overturned the moneychangers' tables and drove them out of the temple. A few years later, many believe, his wealthy detractors caused him to be executed. Perhaps his act against commerce fueled some of their enmity.

To gentiles, the practice of moneychangers conducting their business in and around temples and other public buildings would have seemed commonplace. Greek bankers then were called *trapezitai*. This name evolved from their name for their tables on which these Money traders would pile their various currencies. With a similar etymology, the English word *bank* comes from the Italian word for a bench or a counter: *banca*.

One day the Pharisees decided to try to trap Jesus into making a statement of sedition that would get him in trouble with the Roman rulers of the era. They tried to coax him into telling people that they should rebel against Rome by not paying their taxes. We all know what happens to people today who either do not pay theirs or urge others not to pay theirs. Today tax evaders go to prison for some years, but in Jesus's time the sentence for most crimes against the government was death. It was a simpler time. Instead of falling into this particular trap, Jesus reportedly held up a silver coin to the audience and in one of his famous parables asked the people whose image was on the coin. "Caesar!" some shouted back. He then stated the obvious. He said to give Caesar that which belongs to Caesar and to God what belongs to God. With that, it was as if he took a huge sword and cleaved the ancient word in two. Ever since, it has remained divided: the world of Mammon—Money and commerce—and the world of spirit, which is transcendental and unseen. As the Bible starkly admonishes in Mathew 6:19, "Do not store up for yourselves treasures on earth, where moth and rust destroy, and where thieves break in and steal."

In ancient Greece, as evidenced by ruins one can still visit, there was a noticeable difference in orientation of the cities compared to what we see in our own cities today. Although they were similar to ours in many ways, it is easy to see how the religious temples, governmental centers, and marketplaces were all intertwined, open and adjacent to one another. Church and state were not separate as they are today. Commerce and sacred ritual intermixed. That all changed when Jesus threw the moneychangers out of the temple. Now, for the first time in history, Money was part of the profane, the world of Mammon. People perceived God and religion as separate domains. Money began to attract a shadow. It became associated with the non-spiritual. Money started becoming profaned. In certain ways, this was the beginning of a deep ambivalence about Money in the human psyche and the further emergence of the Midas Complex. Christ reportedly said, "If thou wilt be perfect, go and sell that thou hast, and give to the poor, and thou shalt have treasure in heaven." This implies that those of us who do not do so are not perfect and will not have a bountiful afterlife.

The Bible does not say, however, as many have misattributed over the ages, that Money is the root of evil. In Hebrews 13:5 it actually says that the *love* of Money is the root of all evil. I like Louisa May Alcott's variation on this theme; she says, "Money is the root of all evil, and yet it is such a useful root that we cannot get on without it any more than we can without potatoes." George Bernard Shaw observes, "The lack of money is the root of all evil" and Henry Fielding adds that Money is "the fruit of evil, as often as the root of it."

However we interpret it, many of us inherit complicated ideas about the nature of Money as a good, bad, or neutral substance. Those confusions can lead to various facets of the Midas Complex taking hold in our imaginations. Many people share confusions about the amount of Money received or given and the amount of worth each giver or receiver is expressing. We are told as children, "It is the thought that counts, not the amount." That rarely assuages the disappointment of receiving a pair of socks over a hoped for new toy. The perceived worth of individuals is often tied to how much Money they possess or control as distinct from the quality of their actions toward others. The popular media seldom represents those who dedicate themselves to good works as people of fascination. The lives of the rich and famous more often seem to dominate mainstream media today. Children notice this, and it creates an internalized countertext to the idea that quality and character count more than capital accumulation.

THE WIDOW'S MITE

As is still the case in many temples and churches today, religious leaders in ancient times expected worshipers to give a portion of their wealth to support their religious institutions. Governments tax their citizens and enforce their taxes with threats of serious consequences. Religions use various forms of persuasion and social coercion. Unlike government, however, they have no legal power to enforce the giving, which makes it all the more interesting and complex.

One day, after observing the various gifts left by the visitors to the temple, Jesus gathered his disciples around. In his estimation, beyond the gold left by wealthy merchants and the silver coins, which were the customary, basic contribution for any visitor, an impoverished widow had given the greatest gift that day. She left two tiny copper coins called *mites*, the smallest coins of that era. One is about the size of a slice from the end of a pencil eraser. It would take several to compose a modern penny.

According to the Bible, Jesus said, "Verily I say unto you, This poor widow cast in more than all they that are casting into the treasury: for they all did cast in of their superfluity; but she of her want did cast in all that she had, even all her living." This remains a profound commentary on the relative power of giving, which still enters our national taxation debates today, as will be discussed in chapter 4.

If a poor, working mother drives fifty miles a day to and from her job in an old car that gets twenty miles to the gallon, she uses 625 gallons per year to go to work. If she pays 50¢ in tax for each gallon, she pays over $300 per year in gas tax. If she makes $15,000 in a year, this one unavoidable tax represents 2 percent of her income. A rich man with a $60,000 luxury car that also gets twenty miles per gallon drives fifty miles a day to and from his job and pays the same tax. If he makes $150,000 a year, the gas tax only represents .2 percent of his income. So, not everyone feels the pain of taxation evenly, even if it is "fair." For the same reason, the measure of a gift or sacrifice is proportional to the percentage of wealth it represents, not the total amount. For some the gift of a million dollars is a smaller sacrifice then another's gift of one hundred. The story of the widow's mite is a lesson in relative values. Amounts of Money mean very different things to us depending on what sector of the economic scale we occupy.

THE GODDESS OF WARNING

In 390 BCE, the Gauls attempted to sneak into Rome to attack the city early one morning. The loud honking of geese in the captain of the guard's courtyard awakened him. Consequently, he was able to rouse the troops in time to save the city. Geese are symbols of the goddess of warning—Moneta. Therefore, the Romans built a temple to her. They later made their Money there. Thus, our words *Money* and *mint* both evolve out of this ancient temple and mythos. The myth reminds us that something about Money is inherently alarming. Ever since the invention of Money, people have had to guard and defend it. Now there was something worth stealing and an alarm to be sounded that we all must heed. Soon Money and anxiety became unhappily wedded as a large unsettled complex in the human psyche. Anxiety remains a central component of the Midas Complex today.

In Athens, around this same time, leaders ordered the mints to inflate the Money supply by dipping bronze coins in silver. This was probably the first known debasement of a currency's value. It is not possible to significantly debase cattle or a basket of wheat. As a result, the Athenian public began hoarding solid silver coins as cheap, silver-coated, bronze coins took over circulation. When the United States removed precious metal as the backing for its currency, just as in ancient Athens, silver quickly disappeared from circulation, leaving only the cheap, base metal coins we use today in its wake.

A hundred years after the debasement of the Athenian currency, the Romans were still using heavy bronze bars called *aes signatum* as currency. Harkening back to cattle, they cast this useful metal in the shape of an ox hide. Eventually, the Romans, too, began issuing silver coins, only to debase their own currency during the Second Punic War because they needed so much Money to pay their troops. Enormous inflation was the result. Over the next few centuries, the purity of Roman coinage went up and down.

During his reign in the first century CE, Roman emperor Nero adulterated both silver and gold coins with base metal, thus creating prolonged inflation. By 250 CE, the silver content of Roman coins was only 40 percent. Soon thereafter only 4 percent of coins were still silver. It did not take much longer, historically speaking, for the entire culture to collapse. This Money story repeats itself throughout the ages. Monetary leaders establish confidence in Money and then others erode it through greed and corruption. The currency becomes inflated or debased until it becomes worthless. Then the culture goes bankrupt. After losing its economic and military power to repel foreign invasions, Rome finally fell in 410 CE. The whole concept of banking disappeared with it. It became virtually extinct for about eight hundred years, until the Middle Ages and the advent of the Crusades.

Banking reappeared in Western Europe in the eleventh and twelfth centuries for only one reason: the promoters of the Crusades needed to be able to transfer large sums of Money to support the massive armies fighting in the far-off lands of the Middle East. The Knights Templar became the bankers of the Crusades because of their fanatical loyalty to the church. They, above all knights, could be trusted to not succumb to their Midas Complex and to both guard and transfer large sums to the Holy Land. A huge mythos evolved about them and their fabled hidden treasures. They remain the subject of many novels and Hollywood blockbusters such as the film based on Dan Brown's novel, *The Di Vinci Code*.

THE NEW GOLDEN RULE

After the fall of the Roman Empire, the economic center of the Western world moved east, to Constantinople, along with most of the gold, silver, and other riches of the old realm. The army of the new Christian emperor Constantine plundered the pagan temples and estates throughout the ruins of the Roman Empire. Constantinople became the richest city in the world. Constantine created a new gold coin there called the *solidus*. It represented one month's pay for a *soldier*; this word, to describe someone who serves in the army for pay, emerges from the name of this coin. Incidentally, the French *sou*, predecessor of today's franc, also has its roots in the name of this coin, as does an Italian word for Money, *soldi*, and other currencies, including the Peruvian *sol*.

Thereafter, until the Middle Ages, those who served the church and its military empire were paid in these gold coins. In fact, for centuries the emperor prohibited everyone from trading them outside the empire. This left the rest of the population with various forms of impure coins and trade goods that had irregular, nonstandardized values. Consequently, all those outside the blessed circle of the emperor and his successors were subject to having their currencies debased and inflated. This wiped out stores of wealth, generation after generation. It was the beginning of a different sort of golden rule from the one most of us learned as children from the Bible's admonitions to do unto others, as we would have them do unto us. The new rule was: Those with the gold make the rules. This rule helped allow a European aristocracy to rise in the Middle Ages. They owned most lands and other resources. The aristocracy was supported by a vast population of serfs who possessed no access to a stable currency or capital and virtually no economic means to improve the circumstances of their lives.

Gold has had an enduring and powerful effect on our concept of Money. Gold captures the imagination in a manner that surpasses most other natural elements. Gold and the stories of its pursuit are woven throughout the myths of countless ancient cultures. Numerous films and adventure novels feature it as the Macguffin (an object of desire that drives the plot). Certainly, the love of gold is central to the myth of Midas. Most Christian religious iconography depicts heaven as golden. Gold also adorns the realms of the gods of Buddhism and Hinduism. It illuminates sacred texts. Egyptians buried their pharos with a great deal of gold, which symbolized their sun god, Ra.

Most famously, King Tutankhamen, who died in 1352 BCE, was found resting on a golden shrine, inside a solid gold inner coffin weighing over two hundred pounds, wearing a spectacular heavy golden mask, gold sandals, and a gold dagger. Gold cups, statues, rings, and many other ornaments surrounded him. Excavations reveal gold jewelry, statues, and funereal wear in the ancient tombs of almost every ancient culture that had any access to the substance.

In fifth-century BCE Greece, Pindar noted, "Khrysos [gold] is a child of Zeus; neither moth nor rust devoureth it; but the mind of man is devoured by this supreme possession." His observation predated the similar biblical commentary above from Mathew 6:19. It succinctly heralds the deep psychology of the Midas Complex. In the old European fairy tale "Rumpelstiltskin," the miller's daughter must discover a way to spin straw into gold. In "Tarandafiru," a Romanian fairy tale, the gods aid a distressed princess in search of her husband. They give her a spindle that can spin gold, a gold bobbin to wind the golden thread, and a gold hen that lays golden eggs (an analog of the familiar caution-against-greed fable about the goose that lays golden eggs). Tarandafiru eventually finds her love and then gives birth to two golden children. Jason and the Argonauts searched for the mythical Golden Fleece, which may have actually existed in that ancient prospectors placed sheepskins (wolf skins in Russia) in gold-rich streams to trap gold flecks in the wool. An ancient Buddhist text tells the story of a family blessed by a magical swan with golden feathers, which they could sell one by one when they dropped, but when overly plucked by a greedy wife, only ordinary feathers grow back.

16

The Trojan War resulted after Paris, the prince of Troy, gave a golden apple to Aphrodite, goddess of love and beauty, who then allowed Paris to kidnap Helen, the wife of Menelaus, precipitating the war. Artists often depict Aphrodite as golden and shining, with warmth like the sun. Various mythic heroes from Hercules to Atlas did battle with a dragon, which guarded the tree on which golden apples grew. In German mythology, the goddess Idun's golden apples conferred eternal youth. Gold is like coagulated sunshine, a fundament of life. Gold, perhaps, reminds us the miraculous gift of life. It is virtually imperishable. It is resistant to acids and corrosion. It can spend a thousand years beneath the sea and still shine as new.

Many alchemists attempted to transmute base metals into gold. King Edward II once imprisoned Lully of Italy, an alchemist, in an effort to force him to transmute enough gold to fund the Crusades. Before the European alchemists tried turning lead into gold in the Middle Ages, Arabian alchemists attempted the same thing.

The Inca thought gold was the sweat of the sun, and Europeans believed a mythical golden land called El Dorado existed somewhere in South America. Following Christopher Columbus, Hernán Cortés, Francisco Pizarro, and the other European colonists of the New World, huge supplies of gold began flowing into Spain. In the early decades of the 1500s, this stolen treasure exceeded a ton of gold per year. The natives of the New World did not really understand gold as Money. Spanish soldiers, infected with a virulent Midas Complex, fell on them with a fury and murdered them in untold numbers. They enslaved the rest and cruelly exploited them. Many died from their subjugation and vicious treatment after only a few years labor in the gold mines. This was one of many bloody chapters in the history of the Midas Complex.

Colonists destroyed entire native populations in order to extract more of this resource for the gold-hungry rulers of Spain and other European nations. They imported African slaves to many parts of the New World with the thought that they were better adapted to hard labor in hot climates. As the gold played out, the invaders continued to subjugate their slaves for agricultural work to enhance the profits of a handful of European colonists and early American aristocrats. Of course, it did not always go so well for the conquerors. There is at least one story of native people pouring molten gold down the throat of an invader, a Spanish governor in Ecuador, in vengeful punishment for his insatiable thirst for gold.

The invention of wealth created more hierarchical societies wherein some people labored to produce food and other necessities of life, creating a surplus beyond their individual needs. This surplus could support others who did not labor for their own food but who, by virtue of ruling over the producers, received the means of life by taking a portion of their production. In many parts of the world, the creation of Money accelerated humanity's move from more egalitarian, tribal groupings to more pyramidal cultures, with a few on top and the majority laboring to support them in extremes of luxury. As increasing amounts of wealth got concentrated into the hands of a few, the quest for capital increasingly trumped the spirit of cooperation and mutuality, as demonstrated by the rampant slaughter of innocents in the New World. The jewel-encrusted fabrications of gold from this era are dazzling. Yet, most of them were mortared with the blood of the New World's indigenous people as the colonial era began to display the shadow of the Midas Complex in profound ways.

In 1848, the discovery of gold in California led to a massive increase in the production of gold coins by the US mint. Consequently, in the following decade, the United States moved toward a gold standard for its monetary system. Some Native American tribes in California today refuse to wear gold because it still reminds them of how American colonists forced their ancestors off their lands and even murdered them in pursuit of the riches lying in their streams and hillsides.

In 1851, gold was discovered in Australia. Along with the so-called Gold Rush in California, this led to a huge expansion in the world's supplies of gold for Money. By 1931, France and the United States held 75 percent of world's gold. In 1970, the United States abandoned the gold standard for its currency, went to a silver standard, and then to paper backed only by our faith in the government and God. But that is likely not the end of gold's story. Only time will tell, if as some traders foresee, gold will reign again as the nation's or the world's supreme form of currency. If it does, those who own it will become the foremost purveyors of the new golden rule.

FUNNY MONEY, BUBBLES, AND CRASHES

The rise and fall of valuations are nothing new. Our most recent real estate and stock market bubbles and crashes have many predecessors in the economic history of nations. In 1599, for example, a handful of Dutch traders tried to corner the world's pepper market, and the spice became more costly by weight than gold. A generation later, those clever Dutch scammers created a nationwide frenzy for tulip bulbs, which also soon became worth far more than their weight in gold. This bubble, too—like Florida real estate—soon exploded, leaving the investors with some pretty flowers, spicy soup, and lost fortunes. *Achoo!*

The Mississippi Company was set up to exploit the wealth of French colonies, especially in Louisiana. In 1719, it gained a monopoly of trade with the East Indies and China, and a speculative boom in the value of its shares ensued. The boom, combined with the overissue of notes by the Banque Royale, led to a drain of precious metals from France to London. Then, the boom collapsed—the so-called Mississippi Bubble. This one event set banking in France back by about a hundred years. Contemporary with the Mississippi Bubble was the South Sea Bubble, a speculative boom that took place in the shares of the South Sea Company, originally set up to break the Spanish monopoly of trade with Central and South America. The collapse of this boom undermined the development of banking in both Britain and America for many years.

In 1759, during the Seven Years War between the British and the French in the colonies, General James Wolfe captured Quebec. During his campaign, he complained about being hampered by lack of funds. Similarly, inflation was blamed for the lack of funds that led to the defeat of General Edward Braddock in 1755. Consequently, the British government decided to increase taxation in America, thus spurring the American Revolution. Money policy seems to have had a large hand in our nation's origins.

In 1766, Benjamin Franklin failed to persuade the British Parliament to allow the creation of colonial paper Money in America. Ten years later, before the ink was dry on the Declaration of Independence, the colonials began furiously printing Money to finance the Revolutionary War. They called their new currency the *continental*. Not surprisingly, the continental experienced increasing hyperinflation from 1776 to 1783. At war's end, the new American currency was worthless.

As noted above, centuries ago, Ugandans used cowrie shells as Money. In the early eighteenth century, a man could purchase a wife with just two of them. Then slave traders and other colonial importers began to import large quantities of the shells from places were they were plentiful, making huge profits on these "currency" exchanges. By the end of that century, inflation caused a prospective husband to need a thousand cowries for a bride price.

Shell Moneys were also valued in many other cultures. The early American colony of Massachusetts adopted Native American shell Money, called *wampum*, as legal tender. Wampum persisted as a form of Money for almost two hundred years. But with typical Yankee ingenuity, the European settlers there started a wampum factory where they used machines to shape the shells, which formerly were limited in production by the hand work of native people. Subsequently, wampum met the same fate of the cowrie and other indigenous currencies: it became inflated and its worth as currency collapsed.

During the 1812–14 war between the United States and Britain, inflation ballooned in the United States. As in the US Revolution, during the US Civil War in 1861–65, the Confederacy largely financed its war effort by printing Money. In addition to the Confederate notes, various states, railways, insurance companies, and other companies also issued notes. The resulting hyperinflation rendered Confederate paper worthless for anything but wallpaper in Confederate homes. By comparison, inflation in the North was relatively moderate as the Union government raised substantial sums of Money by taxation and borrowing. This helped the Northern states maintain economic superiority over Southern states for many decades after the war, just as the European aristocracies maintained their wealth over the peasants through the new golden rule.

From 1922 to 1923, after losing World War I, Germany suffered dramatic hyperinflation. At the worst of it, employers paid some workers every day, even twice a day, so they could make purchases before their Money lost more value, causing some goods to cost more than they had the previous day. Reportedly, it could take a barrel full of notes to buy a loaf of bread. Waiters asked for payment in advance because by the time patrons finished a few drinks and their meal, the price might have risen. Postage stamps from that era were repeatedly reprinted going from 5 to 50 to 500, 5,000, 50,000 and even 5,000,000 Marks. Germany suffered hyperinflation again directly after World War II. From 1945 to 1948, ration cards and permits became more important than currency. On the black market, commodities such as soap, tinned beef, chocolate, and cigarettes served as currency, much as they do in US prisons today.

In 1925–26 there was a huge real estate bubble in Florida. When it popped, in 1926, speculators put their capital in the stock market. Through 1928 and 1929, the stock market inflated the next bubble and the government did nothing as the boom got increasingly out of control. The market crashed in 1929, precipitating the Great Depression, seconded by the somewhat similar, less severe crash in 2007 and a multitude of smaller crashes in the eight decades between them. In 1933, Franklin D. Roosevelt became President and implemented the New Deal. This brought with it a great deal of banking reform, including the creation of the US Federal Deposit Insurance Corporation to guarantee repayment of savers' deposits in any further case of default. Similar to the most recent downturn, the stock market continued making Money for the upper ranks while millions of working- and middle-class people remained out of work and out of their homes.

Just as inflation has created multiple bubbles through time, bank failures are also nothing new. They have been happening ever since there were banks. In 1790 there were four banks in the United States. By 1800 there were twenty-nine, and by 1921 almost thirty thousand. Widespread banking failures occurred in 1857 when over fourteen hundred banks had to suspend cash payments. This spread around the world. There was another crash in 1873 and another in 1907, which was also global, followed by the Great Depression and most recently the Great Recession, which also saw many bank failures. Stock market crashes have also often followed large run-ups in stock valuation. We can begin to get a feel for the psychological life of Money: if it were a person, he or she would be severely manic-depressive.

THE END OF MONEY

By the 1960s, most indigenous forms of Money like cowrie shells, sheep-skins, and horses—the latter of which the Kirghiz in the Russian Empire still used as Money until 1910—had largely vanished. Local, fabricated, or collected forms of Money gave way to national printed currencies. As a result, increasing numbers of people moved away from local, subsistence, and trade-oriented economies to larger market economies. Their wealth became increasingly subject to national monetary policies as a result. The population explosion of the mid-twentieth century caused huge inflation, particularly in developing Third World countries in which poverty became increasingly intractable along with rapid environmental decay.

In 2002, the European Union introduced the Euro to replace the national currencies of most European nations. In 2012, however, an economic crisis in Greece had many rethinking the wisdom of all Europe being on a common currency, as Greece's decline weighted down neighbors in the new EU. Money's epic story continues its strange tale of inflations, devaluations, crashes, and revaluations. Money is protean, continually shifting in its forms. Grain and herd animals gave way to gold and silver coins, which in turn gave way to printed currency, paper checks, and plastic credit and debit cards. Despite the shifting forms and fortunes of various currencies, however, something unprecedented and monumental began to occur in the late twentieth and early twenty-first centuries that heralds the end of Money as it has been known for the last two and a half millennia. Money has become digitized and invisible and has learned how to move at the speed of light.

The electronicizing of Money has created a massive, unprecedented shift in our culture's relationship to wealth, commerce, and the concept of Money itself. By 1995, over 90 percent of all transactions in the United States were being made electronically. The high costs of check and coin payments were a strong motivating factor in the development of electronic payment systems both here and abroad. The Mondex electronic smart cash card debuted in 1995, and there are now numerous forms of electronic currency. The latest trend is electronic payment by cell-phone transfer to an electronic receiver at the place of purchase and other digital device–facilitated transfers are proliferating.

The now invisible current of Money is understood by very few, leaving most of us detached from any sort of solid ground or real sense of wealth. Money has transformed from a concrete, useful substance to something of total abstraction. Unseen, mercurial, mysterious, and intensely powerful, it now more closely resembles a god than any other known corollary. Even though electronic commerce and global capital markets have liberated many from the slow pace of bondage to a brick-and-mortar reality, they have also created a sense of unreality, unease, and global anxiety about who (if anyone) is really in control of Money and its future.

Historically, as the above detailed, most Money had some sort of intrinsic worth: it was either biologically relevant to human survival or representative of something that was. Money was a means to the acquisition of needed supplies. Alternatively, it was something beautiful like gold, which, as with all beauty, is a sort of food for the soul. Often Money was a tool for various activities related to survival and human development. Now, for many people, Money has become more of an object of desire itself, far beyond its biological relevancy. In this respect, it has evolved from primarily serving as a tool to being something more like a drug. The phenomenology of Money clearly displays these two major poles—a means to an end (tool) and an endlessly alluring object of desire (drug). Initially, people used Money as a symbol of worth in lieu of trade goods to barter for essentials. Over time, for some people Money itself became the primary goal and essentials became secondary. Just as coca leaves and poppy plants can be refined into the more heavily addictive cocaine and heroin, respectively, recent abstractions of Money may actually facilitate Money behaving more like a drug than a tool for increasing numbers of people.

Most of us in the human sciences have been quite limited in our understanding about Money thus far. The psychotherapist's *Diagnostic and Statistical Manual of Mental Disorders* does not list the Midas Complex. It should. I call it a *complex* because it has many facets. Millions suffer needlessly from this peculiar psychopathology. However, there is hope. First, as with most disorders, we must examine the shape of the wound. Then we will better understand how to proceed with treatment. One of the prevailing fantasies about Money is that a certain amount of it can make anyone happy. Chapter 2 examines that Midas Complex–driven fallacy in detail.

23

CHAPTER 2

HAPPINESS AND THE DEEP PSYCHOLOGY OF MONEY

Money is the most egalitarian force in society.
It confers power on whoever holds it.
—Roger Starr

Midas Myth #2: *More Money creates more happiness.*
Reality: *Money's impact on lasting happiness is very limited.*

MONEY CAN'T BUY ME LOVE

In 1964, John Lennon and Paul McCartney of the Beatles sang

> *Tell me that you want those kinds of things*
> *That money just can't buy.*
> *I don't care too much money*
> *Money can't buy me love.*

Even though the idealism and antimaterialism of the 1960s was just sprouting in the psyche of America's Vietnam era generation, few believed yet that they too did not care too much for Money. Coming as this did from what became one of the richest musical groups in history, I remember this song being followed with a cynical quip from my father saying, "Well it might be true Money can't buy you love, but it sure can rent it for a while." Perhaps contributing to the paradoxical nature of the Beatles' commentary on whether or not Money could make us happy was the fact that only a year earlier, in 1963, the Beatles had rerecorded "Money (That's What I Want)," a 1959 hit single by Barrett Strong that was Motown's first hit record. They made a new hit out of it on their own. In it they sang:

> *The best things in life are free*
> *But you can keep them for the birds and bees*
> *Your lovin' gives me a thrill*
> *But your lovin' don't pay my bills*
> *Money don't get everything it's true*
> *What it don't get, I can't use*
> *Well now give me money*
> *A lot of money*
> *Wow, yeah, I wanna be free*
> *Oh, I want money*
> *That's what I want*

And they got it, but then lamented it could not buy them love. Ironically, this song later became the theme song for the movie *Rogue Trader*, about former derivatives broker Nick Leeson and the 1995 collapse of the Barings Bank. The filmmakers based it on Leeson's 1996 book, *Rogue Trader: How I Brought Down Barings Bank and Shook the Financial World*. This is a true story about how a young man brought down one of England's largest and oldest banks, simply because he was too embarrassed to tell the truth to his friends. He did not want to make them unhappy (while there was still time to save the bank) by telling them how it was all falling apart. In other words, he wanted to be liked and to be happy at any cost. His story forecast the Great

Recession, in which similar reckless pursuits for happiness at any cost brought down numerous financial institutions.

The relationship between Money and happiness is a bit hard to study. Anyone can easily measure Money; all we have to do is count it. But there are no definitive units of happiness. We can quantify how many café lattes we can get for twenty dollars, but not how much happiness we can buy. Nevertheless, the emotion of happiness and the phenomena of Money are often linked in people's minds.

What is true at one level of wealth is also not true at another. The relationship between wealth and happiness is not equally scalable at each level of wealth. It is not a linear or graduated scale. A poor person who doubles his or her annual income may become a member of the middle class, and happiness then expands along with the middle-class privileges of better food, medicine, shelter, and access to education and safer neighborhoods. Money can actually buy some happiness for the poor and lower middle classes. Without access to adequate housing, good nutrition, basic health care, transportation, and other necessities, most of us would suffer. At some point on the wealth acquisition scale, however, there is clearly a diminishing return between increasing Money and increased happiness. Money has a geometrically declining power as status grows on the economic scale, belying French philosopher Albert Camus's comment, "It's a kind of spiritual snobbery that makes people think they can be happy without money."

THE SOCIAL SCALE

As a postmodern academic in psychology, I have often heard the social hierarchy theory of happiness. It basically holds that the higher people rank on the socioeconomic empowerment scale, the happier or more satisfied with life they are likely to be. This theory, however, has proven false in many ways. Sociological theories frequently fail to translate into the psychological realities of life; it is one of the reasons that psychotherapists cannot make good use of some social theory in the consulting room. The majority of us suffer from some degree of the Midas Complex. We do so differently according to our socioeconomic sector (SES) rank. Social theory fails to understand, however, that differences in types of suffering generally do not equate into different *degrees* of suffering. The rich and poor both bleed red.

Extreme poverty, however, is a notable exception to my contention about the relatively equal distribution of suffering from the differing injuries of class. An increase of Money does in fact bring increased happiness for people struggling to meet the basics of life in the same manner that more food for a hungry person brings greater satisfaction. I know from firsthand experience that poverty itself is traumatic in unique ways. Poor people suffer more depression because life for the poor contains greater stressors, many of which are easily ameliorated if one has some Money. Middle-class people do not go to jail because they cannot pay a parking ticket and, until recently, do not usually lose their housing because they cannot make their rent or mortgage payment. Money can eliminate a great deal of suffering for the poor. There is a real limit, however, to the degree of happiness that Money can buy. As people rise on the economic scale beyond survival and basic comfort needs, the relationship between happiness and increased wealth quickly tapers off. Increasing amounts of food for a sated person is more likely to bring indigestion, high cholesterol, and undesired weight gain than increasing degrees of satisfaction.

A wealthy person who doubles his or her income is just *somewhat* wealthier, not inducted into an entirely different class experience. Nevertheless, the Midas Complex drives the fantasy of wealth acquisition as the road to happiness for many people. Erich Fromm states that we all aspire to a "pleasant sufficiency of means." Beyond that, however, another operating system is at play.

How much more do we need? What amount of more will make us happier? At my seminars, most middle-class people guess that if they had double what they had now, they would at least feel secure, if not happier. Many who survived the Great Depression, however, feel as if they can never have enough because, at any moment, a mercurial twist of fate can take it away from them.

Holocaust survivors and immigrants forced to relocate—anyone who has suffered sudden loss of wealth—can be haunted by the trauma. More than others, they may hope to achieve a solid enough economic foundation to withstand the shock of any change in the environment. The Great Recession shocked many Americans and others around the world too young to have experienced the Great Depression. People generally have a hard time adapting to uncertainty and often do not lose much happiness with economic loss, as long as there is a feeling of continuity and future opportunity in their lives.

As with the economic collapse of the early twentieth century, anxiety and depression rose markedly during the years of the Great Recession as the downturn seemed increasingly protracted and governmental interventions seemed to be of little help. The answer to the how much is enough question is very relative to the personal history and psychology of each individual and somewhat relative to the state of the economic environment at any time. The more uncertain life seems, the more some people seek Money as a source of comfort, a shield against uncertainty. When a person's quality of life decreases in pursuit of more than what he or she needs for a comfortable life, however, then the Midas Complex is usually at play.

Researchers Daniel Kahneman and Angus Deaton of Princeton University found that while happy feelings rise with income, they plateau at around $75,000. They note, "Perhaps $75,000 is a threshold beyond which further increases of income no longer improve people's ability to do what matters most to their emotional well-being: spending time with people they like, avoiding pain and disease and enjoying leisure. It is also likely that when income rises beyond this value the increased ability to purchase positive experiences is balanced, on average, by some negative effects" such as "factors in their temperament and their life circumstances." A number of studies have recently developed similar happiness/income correlations.

Research like this points us toward one of the key insights about and potential cures for the Midas Complex. If, in fact, the degree of enjoyment in life is more dependent on social and psychological needs being met than how much Money one has beyond assuring modest comforts and survival, then the formula that more is always better is false. Moreover, it becomes easy to see that when one sacrifices relationships, health, and psychological well-being for the pursuit of more, then not only is the formula false it is toxic. One useful intervention for many of my high-SES clients who feel unhappy is to simply encourage them to spend more time tending to family, friends, health, and philanthropy. Acts such as these rarely fail to increase their happiness.

People with $8 million are not proportionately happier than those with $7 million. A million more does not really make a significant difference to happiness at that level. In fact, at these scales, more does not create any perceptible increase in overall happiness beyond the momentary pleasures of new acquisitions or increases in worth. As the German composer Richard Wagner once stated, "Joy is not in things, it is in us."

Carol Graham wrote an excellent book called *The Paradox of Happy Peasants and Miserable Millionaires*. Her title alone synthesizes the paradoxical content of this section. Some people understand that Money is not the main key to happiness. Nevertheless, this idea remains provocative to many others. When I received an iPhone from my wife for my birthday, I felt happy. Of course, she and I could only afford the phone and its service provider because we have good employment, which also makes me happy. Then I bought her one and was even happier because now we have FaceTime and can actually see each other when speaking on the phone from afar.

Few objects have ever brought me such happiness (and I own no Apple stock). A year later, however, I still like my phone. It is OK. But does it make me happy? Not really. That only happened for a few days around my birthday. I have become habituated to it. In psychology, we call this phenomenon, *hedonic adaptation*. We get used to new things and the happiness wears off.

But my wife still makes me happy, even more so than a year ago. We do not generally become as habituated to relationships as we do to things—certainly not healthy, dynamic, growing relationships. Many studies have shown that marriage and other intimate relationships tend to increase people's overall happiness. The ones that don't tend to wind up in my office.

The amount of Money they make or have, however, only has a modest effect on their positive feelings from day to day. My psychotherapy practice reveals that many wealthy people are unhappy. Most, if not all, however, will say, "I am blessed, or "I am lucky," or "I know I have advantages that most people do not share." Nevertheless, they are truly unhappy, just guiltier about feeling that way, perhaps. Our culture has led them to believe that Money should be making them happier than they are. If you have Money and are not happy, it is easier to believe that there is something wrong with you than if you are poor and suffering from more obvious deprivations.

THE SUICIDE SCALE

If we look at the SES scale alone, one can quickly see how different groups tend to sort out. Black women disproportionately filled the bottom for many decades. In recent years, African American women have made significant educational and economic gains, so most recent studies seem to be recategorizing the bottom more as the province of African American and Native American men. White men, however, highly overrepresent the top, as they have done since the founding of our nation. White women, who now own roughly 60 percent of all stock portfolios in America, fill the second rank. Their wealth is in part due to the enormous economic gains many women have made in recent decades but also to women living, on average, about seven years longer than their husbands do and inheriting their portfolios. With an average life span of eighty years, white women live longer than any other demographic group. By comparison, African American men live about sixty-seven years, which in addition to the poverty gap they face points to a serious mortality gap as well.

Social theory on the power of wealth to buy happiness and satisfaction with life would have us believe, then, that those who have the most wealth and power—white men—are then the happiest or most fulfilled of all social groups. This idea is exacerbated somewhat by a deeply entrenched fantasy of American capitalism: that more is always better. If we look at a more psychological scale of life satisfaction, however, social and economic theory starts to fall apart, at least in this one area concerning what makes life worthwhile. As a therapist with a lot of advantaged clients, it quickly became evident to me that, despite some of the class sensitivities I might have picked up during my liberal education, there was actually a great deal of suffering going on among the privileged classes. As a more reliable indicator of the true psychological well-being of different social groups, I prefer to examine the suicide statistics. Beyond reports of well-being or unhappiness, and social theories of privilege or privation, suicide is a very powerful, objective statement about a person's true state of wholeness or despair.

Who is at the very top of the suicide scale? White males. In fact, white males are heavily overrepresented on this scale; they kill themselves almost five times more often than do white females. The suicide rates for white males over the age of sixty-five take a drastic spike upward. White males in the fifteen- to twenty-four-year-old range also have dramatically increased rates. Who is at the very bottom of the suicide scale? You likely guessed it: black females. In fact, the rate of suicide for African American women is so low it is statistically insignificant.

People who go to church or temple are often happier. It is not clear, however, if this increase in happiness comes directly from religion itself or the social support of belonging to a community. But in the case of black women, it may be one of the factors in their resilience since they are at the heart of their religious communities throughout the nation. Whatever the cause, I believe this phenomenon undercuts social theories that equate happiness with one's rank on the social, political, and economic power scales. Princess Diana once wryly commented, "They say it is better to be poor and happy than rich and miserable, but how about a compromjise like moderately rich and just moody?" She was one of many public figures for whom extraordinary wealth and power did not convey equal measures of happiness.

One of the most constant presentations psychotherapists experience in their consulting rooms are people suffering with varying degrees of unhappiness. Helping clients to make deeper meaning out of their lived experience and ameliorating their symptoms of depression and anxiety consumes the bulk of most psychotherapists' professional attention. One would think, therefore, that we would spend a lot of time researching what actually makes people happy. But this is not the case. One thing that stands out starkly, however, is the clear reality that the power of Money to make people happy is very limited. One might think, "I just wish I just had the chance to prove that more Money will not make me happy." Nevertheless, research reports and the lives of those who do have Money tend to confirm this. On a national scale, if Money made people happy, then the United States would be the happiest place on Earth. Outside of Disneyland, however, which claims that distinction in its corporate motto, this does not appear to be true.

THE WEALTH OF HAPPY NATIONS

The Organization for Economic Co-operation and Development reports that the United States has the highest rate of household wealth in the developed world. However, our nation fails to make the list of the top ten "happiest" nations, even though economic prosperity is generally a strong factor in people's reports of life satisfaction. Various global surveys of national well-being place us at twelfth or sixteenth and even as low as twenty-sixth on national happiness and well-being scales.

For example, people in Denmark, which is ranked first on the global happiness scale, have the most leisure time (including sleep) per day—sixteen hours as compared to fourteen in the United States. So two hours of extra free time a day seems to make a bigger difference than greater wealth. They also have high employment and a very low percentage of citizens who work over fifty hours a week—roughly 2 percent compared to about 11 percent in the United States. Second on the list, Norway, spends more on health care for each citizen than all other surveyed nations. In the third-ranked Netherlands, people report high levels of good health and longer life expectancy. The Swiss are happy about very high rates of employment. Austrians are happy about their high rates of disposable income.

The majority of Israelis, even though surrounded by hostile nations, feel safer walking home at night than do Americans. Sixth on the list, Finland, like Denmark, boasts a very low percentage of employees working more than fifty hours per week. Australians are healthier than Americans, enjoying a life expectancy about three years longer than US citizens. Canadians have much higher rates of high school graduation than students in the United States. Subsequently, they have higher employment rates as well. And Sweden, tenth on the list of happy nations, reports greater leisure time as one of its citizens' claims to well-being.

Beyond wealth, it is health and longevity, strong social support networks, long-term employment and job stability, health and physical well-being, sufficient leisure time (shorter working hours), mental health, educational attainment, and physical safety that seem to contribute to high levels of national happiness. The United States ranks lower in most all these factors. Our average life expectancy, in particular, is lower than all the above and most other wealthy nations as well. This is due largely to our extreme levels of gun violence and high infant mortality compared to other affluent countries. Americans have also become some of the most time-impoverished people in the world. Our affluence has not brought a corresponding amount of leisure time. Compared to other industrial nations where longer vacations and shorter workweeks are the norm, what Americans regret most on many happiness surveys is lack of free time to spend with their loved ones.

According to research by Richard Easterlin, a professor of economics at the University of Southern California, overall levels of happiness do not appear to increase as countries grow wealthier over time, either. He also finds little connection between average per capita gross domestic product and happiness once the populations of formerly poor countries achieve a certain basic level of income. It seems that nations recapitulate the findings about individuals and families. Once minimal standards of comfort and safety are covered, happiness does not increase proportionately with wealth. In the aforementioned *The Paradox of Happy Peasants and Miserable Millionaires,* Carol Graham relates similar findings in her studies of happiness around the world. She notes that wealthier nations generally tend to be somewhat happier, but only up to a point. Then it is the quality of relationships, stability, and the nature of the culture itself that is the greater determinant of happiness, not more Money.

IF NOT MORE MONEY, WHAT DOES MAKE PEOPLE HAPPY?

As psychologist Ed Diener of the University of Illinois, who contributed to a large study on happiness, notes, "People spend most of their time making and spending money, and it is one of the big long-range goals for most people, and so it affects life satisfaction." He found, however, that positive social interactions that further the common good contribute more significantly to happiness than does Money. This is one of the reasons that psychopaths (people who lack empathy for others) are never truly happy—they lack the capacity to work for or even imagine the common good. (Chapter 7 discusses the problem of psychopaths in our economic system at length.)

This research may help explain the above-mentioned inverse relationship between privilege and suicide. In every African American community that I have been in, it is easy to see how deeply embedded in the social matrix the women tend to be. It is as if their hands hold all the threads that weave the community together. They are not only at the center of the lay side of the church but also at the nexus of almost every social and educational program. At the risk of overly idealizing them, I imagine that when one of these women feels a degree of despair sufficient to cause suicidal ideation, their next thought is about all the people in their families and connections in their communities that would fall apart. I know from both their suicide notes and their anecdotal reports in treatment that white men often feel they have alienated so many people on their march to success that no one will really miss them when they are gone.

Gert Wagner, a researcher at the Max Planck Institute for Human Development, theorizes that for people who do report greater happiness from greater wealth do so "not so much from the amount of money they have" but more likely "due to the more interesting and challenging jobs they have. Money is simply a byproduct of good and satisfying jobs. If you want to be satisfied with your life, you must spend time with your friends and your family." Women generally tend to be happier when their mates support family goals over their individual pursuits. Roko Belic, a film-maker working on a documentary called *Happy*, notes that as he traveled the world he found that "the one single trait that's common among every single person who is happy is strong relationships."

Social interaction and exercise are also both associated with greater happi-ness. Working out tends to make most people happier, except for under-weight men and overweight women. Working within a range of truly desired hours of work—that is, not being over- or underemployed—increases happiness, as does sufficient income for basic needs. An attitude of gratitude feeds happiness, as does engaging in activities that help others. This reflex may be encoded into our genetic patterning. Feeling good from helping others positively reinforces our survival as a species, just as the good feeling of having sex reinforces procreation.

Good health has a strong influence on happiness. If health and intimate relationships stay stable, as people grow older happiness actually tends to increase with age. Federal Reserve Chairman Ben Bernanke believes that well-being, which he regards as a longer-term measure of happiness, requires, "[a] strong sense of support from belonging to a family or core group and a broader community, a sense of control over one's life, a feel-ing of confidence or optimism about the future, and an ability to adapt to changing circumstances."

Collecting good experiences and memories seems to produce greater happiness than does collecting any sorts of objects. Researchers Thomas DeLeire of the University of Wisconsin and Ariel Kalil of the University of Chicago looked at various types of consumption. The purchase of things related to leisure, like sporting goods, vacations, and entertain-ment, was the only category they found positively related to happiness. In other words, purchases that produced pleasant and memorable experi-ences, particularly those that strengthen social and familial bonds, tend to create greater happiness than the consumption of material goods alone. For some people, increased wealth may even reduce their ability to experience enjoyment from life's everyday pleasures. I see this problem acutely in the children of some affluent parents. Some of them equate the cost of things and experiences with the value of having or experiencing them, as if there is an increasing scale of pleasure and happiness associated with the increasing expense of anything. Subsequently they often miss out on the simpler pleasures of life.

One of the more evident issues pushing the United States down the happiness scale is that so many people need to work more hours in order to achieve a standard of living similar to others inhabiting the industrial nations on the top ten list. Longer work hours and fewer vacation days mean less time for the above-mentioned quality-of-life elements that do produce happiness. The American dream itself may also have something to do with this. We generally expect more material trappings of success than do most citizens of similar nations. That may drive us to keep sacrificing quality of life to achieve the better car or home to which we feel entitled— or at least capable of owning.

Some analysts have commented that one of the things that drove the Great Recession's housing bubble collapse, which evaporated some $7 trillion in home equities, was the fact that aggressive lenders, who wanted to generate more loan fees, induced many people to purchase homes more expensive than what they could really afford. Consequently, as millions lost jobs, they lacked adequate savings to keep up the payments on their overbought "dream" homes. In 2005 alone, as the housing bubble started to peak before the collapse, homeowners took about $750 billion in equity out of their homes. They spent most of it on personal consumption, improving their homes, and paying off credit card debt previously run up to buy other stuff they could not afford. In many ways, the housing bubble was a culture-wide Midas Complex phenomenon.

In response to the claim that Money can't buy happiness, however, actress Eva Longoria Parker's character on the televsion show *Desperate Housewives* once said, "That's just a lie we tell poor people to keep them from rioting in the streets." Or as comedian and singer Sophie Tucker once said, "I have been rich, and I have been poor. Rich is better." Woody Allen simply declared, "Money is better than poverty, if only for financial reasons." Understandably, these sorts of sentiments underscore the reality that longings for upward mobility remain strong in our culture despite growing evidence that the pursuit of Money on the road to happiness leads most people to a dead end.

THE DEEP PSYCHOLOGY OF ADVERTISING: HOW THE MIDAS COMPLEX TOOK SUCH A HOLD ON OUR PSYCHES

Years ago a wise man in our community named Jiddu Krishnamurti said, "It is not a sign of good health to be well adjusted to a sick society." That has stuck with me through the years. All too often, however, psychologists and other professionals attribute individuals' suffering solely to the decisions and choices they have made and the meaning they create out of past experiences. The sickness of the world we inhabit is another factor that makes us ill. Psychologists in the habit of looking backward, too frequently overlook the crazy-making aspects of contemporary culture. Money in particular defines many key aspects of our world today. Moreover, in many cases, those cultural markers mirror back to us a sense of insufficiency, inferiority, unreality, and even failure. Diverse metaphors of American culture contribute psychological underpinnings to personal issues of enfranchisement, power, and identity as the injuries of class appear in individuals on all points of the economic spectrum. The language and symbolism of class alone can have a profound effect on our psychology, as we will see in chapter 5.

Why are so many people today so fascinated with Money? How did so many of us come to believe that it is the primary road to happiness? An examination of Money's thematic roles in film, literature, television, and popular music readily spotlights the psychology of the materialization and the superficialization of Western culture. It is fair to say that Western culture, and American culture in particular, is a Money-centric one. Money has become a central organizing principle of our cultural identity.

The majority of Americans define themselves as capitalists. That is, our monetary system is a prime source of meaning and distinction from others. In the origins of our nation we defined ourselves more by terms such as *freedom*, *democracy*, *inclusion*, and *equality*. Those adjectives for America are still with us, but increasingly our relationship to Money trumps them as the prime distinction. How did it become so central to most of our lives? Considering that Money is nothing more than an abstract idea, how did it happen that few Americans today can realistically imagine a life without Money? Marketing propaganda has had a lot to do with it.

Through most of history, advertising was largely information-based: "Jacob the sandal maker uses fine leather." While not always accurate or even true, the intent more or less has been to inform consumers about what went into creating products, what use they are good for, where people can find them, and what they cost. The old ethos of American business was "Find a need and fill it," a phrase coined by Ruth Stafford Peale, the wife of Norman Vincent Peale, author of *The Power of Positive Thinking*. With the advent of advertising psychology in recent decades, however, marketing has evolved more into something like "Create a need, and then a product to fill it." That is, create a feeling that a woman lacks beauty or a man lacks sufficient potency or productivity, and then offer a product to assuage the feeling of anxiety that the ads create. A slight variation of this is to create a need for an already owned product for which there is as yet no market—like pet rocks or a medication for the blues, currently only used for deep depression.

Humorist Stephen Leacock once wrote, "Advertising may be described as the science of arresting human intelligence long enough to get money from it." Almost every technique psychologists have developed over the last hundred years to help alleviate the sufferings of mental illness can also be used against people to alter their thinking by design—the science of propaganda. The psychology of advertising started almost one hundred years ago, just as psychoanalysis was beginning to flower in Western culture. Ironically, a nephew of Sigmund Freud started the modern psychological manipulation of consumers through advertising.

The first advertising campaign was quite insidious, setting the tone for a century of increasingly refined technologies for suspending people's common sense and mental balance just long enough to separate them from their Money. Advertising, of course, can have a positive effect. Education about the true nature of products and fair comparisons to similar products allows consumers to make wiser decisions about the products they need. However, much of advertising today is not about informing or better educating consumers. It is the negative, psychologically destructive, driven-by-consumption-and-profit aspect of much advertising that defines our concerns here.

In his 1908 article "On the Sexual Theories of Children," Freud put forth some ideas concerning what he believed was many women's sense of inferiority as they compared themselves to men. He termed this complex "penis envy" and more fully developed this idea in his 1914 work *On Narcissism*. While Freud was lamenting about the state of his fortunes in his letters to his friend Willhiem Fliess, complaining it was "a pity one can not make a living at dream interpretation," his nephew, Edward Louis Bernays, listened to his illustrious relative's new theories with a more jaundiced ear. He apparently thought, "Hey, I think I can make a lot of Money off poor Uncle Sigmund's theories." In particular, he thought he could exploit the vulnerability Freud had detected in women of the era.

Referred to as "the father of public relations" in his obituary, Bernays used crowd psychology, the tenets of psychoanalysis, Ivan Pavlov's theory of behavioral conditioning, and his uncle's theories of the subconscious to manipulate public opinion. He used psychology to sell products and ideas. He took all the technologies that most psychologists were learning about how to help relieve people's suffering and used them instead to manipulate human behaviors. Often—as was the case with the first campaign, cigarettes—this manipulation was to push people toward consuming products that were actually harmful to them and thus initially rejected by intelligent people. Bernays relied heavily on third party "experts" to tout the benefits of his products. They ranged from the tobacco he marketed to young women to bacon (for which he paraded out real doctors extolling the benefits of having a "heavy" breakfast in the morning). They use they same techniques today: a kindly older man in a white coat touts the benefits of the latest pill or pimple cream.

In his 1928 book *Propaganda*, Bernays wrote,

> The conscious and intelligent manipulation of the organized habits and opinions of the masses is an important element in democratic society. Those who manipulate this unseen mechanism of society constitute an invisible government, which is the true ruling power of our country. We are governed, our minds are molded, our tastes formed and our ideas suggested, largely by men we have never heard of. This is a logical result of the way in which our democratic society is organized. Vast numbers of human beings must cooperate in this manner if they are to live together as a smoothly functioning society. In almost every act of our daily lives, whether in the sphere of politics or business, in our social conduct or our ethical thinking, we are dominated by the relatively small number of persons...who understand the mental processes and social patterns of the masses. It is they who pull the wires, which control the public mind.

Bernays worked closely with A. A. Brill, an American psychiatrist who studied with Carl Jung and who was one of the earliest psychoanalysts in the United States. Brill translated a lot of Freud's writing into English. He became famous for labeling cigarettes "torches of freedom" as part of Bernays's cynical advertising campaign to increase the market share of the American Tobacco Company by targeting women as smokers for the first time. Brill helped Bernays to develop this theme, which tapped into young women's psychology of the era.

Bernays hired and organized a group of young fashion models to march in the 1929 New York City Easter Parade. He instructed them to march down Fifth Avenue and had them light up Lucky Strike cigarettes—their "freedom torches"—in front of the press, whom he had assembled for that purpose. He informed the press that they were women's rights marchers demonstrating their freedom and independence from men and male dominance (and penis envy as well, it seems, though that was unspoken). The head of American Tobacco who had hired Bernays, George Washington Hill, was reportedly obsessed by the prospect of winning over the large potential female market for Lucky Strike cigarettes, aka "Luckies." Bernays reported that Hill told him getting women to smoke cigarettes would be "like opening a new gold mine right in our front yard"—a real lucky strike.

Following the parade, the *New York Times* printed, "Group of Girls Puff at Cigarettes as a Gesture of 'Freedom.'" Newspapers around the world published the photos. This single campaign helped to break the previously widely held taboo against women smoking in public. It ultimately brought billions of dollars in previously untapped revenues to the tobacco companies. Millions of women have subsequently died early deaths as a direct result of this act of "liberation." In the year following this campaign, the revenues of American Tobacco suddenly jumped $28 million, which was quite a lot of Money back then.

Calvin Coolidge's 1924 presidential campaign hired Bernays to improve his image before the election. This was one of the first deliberate, widespread media actions for a president. Today the "branding" of political office hopefuls is standard practice. Senatorial and gubernatorial campaigns spend tens of millions while aspiring presidents expend hundreds of millions, even a billion. The largest donations generally come from lawyers, securities companies, investment brokers, and real estate investors. Bernays helped Alcoa and other special interest groups convince the American public that water fluoridation was safe and beneficial to human health. As his career progressed, his manipulative influence on public opinion seemed to grow right along with the size of his retainers.

Bernays argued that the scientific manipulation of public opinion was necessary to "overcome chaos and conflict in society." He shamelessly aided the United Fruit Company and the US government in overthrowing the democratically elected president of Guatemala so that the company could then exploit peasant labor to produce cheaper bananas. His relationship with Freud was never far from his thinking and his counseling. According to author Irwin Ross, "Bernays liked to think of himself as a kind of psychoanalyst to troubled corporations."

The fascist rise to power in Germany demonstrated that national leaders could use propaganda to subvert democracy as easily as they could use it to resolve conflicts. The Nazis used propaganda intensively to justify the abnegation of human rights that led to the holocaust, using images of Jews as subhuman in films, print ads, and posters. Nazi propaganda minister Joseph Goebbels read Bernays's book and became a huge fan of the new American science of propaganda. With thinly veiled savagery, he put it to the then unprecedented use of transforming public opinion about human worth and the dignity of entire populations. Goebbels became one of the primary forces behind the Nazis' attempt to destroy all the Jews—and many other groups as well. It is noteworthy that much of demonization of Jews clustered around false perceptions that they were in some way responsible for the dissolute state of Money in Weimar Germany. Between the two world wars the nation suffered one of the worst economic depressions in the history of industrialized nations.

As it did in Goebbels's Germany, marketing propaganda today, fueled by the power of consumer-focused media, creates or at least exacerbates a great deal of psychopathology. Advertising deliberately attacks consumers' self-esteem, self-image, well-being, and sense of safety, and in its current form is a virulent facet of the Midas Complex. Today, instead of turning public opinion against the intrinsic worth of specific groups, the manipulative science of propaganda is more subtly and insidiously directed toward trying to make people feel worse about their individual worth. Advertisers then promise self-esteem redemption through the products they direct people to consume.

COMMODIFYING WOMEN

In order to help liberate women, feminism deeply analyzed the history of patriarchal culture that denied women equal opportunity and legal protections. Advertisers today, however, following Bernays's lead, intentionally utilize psychological theories about women's internalized sense of inequality in order to make them feel that they are not pretty or thin enough. Men are manipulated to feel that that their car is not cool enough, their penis is not hard enough, or that they are not drunk enough to really enjoy life. Advertisers psychologically manipulate both sexes by intentionally making them feel that they will never be happy or even have the opportunity to procreate unless they consume "the right stuff." They then place products as cures for the very anxieties they methodically induce. Many people then feel they need more Money to buy the products that they have been hypnotized to believe can make them feel better. In this way, the media continually sows new seeds of the Midas Complex. Midas's problem was that he felt, with all his riches, that he still did not have enough. Creating that feeling of insufficiency in people is one of advertising's greatest psychological tricks.

The exploitation of women's psychology in order to market cigarettes to them was just the beginning of advertising psychologists' attempts to manipulate women into consuming more products. For every group of psychologists trying to help people liberate themselves from constraining thoughts and actions there is now another group of theorists trying to ensnare them. Advertisers tell women every day that they do not smell right or look right, that their homes are unfit, and, increasingly, that they do not even have the proper moods or correct behavior. Every aspect of women's bodies has become subject to advertiser's critiques, as has the promise of them conveying beauty power to women through consumption of their product. Advertisers increasingly frame unattractiveness, much less normal appearance, as something abnormal that could subject women to an unpleasant life filled with rejection, lack of appreciation, the absence of love, and even failure to survive.

Women's faces have become objects of microscopic scrutiny and judgment. Eyebrows are too thin or too thick and need color. Eyelashes are too short or too light. They need darkening, lengthening, thickening, and curl. Eyelids need color and liner. The area under the eyes requires the lightening away of any natural shading. Even the eye itself could use a more colorful lens, eradication of any redness, expensive designer eyeglass frames, or even laser surgery to eliminate the need for unsightly frames at all. The injection of a powerful neurotoxin—Botox—can erase brow lines and other lines. This renders the forehead incapable of moving in synchrony with any emotional expression, lending a greater vapidity to women's appearance in accord with a designer ideal for women to display no real inner emotional life. Cheeks are highlighted with color or with cheekbone implants at the more extreme edge of augmentation. Lips need gloss, sun block, and a multitude of colors and sheens.

For the ultimate pout there are now painful and potentially tissue-damaging injections of collagen, which are also used to eradicate facial lines—that is, until they wear off and costly new injections are required. Swollen lips lend a just heavily kissed or even recently beaten look of masochistic sexual submission to women. The entire face needs deep cleansing, special scrubs, defoliants, and moisturizing. Once squeaky clean, women must apply foundation and other colorings to achieve the perfect shade. Blemishes need hiding. Pimples need treatment. Beyond layers of cosmetics, dermatologists and other technicians offer chemical and mechanical peels for facial skin to make it appear more youthful. The cosmetic industry in the United States takes in about $50 billion per year, largely through exploiting the insecurity it has deliberately inculcated into the psychology of women. In 2012, world wide cosmetic sales exceeded $170 billion. This amount is roughly the same as the annual national budget for NASA.

THE BAD BREAST

Breasts in their perfectly natural state have captivated the imagination of artists, and—let's face it—most men and many women, too, throughout time. In recent decades, however, it seems women's breasts increasingly require special bras in order to be properly supported and displayed. These are designed by otherwise out-of-work structural and aeronautic engineers who promise to defy gravity and age through their use of adjectives like *Miracle* and *Wonder* to describe their magical undergarments.

Breast augmentation is the most frequently performed cosmetic surgery in the nation. More than three hundred thousand American women a year voluntarily go under the knife to change the appearance of their breasts, mostly through implants. While there are few medical complaints related to the procedures, several studies note that suicide rates in this group tend to be roughly three times higher than for women not seeking such radical solutions to their self-esteem concerns. Perhaps, as with King Midas, their new gift failed to produce the anticipated level of happiness.

Only 3 percent of women even have the right bone structure to wear the garments modeled on the runways of Paris, Milan, and New York. This leaves the majority of women wondering why, no matter what they buy, they can never quite achieve the beauty standard touted by fashion magazines and other visual media. This puzzlement can affect men, as well, who realize that their girlfriends and wives just do not look like the women in the magazines for some reason. These women, whom my old friend author Warren Farrell, describes as "genetic celebrities," are deliberately out in front of the fashion image makers to make the majority of women feel inferior. As supermodel Cameron Russell candidly admits, "The real way I became a model is I won a genetic lottery." She advises that this is not a carrier path one can aspire to and that, with all their beauty power, "models are the most physically insecure women on the planet."

Feelings of inferiority often lead to a loss of self-esteem, anxiety, and depression. This is exactly the feeling that advertising psychologists want to create. Then comes the promise of salvation: *Buy our product and you will feel much better.* Not only that, you will win the intense competition for the most desirable mate. A reality television show in 2011 featured brides-to-be competing against one another to win otherwise unaffordable plastic surgery makeovers before their wedding day. Even sadder, many of their fiancés strongly approved of their attempt to surgically alter themselves into a more acceptable bridal appearance.

Advertising psychologists know that women have a more highly developed sense of smell than men do. They exploit this genetic, gender difference through the marketing of a huge array of products designed to mask the true scent of women and alter the aural landscape of their environments. The metamessage from advertisers to women is, *Baby, you just don't smell so good*. Moreover, it is implied that if a women does not smell good, she will not mate, procreate, get a good job, have any friends, or otherwise enjoy life. After women shave them bare, their underarms need both perfumed scent and application of chemicals that prevent the natural function of sweat glands. Some researchers suspect some of these chemicals as agents in the rapid growth of breast cancer rates in American women although they have not proven a definitive link.

Men and women both suffer the admonition to tend to their natural under-arm odors and breath as evidence of basic cleanliness. Good hygiene is a basic social requirement, which few can credibly refute. Now, however, women are told along with those underarms, their legs would also benefit from depilation. In fact, hair anywhere except on top of the head has to go. (Well, it is OK to have a little genital hair, maybe an exclamation point's worth, a brief horizontal line running though the middle of her midre-gion.) To smell right, fashion leads us to believe, most women need per-fume. This element is nothing new. Somehow, advertisers infer, the more expensive it is the better it works. Now, however, that ages-old traditional enhancement of a splash of scent on the neck before stepping out is required for their genitalia too.

Advertising loves new frontiers and is forever looking to extend its reach and range of markets. Therefore, in recent decades women's genitalia have increasingly become targets. It seems that women's vaginas are just never fresh enough, and this now appears to have become the perennial women's wisdom that mothers convey to daughters: "Use this stuff to keep your vagina smelling good, because, you know girl, it just doesn't." Following Bernays's attempt to wed women's liberation to smoking, Massengill cre-ated a vaginal deodorant called "the freedom spray." Linger Internal Vaginal Flavoring and other similar products promote a better-tasting vagina, ostensibly to make oral sex more appealing to partners.

In an era when women's rights advocates are valiantly trying to ban the gen-ital mutilation of girls in the name of centuries-old religious and cultural traditions, many young women are voluntarily going under the surgeon's knife to have their labia cut back so that they can have a more youthful, clean, and neat-looking vagina. They are also enduring voluntary episiotomies to have their vaginal walls tightened to increase the sexual pleasure of their male partners. Others simply try to make the outer labia appear more youthful though bleaches and dyes that promise to make it look pinker.

If someone from another country had no contact with America and merely watched advertisements on television, they could easily imagine that American women's homes are all filthy and smell like pigsties. Myriad products promise to rescue women from the scorn of neighbor ladies who, with their innately superior sense of smell, come over and disapprovingly sniff the air. They appear to detect some otherwise invisible-to-the-homemaker scent of last week's fish, a passing dog, child, man, or virtually any other evidence of anyone having actually lived in the home as a violation of their mandate to maintain a sterile diorama of potential but not actual human occupation.

Psychologists know that many women feel that their spouses insufficiently support their needs. This is a reason why Midas complex-driven advertisers frame so many of the household products that target women as gifts of the alpha male. A jean-clad Mr. Brawny with his flannel shirt-sleeves rolled up on his bulging biceps cleans up every possible mess. Mr. Tidy Bowl keeps that unmentionable object in the bathroom sparkling. A heavily muscled Mr. Clean eradicates dirt all over. Just as creatures of the forest aided maidens in distress in fairy tales, Scrubbing Bubbles and other magical creatures are unleashed from cleaning products to aid the twenty-first century homemaker in distress. Psychologist James Hillman observes that America has become obsessed by "gleaming whiteness." Just as the advertiser's standard of beauty is unreachable for most women, their standard of household cleanliness also shimmers on the far horizon, reachable only by five-star hotels with minions of underpaid workers to achieve such dazzling surfaces. Anyone who has ever lived with a child knows that level of cleanliness is like trying to catch a moving bus; you are always a step behind.

In my midthirties, I worked in the feature film business for several years. I was involved in art departments doing set construction, special effects, and building props. My job also involved being constantly present on set from start to finish each day to adjust various settings and manage the props handled by the actors. By virtue of simply being there, I met many actors. I was impressed with how many "beautiful" women I met were actually fairly ordinary, nice-looking people before their hair, makeup, and costuming was applied. Moreover, through the arts of lighting and technical postproduction image enhancements, studio magic turned many normal, pleasant-looking women into extraordinary beauties. I am not knocking movie stars. A few women are genetically endowed with unusual features that make them look more alluring than the majority. Nevertheless, filmmakers create most extraordinary beauty with a lot of smoke and mirrors. "Star" lighting brings out the best, as does good posture, presence, confidence, a great smile, and something ineffable in the eyes for the great ones.

Real beauty is not rare; it is common. Fashion, films, and the whole glamour business have created the widespread illusion that women must take great pains to become beautiful. The beauty mystique, as author Naomi Wolf articulates in her book *The Beauty Myth*, has created untold volumes of misery for generations of women and the men who seek them. Millions of men are manipulated to see unaugmented women as lacking in some essential element that can only be acquired through shopping or surgery.

In recent decades, advertisers have determined that children are increasingly important markets for their products. They are attempting to indoctrinate children into consuming as early as possible in order to develop their brand loyalties for life. Thus, advertising's attempt to demoralize women around feeling good about their natural appearance is now targeting increasingly younger audiences. Most insidiously, the increasing sexualization of prepubescent girls is filling them with the illusion that even as small children they need to have just the right appearances to compete and feel included on the playground.

MOLECULAR BEAUTY AND THE NEW EUGENICS

As one of the products of the rapid growth of the science of genetics through the eighteenth and nineteenth centuries, theories of eugenics started gaining popularity in the 1920s in America. Because geneticists had discovered that some diseases and deformities were passed down genetic lines, some scientists began to tout the idea that the human race would be better off if some people with serious disorders simply did not reproduce. One obvious target was mental retardation. Even with all of the advances in science over the last century, mental retardation remains one of the mental disorders for which there is no cure. Through the 1920s and 1930s, various theorists were successful in convincing medical professionals in the United States to sterilize tens of thousands of mentally retarded people and other people with serious mental disorders.

The underlying idea behind eugenics is that normal is better. People with mental disorders and congenital physical deformities use up a great deal of resources that could otherwise aid the quality of lives of so-called normal people. Normal, however, is a moving target. Normal is a standard that changes from generation to generation and from culture to culture. Normal is the mean of behaviors and attributes in any given population at any given time.

When the Nazis heard about eugenics research in America they thought this was just the idea they had been looking for to advance their fantasy of a superior race of humans who were destined to rule. They combined those theories with the newly created science of propaganda to sell the idea of racial purity to the German public on a scale never imagined by the American academics who got the genocidal ball rolling. Few people seem to know that years before the Nazis advanced their theories of racial purity to rationalize promoting genocide toward entire cultures—like the Jews— they were systematically euthanizing tens of thousands of mental patients in the name of creating a healthier population for all.

The new science of personality and emotional regulation takes the ubiquitous message of abnormal appearance to a deeper and more insidious level. Not only does marketing propaganda today prosper greatly from making women feel insecure about their bodies, billions of product dollars are generated for a few massive pharmaceutical companies through also making women think that there is something profoundly wrong with their personalities and moods. The beatification of women's psyches is now in full force. Ironically or intentionally, pharmaceutical companies that manufacturer psychiatric medications—"torches of freedom" for the soul—are increasingly pitching their products in commercial breaks from depressing and anxiety-provoking television dramas. Advertisers' intentionally inculcated drive for people to make more so they can consume more, through linking that drive to an internal sense of survival, is clearly a Midas Complex phenomenon.

THE ABNORMAL HISTORY OF NORMALCY

Historically, clinicians largely thought of mental illness as a condition that was fundamentally debilitating: a problem that interfered with someone's capacity to work, gain an education, sustain meaningful relationships, or enjoy a range of activities and interests in life. The American Psychological Association categorizes mental illness in a huge text called the *Diagnostic and Statistical Manual of Mental Disorders* (*DSM*). As the range of abnormality has steadily increased over the years in the *DSM*, the range of normalcy has continually kept shrinking.

The first edition, *DSM-I*, was published in 1952. It had three categories with 106 different diagnostic criteria or disorders in it. The *DSM-II* debuted in 1968. It added disorders for children as a new category, was only 98 pages long, and grew to encompass 185 diagnoses. The *DSM-III* emerged in 1980. It represented a radical departure from the previous psychotherapeutic orientation of psychology and ballooned to 482 pages with 265 diagnoses. A later revision brought the total to 297 with numerous new categories. The authors added completely new arenas of psychopathology to bracket the multitude of new individual descriptions. This third edition embraced the medical model of mental health.

Medical doctors now advised therapists to view people with mental or emotional problems as suffering from some sort of disease. In addition, the doctors advocated medical treatments—that is, drugs—as the intervention of choice for an increasing number of disorders. The intertwined medical and psychopharmacology industries began to demean psychotherapy as unscientific. Of course, they had a strong stake in selling their products. Mental illness became very big business. Doctors can make a lot more selling prescriptions than they can by providing psychotherapy by the hour, one doctor to one patient at a time. A Midas Complex drive for steadily increasing numbers of patients and fees took over the field. Mental health provision suddenly became big business.

Since the advent of the *DSM-III*, a disturbing number—at times even a majority of the scientists on the development workgroups and panels creating these diagnostic categories—have had close ties to pharmaceutical companies. Once the manual's authors categorize and codify some aspect of human behavior as a legitimate mental illness, they give it a code. Researchers use these codes to tabulate their research. More significantly, these codes inform insurance companies that the therapist is treating the client for a "real" disorder, not just the general problems of life for which so many people legitimately seek assistance from psychotherapists. While not all disorders benefit from medication, many do. The Money at stake is enormous. Once they code a new disorder, physicians can prescribe the appropriate drug and insurance companies with drug plans are then obliged to pay.

A new disorder can be worth hundreds of millions of dollars in medications, new clinics, treatment specialists, and other professional services dedicated to ameliorating it. However, new mental diseases are not like physical ones. This is the great fallacy of the medical model of mental illness. For example, attention deficit disorder (ADD) is not at all categorically like tuberculosis or strep throat. No blood test, or any other objective medical test, for that matter, can prove or disprove whether or not a person has ADD. Many other new disorders also fall into this paradox. A subjective discernment by a clinician, or even a school nurse, can result in a patient receiving a "scientific" label and treatment regime.

Many disorders are merely cultural or lifestyle differences between an individual and the dominant mores of his or her culture. For example, until the mid-1970s diagnosticians categorized homosexuality as a mental illness; now it is just another orientation. This is one of the very few diagnostic categories that clinicians have actually removed as the manual has evolved. Mostly, the range of pathology has steadily increased, which in turn means that the range of describable normalcy has steadily decreased. The *DSM* is like one of those nightmare rooms in which the walls keep moving closer and closer and the range of available space in the middle keeps shrinking.

In the nineteenth century, most people viewed alcoholism as a moral failing, an issue of character. Now most of us believe it is a treatable mental illness. The point is that many of these categorizations are fluid depending on the time and culture in which the designated ill persons find themselves. Until recently, anyone arrested for smoking marijuana was likely to be charged as a felon and could then go to prison for a long term. Today, in a steadily increasing number of states, for those with a prescription filled in one of thousands of legal medical marijuana dispensaries, it is no longer a legal issue. Any student of history would have to assume that many of the symptoms we imagine to describe mental illness today will be as laughable a century from now as is the practice of bleeding people to cure their fever or headaches today.

The *DSM-IV* launched in 1994. By this time, the medical business model had fully taken hold of the mental health treatment field and this Midas Complex–driven view of mental health and illness has steadily grown since. This fourth edition of the book, slightly revised in 2000, thudded unto our desktops at 886 pages. More than seven times longer than the *DSM-II*, it included 365 diagnoses. The *DSM-V* is slated to arrive in mid-2013. Rumored to exceed 900 pages, it appears to corral many more Americans within its mental illness rubrics. Just as Bernays delivered millions of healthy women to the slaughtering pens of the American Tobacco Company, one of the more troubling aspects of the *DSM-V* is how widely it is targeting women. It is not hard to critically view it as a blatant attempt to ensnare millions more into the net of described metal illness in order to convert them to consumers of psychiatric products.

SELLING NORMAL

Almost a century after the invention of "torches of freedom," psychoactive chemicals are the latest enhancement products to target female consumers. One of the mystiques many officially beautiful women project is an image that they are happier and more energetic than normal women. The latest range of human experience to fall out of the normal spectrum and into the expanding basket of psychopathology is subsyndromal symptomatic depression (SSD). What is that? Therapists have well known the criteria for depression and its milder form, dysthymia, for over a century. The description of these disorders is somewhat universally recognized and there is a range of psychotherapeutic, behavioral, and chemical treatments available. What is a patent owner of one of these chemicals to do when it has pretty much reached the full range of the available market? To keep to the business driven axiom of greater success through locating ever-expanding markets, there is nothing like a new mental disorder to help further expand the marketability of pharmaceuticals.

The volume of antidepressant medication prescriptions has risen over 400 percent in the last two decades. Without the expenditure of hundreds of millions of dollars on research for new drugs that perform better than the old ones, drug companies have pretty much saturated the market for ordinary depression. It is much cheaper to merely create a new disorder for an existing medication than to create a better medication for an existing disorder. *Subsyndromal* means this new disorder is beneath the threshold of describable depression or dysthymia. *Symptomatic* means there are, however, some symptoms. *Depression* means that it is some kind of depression, implying that the treatments for previously described depression may apply here as well. Pharmaceutical research estimates that as many as twelve million people, mostly women, suffer from SSD—now classified under *other* specified depressive disorders. What we now call SSD is pretty much just what it sounds like—sadness. Sadness is less than depression, more mild than dysthymia, but still not normal—if normal is described as peppy, pretty, and perky. We now welcome the minions of previously neglected sad women to our consulting rooms. How did they get by all these centuries without our professional care?

The next category of mental disorder for women that psychiatrists and their pharmaceutical comrades in commerce have proposed for inscription into the latest edition of the *DSM* is premenstrual dysphoric disorder, which only affects women—also around twelve million per year. Thus, with a few pen strokes and some big pharma–supported studies, existing medications such as Prozac, Zoloft, other selective serotonin reuptake inhibitors, and related medications have found twenty-four million potential new customers. Medical professionals may now freely lead some previously "normal" women to think that they are ill. This new base represents the potential for billions in profits for a few companies over the coming years without the need of any expenditure for research and development; only advertising dollars need apply. When companies can just make up new illnesses by moving the normalcy goalpost and doctors can treat them with already developed and trademarked products, the result is pure profit.

One of the most controversial proposed additions to the panoply of new psychopathologies is sexual interest/arousal disorder in women. The preliminary text of the disorder reads, in brief, as follows:

A. Lack of sexual interest/arousal of at least 6 months duration as manifested by at least four of the following indicators:
Absent/reduced interest in sexual activity.
Absent/reduced sexual/erotic thoughts or fantasies.
No initiation of sexual activity and is not receptive to a partner's attempts to initiate.
Absent/reduced sexual excitement/pleasure during sexual activity (on at least 75% or more of sexual encounters).
Desire is not triggered by any sexual/erotic stimulus (e.g., written, verbal, visual etc.).
Absent/reduced genital and/or non-genital physical changes during sexual activity (on at least 75% or more of sexual encounters).
B. The problem causes clinically significant distress or impairment.
C. The sexual dysfunction is not better accounted for by another Axis 1 [mental] disorder (except another sexual dysfunction) and is not due

exclusively to the direct physiological effects of a substance (e.g., a drug of abuse, a medication) or a general medical condition.

This disorder seems to suggest that a woman is mentally ill if she does not meet her partner's demands for sex or is not turned on by pornography. These criteria appear to imply that unless a woman has a porn star's standard for her sexuality, there is something wrong with her. Not surprisingly, the majority of the doctors on the panel making up this new disease were men. The more successful the marketers of products designed to enhance women's lives are in convincing them that there is something wrong with them just the way they are, the more Money they make. Bernays, who started this all, relied heavily on "experts" to convince people to purchases products they did not need. He used experts to convince people in the 1930s that Dixie cups were "more sanitary." Thus, disposable paper products made their big debut and have been contributing to landfills across the nation ever since.

SEPARATING THE MEN FROM THE MONEY

In similar ways, advertisers also use behavioral, depth, and symbolic psychology to manipulate the minds of men and get them to spend in specific ways. Many concerns of life somewhat equally overlap the domains of men and women. Yet advertising psychologists know that, even in this postfeminist era, men's earnings still represent approximately 75 percent of household income. Whereas they know they can be more successful targeting the psychology of women for household, health, beauty, and now even mood-care products, men still tend to be in charge of large-ticket purchases. Subsequently, men are the prime targets for automobile ads.

Ads for cars, and luxury cars in particular, try to tap into male fantasies of unlimited freedom, escape from stress, and acquisition of the same mythical attributes of beauty that advertisers manipulate women into mimicking to attract men who can afford such large-ticket items. Where prowess as a hunter may have once been a symbol of male virility, an expensive car today broadcasts a man's earning power. At least it appears to, since the car may be leased or about to be repossessed. Nevertheless, while a man is in possession of a luxury car, the metamessage advertisers are broadcasting is that it will include a beautiful woman for the purchaser.

Years ago a wonderfully funny movie, *Crazy People*, featured Dudley Moore as a burned-out advertising executive who winds up in a mental hospital. He then enlists the other patients as his new advertising team who conspire to only tell the truth about products. The ironic premise of the film is that only truly crazy people would tell the truth in advertising. One of the ads they produce is for Jaguars, and the slogan is "For men who like hand jobs from beautiful women they hardly know." I once heard that an earlier draft of the script said *blow-jobs*, but either way the message is clear: buy this car and you will have fantasy sex. At over $5 billion per year, advertising for automobiles outstrips all other categories by far—seconded by the pharmaceutical industry, which spends about $3 billion per year.

Like women's vaginas, men's penises are also subject to increasingly intense marketing efforts to make them larger, harder, longer, and more or less sensitive. Surgical augmentation is on the rise, and sexual performance–enhancing drugs like Viagra have annual sales exceeding $3 billion. Testosterone replacement therapy for men is growing rapidly and sales are approaching $1 billion dollars per year. I wonder what Freud would say now?

Men are also the prime consumers of alcoholic beverages. In the United States this $120 billion-per-year retail industry spends roughly one billion dollars per year advertising its products. About three quarters of their advertising budgets and revenues are for beer. During the course of a year, roughly nine out of ten men see at least a dozen ads for every major brand of beer. Ads do not just promote alcohol on television. It is also sold through sponsorship of cultural, musical, and sporting events; Internet advertising; window and interior displays at retail outlets, bars, and restaurants; distribution of branded items such as T-shirts, hats, watches, and glassware; product placements in movies and TV shows; catalogs and other direct mail communications; price promotions such as sales, coupons, and rebates; and trade promotions directed at wholesalers and retailers.

For many men, consuming alcohol is an integral part of business culture. I have treated several high-powered executives who became alcoholics as a direct result of their employment-required entertainment of clients (the old three-martini lunch) and the need to demonstrate membership in the business culture by drinking with associates. My first book, *Knights without Armor*, explores this dilemma of male culture in some depth for readers interested in the numerous links between Western codes for masculinity and alcoholism.

CANDY IS DANDY BUT LIQUOR IS QUICKER

Just as Brill targeted women's psychology to convert them into avid cigarette smokers, advertisers play on male insecurities and psychological stressors to target them as alcohol consumers. Any practicing psychologist today is aware of the ways in which most men feel more socially isolated than do women. In divorce, much of the social network tends to leave with the woman. Men retain more Money but fewer friendships, and subsequently their mental health generally takes a more significant dive after separation than women's mental well-being does. As noted above, suicide statistics show men killing themselves almost five to one over women, which gives sad testimony to the largely silent epidemic of male depression in our culture.

Advertising psychologists play on the deep-set feelings of social isolation and alienation that many men secretly feel—even those who are seemingly successful and outwardly socially engaged. Once they have dropped their shuck-and-jive heroic male bravado in their private work with me, my male clients often say, "I feel alienated, isolated, and alone." Advertising psychologists know this; hence, ads for alcohol usually display some theme of social inclusion and engagement. By drinking the right stuff, suddenly a man has the right stuff that will attract a whole group of happy and playful friends who want to dance, swim, ski, and play small-team sports with them.

Another aspect of male insecurity that advertising psychologists cynically exploit is the knowledge that in this twenty-first, postfeminist, century many young men feel unclear about dating/mating rituals. After decades of political correctness, many young men are uncertain about what it is that women really want from them and how to go about meeting and sustaining connections with women in whom they are interested. But why worry when you can have a buxom St. Pauli Girl simply by making a small purchase at a liquor store? In the ads, she comes to life and displays her desire to please him when a man drinks from her bottle. In addition to friendship, fun times, and social inclusion, the alcohol ads, like many of the automobile ads, also promise intimacy with a desirable woman.

Apparently, very attractive women just cannot stay away from men who drink the right booze. Capitan Morgan rum gives men an irresistible confidence imaged by a silly raised knee posture. Dos Equis beer depicts the "most interesting man in the world" (to women) in evocative and adventurous scenes, drinking its product. Beautiful women, it seems, cannot resist James Bond, whose mystique is magnified by a martini, which is shaken, not stirred. And, as with the St. Pauli Girl, if a real woman does not find a man attractive, then he does not have to feel bad—lonely, rejected, and loveless. He can just grab another drink and she magically appears. A young fashion model languidly sucks on an ice cube virtually promising oral sex to an otherwise vapid bar tender who serves her Disaronno "on the rocks." Metamessage: "It's the booze, honey, you don't really need a personality to get me."

Look at almost any liquor ad in a magazine and try to read the subliminal message. Most of the time it simply says, "Drink this." Beautiful women will adore you and/or you will have many happy friends. Either way, the psychological metamessage is that alcohol consumption is the cure for loneliness. One of the dating proverbs I heard as a teenager was, "Candy is dandy but liquor is quicker." Advertisements promise that if you drink the potion you will feel as if you actually have the girl without all the hassles of dating, courting, and trying to understand interesting people from a gender culture different from your own. The more insidious flip side of this message is that if you get the girl drunk enough she will overlook your personality deficits and have sex with you. The retreat from courting anxiety is awash with alcohol.

It is obvious that the outcome of tobacco marketing to women has taken a monstrous toll on women's health since such efforts began in the 1920s. Similarly, annual health care expenditures for alcohol-related problems in the United States now amount to about $22 billion. The total cost of alcohol problems is $175 billion per year compared to $114 billion for all other drug problems and $137 billion for smoking. Untreated alcohol problems waste an estimated $184 billion per year in health care, business, and criminal justice costs, and cause more than 100,000 deaths. The US Bureau of Labor Statistics reported in 2011 that the average American family spent over $400 on alcoholic beverages. Many of these families cannot afford the most basic of health care policies. Such is the power of the Midas Complex to drive advertising.

With total annual spending on advertising exceeding $150 billion in the United States, it is no wonder many of us feel visually, audibly, psychologically, and emotionally assaulted by hundreds of thousands of messages with deep psychological embeds saying, "You do not have enough; you do not do enough; you are not good enough, attractive enough, productive enough, or happy enough." The feelings of anxiety and emptiness this propaganda produces are prime elements in which the Midas Complex takes root.

Subliminal advertising in alcohol ads used to embed images of skulls and other scary symbols to produce anxiety or hidden images of women's nude bodies to create desire and stimulate the desire to drink. This blatant practice was banned in the 1970s but continues today in various forms. Now the use and abuse of symbolic language has gone way beyond inserting a fast flicker of words into a few frames of a film saying something like, "Drink Coca-Cola" or "Hungry? Eat popcorn" to drive viewers to the snack counter during intermission. Today's advertisements use mythic imagery to promise that if you buy the right product you will feel young, sexy, and vital. If the beauty creams and shiny new cars don't work their promised magic, then there are a galaxy of new molecules to consume that will change the way your brain works. All of these harangues are about one thing: the promise of happiness. There is only one problem—this is just another refrain in the siren song of the Midas Complex. As this chapter contends, things do not make us happy; they merely enhance our innate capacity to enjoy life.

What is the net effect of this hurricane of imagery and sound dedicated to making people feel as if their lives are not complete unless they can acquire the whitest teeth and bathroom porcelain? The effect is greater than just the loss of Money we suffer from buying needless things, the disappointment of learning that the pleasure they produced was transitory and limited, and that they ultimately just created more clutter in our lives. The dark side of all this corrosive, self-esteem-eroding chatter is that many people today feel a ubiquitous sort of free-floating anxiety that comes from unknown quarters. Out of this, many consuming compulsions arise like *shop till you drop!* In recent years, increasing numbers of injuries and even several deaths have occurred in shopping stampedes at holiday season sales at big-box shopping marts. One of my students actually camped out at one to help prevent injury to her young nephew seeking a deal on a new TV. She used all her graduate training in psychology and international conflict resolution to help prevent riots from breaking out in the days-long line of agitated shoppers waiting to get into the sale.

With the advent of the Internet, advertisers have become much more sophisticated in their niche marketing. Gender specificity was just the beginning. People's interests are increasingly subcategorized into age group, political orientation, economic strata, neighborhood, race, culture, reading habits, hobbies, religion, sexual orientation, and other affiliations that give advertisers some leg up into targeting a person's specific interests. To some degree this has gone on for years, with the creation of massive data banks that track people's purchasing interests though surveys and analyses of past shopping patterns through coupon use, warranty cards, and other records of purchases. The Internet is tracking information in unprecedented ways. Some consumers are noticing that as they surf the Internet, the same ads recapitulating their interest categories seem to appear on different pages in otherwise disconnected places. You can block that, by the way. Regardless of how the psychology of advertising is working, from targeting our gender psychology to our income level, the aim is always the same: to separate us from our Money by creating a previously unfelt need within us.

THE EMPTY SELF

One historical foundation of the American dream is the fantasy of endless expansion and limitless geographic frontiers. Philip Cushman, the author of a cultural history of psychotherapy titled *Constructing the Self, Constructing America*, believes that as we ran out of geography we began to mine the collective unconscious as a new virgin territory from which to exploit resources. The advertising industry discovered, through Freud and his nephew, that we had an unconscious mind that could be manipulated to act in ways that were not necessarily consistent with the conscious mind. For example, as previously discussed, we could become motivated to consume things that destroyed our health or even killed us. I cannot count the times people close to me have kindly offered me cigarettes, alcohol, and even drugs over the years, not to mention countless helpings of food packed with refined sugar and trans fats.

Cushman notes that consumerism and capitalism, which is the engine behind much of our consumerist activity, results in the psychological creation of what he calls an "empty self." Because it feels so terrible to be empty, we can then feel compelled to fill up these lacunae in the soul with more and more products, media experiences, and other stimuli. This is the Midas Complex; the rich old king just could never get enough gold. We even acquire things we do not really need but hope will somehow, like wall-to-wall carpeting, dampen the hollow echoes of the bottomless cavern within. The psychology of consumerism represents a collective trauma, which fuels the psychodynamics of an empty self hollowing out the inner lives of many Americans today.

One little, visible feature of this growing problem is that, in recent years, women's purses have kept getting larger. On average, women's purses today weigh as much as fourteen pounds; twenty pounds is not uncommon. Women are carrying around more and more stuff they think they must have with them at all times. "Man-bags" are beginning to grow, as well as the average weight of briefcases and other over-the-shoulder stuff-totes. Storage lockers are proliferating. Cars and houses were growing larger and larger for decades up until this era's downturn, all to accommodate more goods and a growing sense that in every possible circumstance, more is better. Also growing are our landfills across the nation. Many communities are actually running out of space to throw away all the stuff they do not need and are having to export their trash elsewhere.

Cushman describes a uniquely American self that, while it has many similarities with other socially constructed Western selves, is acutely emptier than most. He notes that the American psyche today lacks an internalized sense of community; that consumerism has shorn us from traditions and shared meanings. Cushman understands psychic emptiness, meaninglessness, and the lack of interiority, inner sense, fullness, or completeness as a psychological state of chronic hunger—what I am calling the Midas Complex. This results in a profound desire to consume products, intense experiences, and actual substances such as food, drugs, and alcohol in an attempt to fill this perceived hole in the soul. Moreover, the need to soothe the anxiety of an empty self that cannot generate self-soothing from within drives increasing degrees of substance cravings.

Most of us in the helping professions are acutely aware of this destructive process and daily deal with its after-affects in the lives of our suffering clients. Whether they realize it at first or not, many of them are seeking to recover from an internalized sense of worthlessness and emptiness based on status. They long to move toward a more complete sense of self based on other-than-monetary values.

One the world's experts in the treatment of narcissism, Otto Kernberg, characterizes the empty self as "malignant narcissism." Kernberg understands this as a spectrum disorder with varying degrees of narcissism, the ultimate being a destructive state of self in which a person possess no empathy for others. In chapters 6 and 7, I will discuss the impacts growing numbers of people in this psychological state are having on the world we all inhabit. Next, however, we will examine the more direct effects of the Midas Complex on our mental health and interpersonal relationships.

CHAPTER 3

MIDAS IN RELATIONSHIPS: SECRETS, COMPULSIONS, ADDICTIONS, AND LIES

Money, it turned out, was exactly like sex:
You thought of nothing else if you didn't have it and thought of
other things if you did.
—James Baldwin

Midas Myth #3: *It's not about the Money.*
Reality: *It's about the Money.*

FAMILY VALUES

Our personal understanding about Money often has its roots in our families of origin. Financial skills and deficits, complexes and fears, confidence or insecurity often begin during our developmental years with the overt and covert messages we receive from parents and other influential adults. We inherit much more than heirlooms and photo books from our parents. Our inherited beliefs about Money, in many cases, have a stronger impact on our lives than the material wealth they may pass along to us.

The expressions we hear as children and other common traits in our personal Money histories influence our adult relationships with Money. Families can use Money to liberate and empower or enslave and control their members. Many of us, at some point, have to decide whether or not to embrace our family values or to carve out our own Money code. Doing so can be a process of awakening and liberation, yet it is often fraught with a certain amount of distress as well. When people feel that their family's code does not really serve them, it can feel like a betrayal to adopt new monetary guidelines, similar to embracing a different political party or religion than that of our parents.

It can take an unflinching self-inventory around our Money beliefs to discern the differences between what is valuable about our inherited ideas and what might be getting in our way. Many people, however, never even question their inherited Money codes, taking them as foundational truths about life. Similar to the ancient family crests and heralds associated with ruling-class European families, most families hand down some core phrases about their Money philosophy. For example, some of the sayings shared at my Midas workshops over the years are:

Money doesn't grow on trees.
Poverty is no disgrace, but no honor either.
Money grows between my toes.
Spend it today because you might die tomorrow.
Put your Money where your mouth is.
It is just as easy to fall in love with a rich man as a poor one.
Poverty is no sin, but terribly inconvenient.
With Money you are a dragon; with no Money, a worm.
When someone says it's not about the Money but the principle of the thing; it's about the Money.
You need Money to make Money.

Life is like a manure sandwich, the more dough you have, the less shit you eat.

And my own motto:
Live below your means and you will always feel wealthy.

I invite you to think about your own family beliefs. What slogan was inscribed on your family's invisible Money crest? What did your parents tell you about Money? Did you and your spouse inherit different slogans? How does that affect your relationship? What Money wisdom would you inscribe on your own heraldic coat of arms? What are you telling your own children about Money?

THE HEIRESS

One of my clients was the sole heiress apparent of a European estate. She fell in love with an American man who, as a public service attorney, earned about $65 thousand per year and owned few assets. As she prepared to marry him, her family disinherited her and evicted her and her two small children from a home they owned in Santa Barbara. Because of her family's wealth she received no support from her previous spouse, nor was she educated or occupationally prepared to make a decent living on her own. Her family had always told that her job would be to manage the family business when her parents retired. Her parents now told her that they still loved her deeply but in order to prevent her from the mistake of marrying a man so far below her class, they had to force her to return home by making her financial circumstances unbearable.

Rather than submit to her family's tyranny, however, Alexandria married the man she adored. The four of them moved into a small apartment in a more colorful part of town with substandard schools. Her husband-to-be felt compelled to quit the job he loved to take a position with a corporate firm. When her family realized that their manipulation had failed to create sufficient desperation to drive her back to France, they again tried to return her to the fold, going so far as to attempt undermining her husband's career. This gambit also failed.

A few years went by and the parents began to lament the loss of connection with their grandchildren and the estrangement from their daughter. Although they never embraced their new son-in-law as one of their own, they begrudgingly admitted to themselves that their daughter was happier than she had ever been and well cared for even though she was living like "a peasant." They gave her the title to the house from which they had evicted her and, while she still refused to come back to Europe to run the family business, they remained in contact with each other and allowed the grandchildren, who were thriving in the new marriage, to visit each summer. By sticking to her principles and being willing to walk away from a guaranteed fortune, she found real love and happiness. Moreover, in the end, she retained her parents' love as well. She had to find the courage to walk away from her family's Money code that said, "Always marry up [to a man who has more than you do]."

DANGEROUS LIAISONS: THE TRICKY BUSINESS OF MARRIAGE

An old expression states that whoever marries for Money is sure to earn it. Money, nevertheless, often figures into some aspect of mate selection. In my experience as a therapist, the more important role Money has in the choice of a spouse, the more likely the marriage will suffer or fail. This is not always true, however. Some marriages endure surprisingly because they are successful business arrangements. Some cultures view romance as highly overrated as an organizing principle for marriage. Nevertheless, when Money takes the center stage in a marriage or other intimate pair bonding, it often points toward a serious problem.

As Aristotle Onassis, one of the richest men in the world in his time, said, "If women didn't exist, all the money in the world would have no meaning." After having been previously married to President John F. Kennedy,

Jacqueline Kennedy married Onassis. This was hard for many people to understand since he did not appear anywhere as handsome, charming, or charismatic as her former husband. Studies show, however, that most people perceive wealthy people as more physically attractive than similarly appearing poor people.

Money issues can affect every aspect of intimate relationships, from the bedroom to the broader social realm that couples occupy. In intimate partnerships, Money provokes issues of equity and equality, survival and freedom, cooperation and autonomy, as well as shared and opposing economic values. Money can be held as secretly as sexual affairs and be just as potentially damaging in both heterosexual and same-sex relationships. As with family secrets, secrets about Money can have a particularly corrosive effect on couples.

Differences about Money are the number one reason most couples divorce. Couples argue more about distribution of labor and child-rearing issues, but Money conflicts are the most lethal to long-term viability of marriage. On the other hand, millions of couples remain in destructive marriages or dysfunctional family systems because of economic fears. One of the great achievements of feminism was to liberate many women from economic dependency as a reason to remain in abusive relationships.

One major reason for marriage failures is that couples often fail to discuss Money in useful and meaningful ways. As Washington, DC, divorce attorney John Thyden notes, "Financial issues are the primary reason for 90 percent of divorce cases I handle. But, it isn't necessarily the amount of money a couple has that tends to trip them up. It's the differences in their spending habits and especially their lack of communication." The establishment of transparency in all financial matters for a couple usually helps deepen the bonds of their intimate partnership.

Couples can take various steps to help prevent Money from becoming a corrosive element in their relationship. Through regularly telling the exacting truth to one another about their financial issues and dealings, it is less likely for economic tensions to mount. Honesty is particularly crucial when one has made some mistake or suffered a loss without consulting the other. Openness about Money builds resilience to face the inevitable challenges it periodically brings to most of our lives. Since reporting every detail can be cumbersome, another way to keep Money peace is to set a limit for what each can spend without consulting the other. Business partners do this; why not couples?

Retirement discussions must include where both would like to live and what each spouse really wants to do with each one's time. Investment planning needs to seek shared values around risk tolerance and financial goals. A large Money issue for many parents concerns how and where they are going to educate their children. Just as flight attendants advise us to put our own oxygen masks on before assisting children, planning for retirement should generally take precedence over saving for college. Spending on a spouse or kids does not necessarily equal love, particularly when spouses are not in agreement or perceive one's spending to be at the expense of the other. Setting a clear budget for vacations and other luxury items helps keep the necessities budget in line. For most couples, getting these sorts of issues out in the open early on can help prevent many years of tensions.

Since talking about Money is often anxiety provoking, it is usually best to have Money talks when neither partner is especially tired or upset. Setting aside regular meeting times, like business partners, is a good way to keep Money sanity in the relationship. It is helpful to try and hold a blame-free sprit of compassion for the anxiety, stress, and awkwardness a partner may feel around talking about Money, particularly either one's emotional, even irrational reactions to monetary issues. Some couples and families in my office admit that their discussions with me have been the first times in their lives that they have ever had open, frank, and substantive talks about Money.

I try to notice each family member's styles about discussing Money. Who leads the conversation and who follows? Who dominates discussion and who shares more openly? Once I get a sense of the patterns, I often suggest they change roles, with the more dominant spouse or parent listening and the more silent or supportive one speaking about his or her own needs for a

Midas in Relationships: Secrets, Compulsions, Addictions, and Lies

while without interruption. Readers can practice this without help. When seeking professional assistance with psychological and emotional issues around Money, however, people should seek out a therapist who actually knows something about it. As someone who has trained thousands of therapists over the last few decades, it is clear to me that many are unprepared to host Money-talks with their clients.

Most therapists never receive a single seminar about how to work with their clients' hopes, fears, aspirations, fantasies, and frustrations about Money. One of main reasons I wrote this book was because so many therapists who took my Midas seminars urged me to write it all down. As with discussions about sex (something most therapists do have some training in), just having a third party present, who can unabashedly host the charged topics, has a way of making it easier to talk about Money. This means working with someone who has reflected upon and come to terms with some aspects of his or her own Midas Complex.

Several of my past books explore gender differences in communication and sense of self; Money issues also often host some gender-based influences. Some couples come together with huge differences in their financial literacy and comfort levels in speaking about Money. In many couples, the partner with the most comfort or familiarity with finance takes responsibility for all financial records and transactions. While division of labor can be an efficient use of time in a relationship, a financially perceptive partner is not really serving the less knowledgeable partner by taking over the whole responsibility for financial planning. Particularly in couples from my generation and older, the man is often more dominant around finance. When this is so, it is imperative for women to gain skills and for their partners to take the time to help them achieve them.

After the death of a spouse, a less financially literate survivor can become very depressed, even desperate if not able to pay the bills, balance the checkbook and understand all the instruments of household finance from retirement accounts to mortgages and insurance instruments. Men are not really doing wives any favors by taking it all on themselves. The reverse is just as true, of course. All stakeholders need to be included in discussions and

71

planning around insurance, disability, death, illness, making and receiving wills, creating trusts, and the like. This means getting the discussion about the inevitability of death into the open. To hold these issues in discomfited secrecy is to underserve the soul of the relationship—the deep emotional bond between couples.

Money stresses can take a toll on a couple's sex life as well. Men, in particular, often have a great deal of self-worth and self-identity tied up in their economic productivity. When a man cannot provide for his wife and family he may feel less masculine, less confidant, and even less aroused. In a discussion below about stock traders, I mention a study showing a link between testosterone production and inner feelings of financial success. In this era, many women are the primary earners. Decreased libidos from decreased earning can swing both ways.

In both same-sex and heterosexual couples one spouse may unconsciously view their unemployed or underemployed spouse as less desirable. Many people perceive monetary success as sexy and exciting. Moreover, reduced finance can diminish pleasurable activities that can lead to intimacy—dining out, a weekend retreat, a special gift, a nice hotel, or an evening on the town. During the financial downturn of recent years, there was a dramatic increase in sales of sex-enhancing pills and antidepressants. However it occurs, Money loss can lead to lowered libidos. Couples need to be attentive to the ways that restricted income can restrict eros. They can work against this tendency by finding less expensive ways to be romantic and by being compassionate about the ways in which Money worries and anxiety can affect their spouse in the bedroom.

Various studies on "financial infidelity" indicate that anywhere from one-third to one-half of all couples lie to each other about their finances. One in ten spouses may have hidden bank accounts. According to survey results by CESI Debt Solutions, a nonprofit debt management company, roughly 20 percent of spouses use a secret credit card to make hidden purchases. About a third admit they have hidden some purchases from their spouse. Paradoxically, however, most people rank being honest about Money as equally important with remaining sexually faithful. As one survey site's editor, Martin Wolk, says, "It's one thing to fib about a new pair of shoes, but keeping serious money secrets from one another—about problems with debt or spending—can be a recipe for disaster."

Many people fear that financial infidelity can lead to sex outside the marriage or that Money secrets may themselves be indicators of sexual secrets. More than any other factor, intimacy in marriage is based on trust. In essence, if you cheat your partner in an intimate relationship, you are cheating yourself. So, during times of Money stress, when one spouse may feel more tempted to lie to the other, couples need to consciously spend more time maintaining the foundations of their marriage then usual.

CHILDREN AND MONEY

Family secrets can take a particular psychic toll on children. Our unconscious attitudes toward Money, our Midas Complexes, affect them as well. Parents with or without Money leave specific and detectable influences on their children. As parents or educators, we want to carefully consider what to teach children about Money and how to avoid mistakes that can turn a child into a Money addict or induce other forms of Money madness later in life.

In my past relationship, we gave my stepdaughter a checking account with a modest balance when she turned sixteen. We were trying to prepare her for independent living in a few years. Some weeks later a number of overdraft notices arrived in the mail with considerable bank fees attached. When we asked her what happened, she replied, "That can't be true, I still have six checks left." Obviously, we had not done such a great job of educating her at the time.

Parents periodically ask me how much I think they should give their children for a weekly allowance. For most middle-class families, roughly half a dollar for each year of age is a reasonable guideline at this time. This adjusts, naturally, according to economic status and regional differences but it is a good average for setting a standard, which is often very hard for parents to figure out. Regular conversations about the real cost of things can go a long way to inculcate Money literacy in our children. My mother used to calculate the per-person cost of each meal she put on the table. Although this occasionally annoyed me, by the time I was a teenager living on my own, I was fully capable of maintaining and living within my own household budget.

Optimism toward Money tends to breed a more relaxed and hopeful attitude toward life in children. The economic strain we feel, and fears we express, also influence our children's psychology. Parents with increased financial pressure often show more depression and may even feel less connected with their children during those times. Children report it is not so much reduced spending that bothers them as much as it is the fact that their parents are more distracted, have less leisure time, and are less easygoing or fun-loving when they are under financial strain. Children, in turn, can then show less evidence of supportive behaviors toward others, becoming less generous and positive toward them.

Velma McBride Murry, a professor at Vanderbilt University, notes, "If you entered [the downturn] having an increased vulnerability to depression and anxiety, economic strain elevates it, or sets it off to where you are more likely to experience greater devastation than people who are much more mentally stable." In my experience, family therapy can go a long way to help ameliorate the effects economic instability often has on families. It can assist spouses and children in better understanding how family finances are impacting their mental health and emotional well-being. Secrets tend to be less helpful. Kids often sense something is wrong but do not know what it is. In many cases, what they start to imagine is worse than what is actually occurring. So, more openly talking about budgets, losses, and gains can help normalize family dynamics rather than, as many seem to fear, worsen psychological states.

Beyond the need for couples to practice regular open and frank discussions about finance, it is also essential for extended families as a whole to have

74

similar talks about their intergenerational issues. So often there is a great deal of consternation and needless suffering after the death of elders that could have been ameliorated by whole family meetings while all stakeholders were still alive. Compassionate estate planning is much more than just having great instruments drawn by good attorneys. While that is important, so is giving everyone an opportunity to discuss inheritance and other family finance issues while everyone is still alive, even though such dialogues can feel awkward and uncomfortable at first.

THE FOUR GENERATIONS

A few years ago, a large family that was trying to sort out its monetary issues asked me to provide an intensive consultation with three generations of the family gathered at a private retreat. My job was to help them heal a deep rift concerning inheritance of the family business. The now deceased parents of the oldest generation present had started the family business in the nineteenth century. It grew steadily and they groomed their three children to take over. Those three, now in their sixties and seventies, had grown the business into a corporation. They dedicated their entire lives to it. Now they longed to retire. Just as their parents had done, they wished for their own children, who were in their thirties and forties, to take over the business.

They did not want to trust their heritage to outside management. They felt that since their children and grandchildren (the fourth generation) had benefited from the significant wealth the business had created, it was time for the children to put aside other pursuits and take over the business, just as they had done. There was only one problem: not one of the seven children wanted to run the business. In fact, none of them wished to even work in the business. This troubled, even insulted two of the three second-generation parents. The other, the eldest and president, was more relaxed about the situation. He had, most of all, always wanted for the children to be happy.

As a first step, the parents all needed to understand right away that their offspring were no longer children. Even though none of them ran a large business the way the first and second generation had, they had legitimate lives of their own. Five of the seven had pursued higher educations. One was a teacher, and another had a small ranch where she bred horses. All had generous preinheritance gifts and so none really *had* to work. Nevertheless, all but one of the third generation did have occupations, which they valued. One significant feature of this group was that they all had children of their own, ranging from a newborn to those in their late teens and early twenties.

The whole family of twenty-two was present at this gathering, and they were a close-knit group. There were, however, some deep-seated resentments. These feelings had simmered for years and were finally coming to a head as the parents announced their impending retirement. Through the course of the discussions, it became increasingly clear that none of the third generation wanted to step up and run the company. They weren't really businesspeople and they enjoyed the lives they had. One young man in the fourth generation showed interest. He was really too young to take the helm of this multistate merchandising group, however, and the parents wanted to step down in the following year.

The other large issue was inheritance. By virtue of previous marriages in the first and second generations, and other complex issues of the past, each member of the second and third generations did not have equal shares in the company. This had created some tensions among the siblings and cousins for many years. We discussed these issues at length.

Many in the third generation were unhappy that their parents had spent so much of their lives running the business. They regretted that they were not there for them in personal ways, as they grew up with tutors and nannies while their parents toiled twelve hours a day, six days a week except for Christmas and two weeks in the summer. Several of the parents felt their children were ungrateful for the privileged lives they had created for them. One of the second generation, a now divorced mother with three children, talked about how she could think of nothing more important or delightful than spending as much time as possible with her children, going so far as to homeschool them. Her mother pointed out that was only possible for her because of her trust fund.

This was a profound moment in the dialogue. What was emerging was a generational difference in values. Most significantly, the members of the third generation had missed and still missed life with their parents. Apparently, this annual retreat was one of the only times of the year when most of the family saw one another. Almost to a person they longed to spend more time together.

Then Jacob, a fifteen-year-old in the fourth generation, asked, "If the business were sold, what would the smallest family share amount to?" In fact, all knew that his parents would be the recipients of the smallest share.

Their grandfather did some quick calculations on a paper napkin—"Well, with taxes and after all the smoke cleared, we should be able to walk away with about 350 million dollars. That means your family would receive around seventeen and a half million." That just hung in the air for while.

While all knew they had wealth, up until this moment, none of the younger generation realized just how large the estate was. The parent's generation had played their cards pretty close to their vests. But my contract for working with them to help solve their family conundrum was to create an atmosphere in which there would be no secrets, at least to the extent that the telling of any secret was not significantly harmful.

This $350 million, of course, was just the share of their inheritance that was in the company. The second generation also had assets outside the company, which, to varying degrees, could also pass on to their children after death. In addition, the grandparents had set up trusts for all the children. They were already comfortable, though not living lavishly.

"So why don't we just sell the thing and all enjoy the rest of our lives together?" Jacob asked.

This was a shocking and patently brilliant solution. However, it violated the basic precepts of the first generation that had felt they had created a legacy in the business for their children. The second generation had dedi-cated themselves to that dream to the exclusion of developing their other talents and, at times, even sacrificing the joy of family life with their chil-dren. The second generation felt that to sell would be to betray the mem-ory of the first generation. The third generation repeated their unwavering unwillingness to become businesspeople. They wanted to enjoy the rich-ness of life that already had been created for them and that they in turn had created for their own children. It made sense, but the family remained at loggerheads. They were stuck.

What was the sticking point? All the discord had made the older genera-tion feel unappreciated for the sacrifices that they and their own parents had made. So, we spent some time going around the circle, with each of the third and fourth generations speaking about what they loved and admired about the first and second generations. In that spirit of love and valuing, the way was clear. The substance of their message was, "Mom and Dad you created something wonderful for us and all who will follow. You have done enough and now we want you to have more fun with your own lives and to be a greater part of ours."

As I changed the direction of the circle and the second generation shared their love and appreciation of the third and fourth generations, they clearly stated that what they wanted most of all was for their children to be happy. In the following months, the elders sold the company for a little more than the grandfather, George, had estimated. I later learned from George that this outcome was what he had always wanted. He knew that none of the younger generation was interested and, more troubling in his opinion, none of them was really capable of running the company. He regarded this as his own *mistake* in encouraging them all—his children, nieces, and nephews—to get the education that he never had the opportunity to pursue. This was a good outcome, but it could have gone quite differently had the family never found the courage to hold an open, honest forum in which they could face the deep, long term issues of their collective issues with the family wealth. I need not detail the counterpoint. The daily media are full of the sordid tales of families torn apart by their inheritance disputes once the primary wealth holder passes on.

SHAMEFUL MONEY SECRETS

One of the exercises I often utilize in my Midas seminars involves exposing long-held Money secrets in the service of depotentiating the psychological charge such hidden memories can carry. I ask the participants to write on a small piece of paper the worst, most embarrassing, difficult, disturbing, or shameful thing they have ever done for Money. They then put the folded paper into a basket.

We sit in a circle. The basket goes around the silent room from person to person, each in turn adding his or her revelation to the growing harvest of long-held secrets or simply passing it to the next person. We do not put anyone on the spot, and participants can always opt out. The invitation is an opportunity, not an obligation. Those who decline to add a note simply do not read one at the next stage. There is often great value in simply bearing witness to others. After the participants fill the basket with folded papers, it goes around again. Once all participants who wished to do so have withdrawn a secret from the basket, they take turns reading the notes aloud. The mood is usually somewhat anxious. Many people have buried these stories for years, some for decades.

Discussion then follows in which the group tries to compassionately imagine what issues may have precipitated the act, while the note's author has the opportunity to listen into the conversation with anonymity. In some cases, the authors then come forth and reveal themselves, to bring their own lived experience into the discussion. Either way, the results are often personally liberating. Following are samples from several workshops:

> When I was a teenager I was really upset one day over something I do not even remember now. I went into a drug store, put on an expensive pair of sunglasses, and then just walked out with them as if I had been wearing them the whole time. I remember how exhilarated I felt. Whatever ways I felt that life had been shortchanging me suddenly felt rectified. I felt I had some payback and had somehow taken control of my life. Many years later, I became a small business owner. I have always felt bad for that storeowner and all the other hardworking merchants who have to guard against teenagers and other petty thieves like me.

I stole money out of my mother's purse when I was a child. When she confronted me, I lied. She then blamed my sister, who also denied it. However, I was such a convincing liar she suspected that it was my sister. My sister hated me for that for many years.

When I was in my early twenties, I worked as a prostitute for about two years. I was desperate. I had two abortions then. Today I am married to a very successful and respected art dealer. I have never told him about this and fear that if he knew he would be disgusted and think I had cheated and lied to him about my real past.

I sold drugs when I was in high school and in college. Now, I am in an internship at a drug-counseling center and am seeing real lives destroyed by drugs. I have a lot to account for.

I cheated on my taxes and have worried for years that the IRS will find out and arrest me or fine me more than I can bear.

I went to law school for three years because I was afraid my father would disinherit me if I did not do as he wished. I never took the bar exam and am finally doing what I wanted to do with my life. All those years I hated studying the law but did it anyway...for the money.

I worked in Sacramento as an aide to a state senator. I handed over envelopes of cash to designated bag men in elevators, underground parking lots, and once in the back row of a daytime porno movie theater. On one level, the whole thing felt exciting—sort of like a movie. On another, and more lasting, it felt sleazy. Even though I played a small role, I had a hand in perpetuating government corruption.

I married a woman because she had money. I liked her, but I was not in love. Honestly, I was more attracted to her money than I was to her. After a few years, I could not have sex with her anymore. We spent many years in a somewhat loveless arrangement. I feel like I sold a large part of my soul for her money.

I lied extensively on a loan application to get a mortgage. I made up tax returns, created a phony business with a real phone number and paid a person to answer it to verify phony income. Later I had to default on the loan and lost the house. In effect, I robbed a bank with pen and paper.

I never confronted my mother about her alcoholism because I was afraid she would cut me off financially and remove me from her will if I did.

I let my husband ruin my credit with business deals that I knew were deceitful but I was too afraid of rejection and his anger to say no.

We read slowly, with pauses. The looks on people's faces are profound, serious, and intent. We continue until all have had a chance to speak:

I stole drugs out of the medicine cabinet at my grandparent's house and sold them to other kids at school.

I stole a valuable diamond ring out of a jewelry box when my stepmother passed away. She did not designate me in her will. Her estate went to her birth children, and for reasons of childhood resentments I stole a valuable part of their estate to get even with them somehow.

I faked my résumé to get a good-paying job for which I was basically unqualified.

I stole books out the bookstore this quarter. I was so mad that these textbooks were so expensive on top of our huge tuition."

I was driving a cab and someone left her purse in it. There was a lot of money in the wallet. I dropped the purse in a mailbox but kept the money.

I padded my household expenses to take money from my husband that I spent on frivolous things.

I shoplifted clothing that I did not need and which I could have afforded to pay for.

I spent money on drugs while my family was not even getting their basic needs met.

After receiving a small inheritance I lost the entire amount gambling in Las Vegas trying to parlay it into a lot more.

When I was a teenager I got stranded at a party one night without a ride home. At two in the morning, I called a cab. I told the driver that I had no money on me and that when we got home my parents would pay him. I directed him to a house a block away from my house. I told him I had to go around through the back door and would be right back with the money. When out of sight, I vaulted the fence in the backyard and then another behind my house. All I proved was that you can take advantage of an honest person with a good lie. I hope the generous tips I now hand out to drivers will pay it back in some sort of indirect way.

I traded sex for money with men. I also manipulated men to buy me expensive gifts with the subtle promise of giving them sex if they did it. Many times, I failed to deliver my part of the bargain and felt pretty good about myself for tricking them out of their money.

In almost every group I have hosted over the years, among the many provocative secrets revealed, at least one and sometimes several women admit to having committed acts of prostitution. Occasionally a man will also raise this revelation, usually from his youth. In the United States, over a million girls and women along with tens of thousands of boys and young men will trade sex for Money at some point in their lives. Most of us will engage in some fairly atypical behaviors when faced with hunger, cold, lack of shelter, addiction or danger. There is no shame in this. However, many people carry deep underground currents of guilt around past devil's bargains they have made in order to survive. This is particularly acute for many who have traded sex for Money. Moreover, many people who would never enter the sex trade feel similar shame about more prosocial arrangements they've made to bargain their intimacy for another's wealth and protection in intimate partnerships.

The discussions that follow our basket of secrets are inevitably poignant and potent. We try to understand what might have driven seemingly honest, intelligent, and caring people to commit these crimes and moral violations. Treatment for Midas Complex wounds requires recovery from the traumas induced by self-betrayals undertaken in the name of economic and social survival. Opening the bag of Money secrets in a safe container, with a private counselor or compassionate group, can go along way to ameliorating the long-held shame many of us carry around our past shadowy bargains. One of the biggest long-term bargains most of us make is an agreement to sell our time and talent for Money—our jobs.

CAUTION: MONEY AT WORK

Buddhist teacher and author Stephen Levine has spent decades working to help people more consciously confront death and dying. He recently commented that one of the top three regrets people expressed at the end of life was working in a job just for the Money instead of doing what they loved. The other two were staying in a marriage they should have left and not having had more fun in life. Various surveys of job and life satisfaction indicate that as many as 80 percent of Americans work at jobs they dislike.

Human motivation theory reveals that Money is a prime motivator of human behavior, perhaps the most powerful behavior-affecting force in the world today. John D. Rockefeller once commented, "I know of nothing more despicable and pathetic than a man who devotes all the hours of the waking day to the making of money for money's sake." Money appears to be as powerful an influence as fear of abandonment, injury, and, in some cases, even the fear of death. The risks and rewards of following a calling or vocation versus getting and maintaining a job are a difficult calculus for many. At the end of life, however, very few people say, "I wish I had made more Money." A visit to any graveyard in the world gives stark and poignant commentary on what was really important to all—their relationships—who loved whom and who is missed; not what they built, owned, or had in the bank.

Some time ago, a researcher named Schwab reportedly conducted an experiment on Money as a motivator of human behavior. He asked his subjects to hang from a horizontal bar as long as they possibly could without letting go. He timed them with a stopwatch and found the average time they could endure the task was about forty-five seconds. Then he threw at them all the different techniques that psychology knew could enhance human performance. These were interventions such as suggestion, motivational coaching, (i.e., "You can do it if you really try"), visualizing, and hypnosis. Coaches use similar techniques to help athletes reach their full potential. The use of these psychological techniques for reaching the upper limits of performance increased the average hang time for participants to about seventy-five seconds, which is in itself pretty remarkable. Then he offered them Money if they could increase their time on the bar even further. The reward, figuring in inflation, would roughly equal fifty dollars today. With this additional motivation, participants increased their average time to 110 seconds. This average was more than double their first attempt, in which they had tried their very best to hang on as long as they could.

This experiment merely underscores something that those who utilize human labor for their own profit have known for centuries: Money is a prime, and in many circumstances, the most prime motivator of performance and the capacity to endure difficulty or hardship. The hang time that the participants in this experiment achieved is particularly significant due to the fact that 110 seconds represents the absolute limit of time that most people can hang on to a bar, rope, ledge, or other precipice, even when the consequence of letting go will result in their death. In fact, the longest recorded time for such a feat by a trained athlete is merely 135 seconds. So, in this one circumstance, one could say that fifty bucks represents a power of human motivation roughly equivalent to the consequence of sudden death for failure. It is little wonder that so many of us feel anxious at our jobs.

Money affects people of all races and cultures across the full spectrum of economic and social status. The ways we choose to make Money often have a significant effect on both our personal sense of identity and the ways others perceive us. The initial social query, "So, what do you do?" is generally not expressing curiosity about our hobbies. Implicit in that query is, "How do you make your Money?" We might try asking a new acquaintance something like, "So what is exciting in your life right now?" or, "What are you currently most passionate about?" That answer might not say much about someone's economic status, but it will say a lot about him or her.

When we reply to the "What do you do?" question with, "I am a barber," "I am a baker," or "I am the CEO of a multinational corporation," it appears to convey a great deal to the others about our education, values, social standing, and economic status. They then may feel that they know roughly where we operate within the socioeconomic hierarchy and, for many, a whole pattern of mostly unconscious social calculations proceed from there.

Some people with seemingly successful careers wind up in my psychological consulting room concerned about their so-called workaholism, overworking to the degree that they are trading their quality of life to make more Money than needed. This disorder often includes growing alcohol and drug abuse, depression and anxiety, failing health, alienated children, and estranged spouses. The workplace is clearly another arena in which the Midas Complex captures people. Many of us question just how we can free ourselves from unhealthy relationships to work without winding up impoverished or socially isolated. It is possible to make a living and make a good life at the same time; however, it requires some critical reflection on the values put forth to workers by some leaders of our economic institutions who value economic productivity above worker's health. Conversely, some organizations today are radically dedicated to their workers' mental and physical well-being. Chapter 8 discusses some of the values that make such organizations different from the majority of workplaces today.

Many psychotherapists, I am sad to say, unconsciously collude with some employers' attempts to mine the libido of their workers at a nonsustainable rate. Often the aim of psychotherapy is to return someone to a previously higher level of functioning. When this is undertaken solely so that clients can resume work at jobs they despise and/or jobs that continually demand they sacrifice their physical and mental well-being as the price of continuing employment, the therapist is then in primary service to the organization. That is not entirely a bad thing as long as it is clear that serving those institutions is the primary aim of the therapy and in the best interests of the clients. For some of us, learning how to function better at a job we hate is necessary to our immediate survival. I believe, however, that the central goal of psychology should be to aid the souls of the clients—their deep inner lives. If one of the goals of therapy is to help free clients from whatever sort of bondage holds them fast, then serving this goal can bring therapists into a more critical, even confrontational relationship with the dominant economic ethos of our culture and our era.

In my view, psychotherapy is ultimately a radically subversive undertaking, a process of liberation in which clients systematically free themselves from the internal and external structures that prevent them from becoming whole people. From this point of view, symptoms generated in relationship to one's work must be examined as a call to deeper reflection about the real reasons, beyond obvious economic necessities, that one has chosen their particular line of work. This inquiry then asks how they might reimagine their lives in a way that brings greater satisfaction and fulfillment. Through understanding the full range of psychopathology associated with Money, we open the doorway to various ways to recover from the miseries that Money traumas can bring.

MONEY MADNESS

A wide range of diagnosable psychopathologies is associated with the Midas Complex. A variety of approaches can also help ameliorate the depression, anxiety, obsessive behaviors, and other ills that an out-of-balance Money relationship can precipitate. Money and self-image are often profoundly linked. Some years ago, the government indicted a successful American businessman as an international narcotics trafficker. His legitimate business produced a seven-figure income for his family. He owned an estate in Malibu. The house contained a multimillion-dollar art collection and other valuable artifacts. He was married to a lovely, devoted woman, and had three school-age children. The local community respected him as a patron of the arts and various cultural programs. He achieved all this before engaging in any criminal activities.

When a friend of mine asked him why he put his beautiful life at such risk when he was already a very wealthy man, he replied,

> Yes, it is true I am rich by most people's standards. But, as you know, there are many multimillionaires in this neighborhood; anyone who owns a home on this beach is worth a few million, at least. But, some of my friends and my wife's closest associates are *cien*-millionaires. They have hundreds of millions of dollars and are in another class altogether. They can afford 200 foot–long yachts, a string of polo ponies and, more importantly, they have access to the highest levels of political and cultural influence. I felt socially inferior to them and wanted desperately to be able to comfortably occupy the same realm of influence and international social spheres that they inhabited.

His life as he knew it was ruined by the scandal and legal battles that ensued, although he regrouped and managed to live a more simple, comfortable, largely anonymous but more fulfilling life. He got over his Midas Complex the hard way.

Money creates a range of psychological traumas for many people, through either its presence or its absence in their lives. The things people do to acquire it and the feelings they have when they lose it result in varying degrees of trauma. When we are traumatized by the impact of a strong stimulus in our lives, certain neurological and chemical reactions take place that can create symptoms of anxiety, depression, and even the distortions of reality that accompany psychosis. Money madness is a real and potentially dangerous disease. When Money pressures are too great, people can feel driven to self-destructive acts and violence toward others. Money madness can drive people to drink, use drugs, engage in sexual obsessions, and take other high-risk flights from reality.

Throughout history, there has been a range of commentary about the deep psychology of Money. From Jesus's parables concerning homage paid to the soul versus the state, to Sigmund Freud's analysis of links between filthy lucre and feces, there is no shortage of opinions. One of the many metaphors that hitchhike along with Money is the internalized connection many people make between finance and health. Like blood in our bodies, Money *circulates* in our economy. When it does not circulate, financial reporters say that the economy is *stagnant* and that institutions are *starving* for credit or *strangled* without it.

Parallels between Money and mental health readily emerge through metaphors that effortlessly glide from one domain to the other, such as inflation, depression, mania, value, allure, debt, obligation, uncertainty, worth, deficit, loss, gain, attachment, promise, confidence, stability, failure, and trust. Moreover, many people somaticize their emotional relationship to Money, equating it with biological tropes and even creating actual physical symptoms. Lose your wallet and you might feel sick to your stomach. New capital is an *infusion*, companies and economies are *healthy* or *sick*, currencies are *weak* or *strong*, family finances can be *flush* or *depleted*.

When our retirement fund suddenly loses half its value, we might feel a pain in our hearts or dizziness in our heads. A sudden gain may leave us breathless. We associate our Money with physical and mental health and suffer physical and mental maladies in reaction to the state of our Money affairs. Even good fortune can cause tremendous stress, as was seen in a number of so-called dot-com millionaires a few decades ago. They suffered from what came to be called *sudden wealth syndrome*. This was followed years later, for many more people, by *sudden loss syndrome*. Both take a toll.

Money, however, is not really medicine or nutrition. It cannot heal us or even make us very happy for long. Money as a substance is inert. It will do what we tell it to do. Money as a psychological complex, however, is deeply embedded in our unconscious. It can just as easily control us as we can control it. As was discussed in chapter 2 regarding happiness, we can think that if some Money made us feel better and enhanced our quality of life that more of it will give us even more good feelings. One drink feels good, three are even better; but ten make us sick. With drugs, a little cures or eases pain, a little more kills.

So if Money cannot really buy happiness, how is that some people can actually become addicted to it? In short, the answer is that Money can and does behave like a drug in many ways. Most people can have glass of wine with dinner and not have the desire to drain the rest of the bottle and then open another until they pass out. Alcoholics, however, cannot resist. Money does not have a direct chemical affect on our nervous systems in the same way that alcohol, cocaine, or heroin does. However, the emotions associated with its acquisition and loss can create a complex cascade of hormonal and endocrinological activity that mimic the sorts of responses associated with addictive substances. As the actor Robin Williams once said, "Cocaine is God's way of saying you're making too much money." When we get excited, fearful, angry or sad around Money, the same sorts of psychological and biological responses associated with those emotions can come into play. In addition, we can get habituated to those responses and then start craving them. This may actually create a quasi-biological basis for Money addictions.

An anonymous text, often misattributed to the Dalai Lama asks, "What surprises you the most about humanity?" The reply is, "Man.... Because he sacrifices his health in order to make money. Then he sacrifices money to recuperate his health. And then he is so anxious about the future that he does not enjoy the present; the result being that he does not live in the present or the future; he lives as if he is never going to die, and then dies having never really lived." Two thousand years ago, the Roman philosopher Seneca similarly observed that many people are so busy with their roles and possessions that they lose the simple joys and meaning of life. As someone who lived among the wealthiest and most famous people of his era, he noted, "You can hear many who are burdened with great prosperity sometimes cry out, 'I have no chance to live.'"

Although we all have aspects of our identity defined by Money, most of us also embrace values that transcend our economic status. Money-mad people feel their changing financial fortunes in their bodies and their souls.

Shifting bank balances do not overly define Money-sane people. For those of us under the spell of the Midas Complex, however, the amount or flow of Money in our lives deeply affects our personal sense of well-being and identity as whole. Sadly, most of us are in this latter category. Few of us have achieved a state of wholeness around Money to the degree that our changing fortunes do not affect our state of mind. Yet our capacity to understand ourselves as something more than our income or our wealth is one of the things that keeps human culture whole.

Freud talked about this life-affirming quality as eros—the capacity to love. People lacking eros exist without an inner richness; it is almost as if they lack a soul. Jungian psychologist Adolf Guggenbühl-Craig keenly notes, "Those who cannot love want power." Since most people equate Money with power, another way to understand this would be to note that those who cannot fully love might want more Money as a substitute. However, Money itself can never fill the emptiness that drives Money-mad people into their quests for more and more. The roots of this condition are complex, but its symptoms are quite clear and understandable.

The more Money represents a person's unfulfilled needs and desires, the less it satisfies them. The less it satisfies, the more likely one is to become addicted to Money as a symbol of all that is missing in life. Then, a profound fantasy may be generated: that all the missing elements in life can become supplied through an increase in Money. Once this idea takes hold in a person's psyche, the road to psychological ruin is well paved.

MIDAS FANTASY AND THE LOTTERY

For most people Money can fuel the production of fantasy more intensely than any other object or idea. It is an equal opportunity stimulant of the emotional and psychological dimensions of the self. Because of its powerfully protean nature, Money can be converted into almost anything else.

Conversely, of course, people can convert almost anything into Money just as Midas converted all his real wealth into gold—a protean fantasy. Everything, it is often said, has its price. Wherever we are on the economic scale, we make regular conversion calculations throughout our day; can we afford this or that?

What fuels the billions spent on lotteries throughout the world each year and billions more spent in casinos and other gambling venues? The fantasy of acquiring Big Money is a major driving factor by which gambling establishments separate us from our hard-earned and limited supplies of Money. At one end of the economic spectrum there is a highly leveraged play in the stock or commodities markets—at the other end is a scratch-off lottery ticket purchased at the local convenience store.

Once mostly the province of the underground gambling world—the numbers racket—the majority of the states today have some form of a lottery. Annual lottery expenditures in the United States are roughly $60 billion. A study by the Commission on Thrift reports that households making less than $13,000 per year spend 9 percent of their income on lotteries, while households making $130,000 spend merely 0.3 percent. For the poor, lottery spending is often at the expense of food and other necessities.

Average spending on lotteries is about $525 per year in the United States, more than the average spent on reading materials or movies. If a lottery player instead invested this much in the stock market, over time he or she would likely have a significant nest egg. On average, the stock market returns 800 percent more than the average lottery, which only returns about half of what it takes in. In chapter 8, I discuss how some of the poorest people in the world are successfully investing their way out of abject poverty through pooling very tiny sums as a group.

The National Gambling Impact Study Commission finds that those with the least education spend the most on lotteries. One significant factor along the economic spectrum is the fact that the lower one is in the socioeconomic sector the greater proportion of wealth one is likely to spend on the lottery. In other words, lotteries are designed to attract people who lack other options for wealth accumulation or perhaps just have never had the opportunity to learn statistics. Lottery organizations exploit the psychology of the poor, who are longing for the relief from suffering that they imagine wealth can bring.

GAMBLING WITH THEIR LIVES

Although lotteries take their toll on family finances, few lottery players wind up in treatment after destroying their wealth, health, and relationships. Gambling addicts do, however. Gambling addiction is perhaps the most obvious and easy to understand of Money addictions. The gambling industry has grown dramatically over the last few decades. Once more of an underground or side pocket of American culture, it is now widespread and socially accepted in most circles. With forty-eight states now having some form of legalized gambling, about 80 percent of US adults have gambled in the past year, spending over $70 billion. This is more than the amount spent on movie tickets, spectator sports events, vacation cruises, recorded music, and theme park admissions. Illegal gambling accounts for untold increased amounts. It is likely in the billions. In 1978, there were no US casinos outside Las Vegas. Now there are over 260 casinos nationwide on Indian reservations alone.

The majority of cash spent at casinos is withdrawn from ATMs, either from personal accounts or as cash advances from credit cards. Internet gambling has created a completely new venue for people to gamble from the privacy of their home.

The Internet has over a hundred sports gambling sites alone. Many other new forms of virtual gambling are emerging as online gambling proliferates at exponential rates, roughly doubling each year in the last decade or so.

New technologies are trying to bring slots and other games of chance to the Internet as poker and other online multiplayer games proliferate. Many sports bars are attempting to add Internet portals for customers to play in areas where on-site gambling would otherwise be illegal. The American Psychological Association speculates that the Internet alone could be as addictive as alcohol, drugs, and gambling. Increasing numbers of interactive video game players are becoming addicted to these games, trying to gain intangible virtual assets at the expense of real life. When we add real-life gambling to the mix, the Internet becomes a much more potently addictive phenomenon.

For many people, gambling is just a form of entertainment. They are like social drinkers who can go out to dinner, enjoy some fine wine, and then not even think about drinking the next day. Alcoholics cannot stop with one drink. Gambling addicts cannot stop with a single bet. The influence of alcohol and other addictive substances also fuels gambling behaviors. Those Las Vegas casinos do not keep giving free drinks to high spenders just to be generous hosts to their customers. They know that the more their customers drink, the less they will worry about loss, the more they will spend, and the more recklessly they will gamble.

The National Gambling Impact Study Commission estimates the annual cost to society of problem gambling at about $5 billion. By various estimates, as many as fifteen million people show some sign of gambling addiction. Most gambling addicts who wind up in our psychological consulting offices owe as much as $100,000 in gambling debt by the time they seek our help. Women, who represent a small minority of gambling addicts, tend to have debts closer to $20,000 when they realize that they need help. The divorce rate for pathological gamblers is roughly double that of nongamblers. Their suicide rate is twenty times higher. Two out of three gambling addicts wind up committing crimes to feed their "habit." Not surprisingly, crime rates often steadily begin to rise in a local radius after casinos open in areas were they were previously absent. By some reports, Atlantic City area crime rates doubled after casinos opened there.

Here are some key signs of gambling addiction:

- Gambling becomes more important than family, school or business.
- Turning to crime to support the gambling habit, often to the point of run-ins with police.
- Betting larger amounts on all forms of gambling than casual gamblers would.
- Gambling more frequently and spending more time gambling than casual gamblers.
- Using gambling to escape problems or relieve depression and often having wide mood swings.
- An inability to stop gambling regardless of winning, losing, or constant promises to stop.
- Being preoccupied with gambling and becoming restlessness or irritable if trying to stop.
- Using alcohol, sleep, or drugs to escape.
- Lying to family members or friends to hide the true level of gambling; impatience with family and friends.
- Asking others for Money to pay gambling debts, or borrowing against assets.
- Missing work and neglecting other responsibilities.
- Risking the stability of romantic relationships due to gambling.
- "Doubling down": trying to win back Money lost on gambling by betting even more.
- Having magical beliefs (despite statistics) that the winning streak will not stop.

MONEY ADDICTS

We can properly call the most common example of Midas madness an addiction to Money. It takes a variety of forms. The already mentioned obsessions with gambling are the most obvious. Less clear but equally pervasive are fixations on pursuits such as stock trading and other all-consuming, intensive "investment" activities *to the exclusion of relationships and health maintenance.* There are a number of common traits associated with Money addiction. Money addicts all think about and pursue Money to the exclusion of other healthy activities.

Money-seeking behaviors intrude on normal life and are in excess of what is reasonably required to satisfy one's true economic needs. In the Money addict, Money becomes an object of desire greater in significance than the needed goods it can purchase. Individuals with Money addictions are consumed with anxiety, and often suffer depression or engage in high-risk behaviors that would not be otherwise considered normal for a person simply seeking what Erich Fromm calls a "pleasant sufficiency of means."

First, there is an object of desire. Midas wanted more gold. Today it could be gold, clothing, the latest computer, a new car, a pile of cash, a pile of drugs, food or alcohol, winning the lottery, or even a new pair of sunglasses. The objects of desire all differ according to the psychological makeup of the addict. What is common to most Money addicts, however, is the feeling that precedes the longing for Money or the stuff it can buy. That feeling is usually a profound sense of emptiness. This can manifest as boredom, depression, low self-worth, restlessness, anxiety, and feelings of inadequacy. The fertile ground in which the Midas compulsions grow is a barren field in which inner riches, inner joy, and inner satisfaction with life have been lost.

As the section on the empty self in chapter 2 discussed, it feels terrible to experience oneself as empty. Therefore, the Money addict futilely tries to fill that emptiness with more and more and more. When spending or acquiring the object of desire, the addict shortly feels a greater sense of power and control. He or she might feel more attractive or vital when in possession of a new object or when experiencing the thrill of Money flowing in, even if that Money has been borrowed, sometimes with no intention to pay it back. The fact that the emptiness of the Money addict is bottomless illustrates the severity of this problem. No amount of stuff will ever fill that emptiness, just as no amount of alcohol ever fully satisfies an alcoholic.

The addict might feel sated for a moment by the latest acquisition or increase in income, but soon the emptiness returns like more bad weather after a short break in the storm. Most of us feel happy when we gain a windfall and disappointed when an unexpected expense comes our way. However, Money addicts' losses or gains significantly alter their moods, sometimes to a degree that the intensity of these feelings disables them. When gambling or spending they feel a rush, excitement and intensified enjoyment bordering on sexual pleasure and anxiety at the same time. Their senses seem heightened. They feel more alive.

Most of us think about Money from time to time, but Money addicts think about it much of the time, most of the time, or even all of the time. Money worries and concerns invade the addict's sleep and waking activities. These thoughts can be obsessive and intense. Having Money provides no immunity to these excessive worries; even people with significant wealth can suffer loss of peace of mind and intrusive thoughts about Money. Money addiction affects people at every level of the economic spectrum. Men are somewhat more likely to suffer from gambling addictions and women from shopping compulsions, but they affect both sexes in similar ways.

Money addicts' losses and gains significantly affect their behaviors. The rise and fall of economic success and failures can trigger other sorts of addictions as well. Difficulties and disappointments in daily life or relationships can also provoke Money binges—buying or stealing things that are beyond their means, even things they do not even need.

After a period of overspending—a binge—Money addicts often experience a period of remorse, sadness, shame, guilt, fearfulness, self recrimination, distress, feeling out of control, confusion, and disorientation. They may engage in kiting (borrowing from one account to pay the bills in another) and otherwise juggling accounts, creditors, credit cards, friends, relatives, and employers with advances on wages—just like drug addicts do to keep the flow of expensive substances flowing beyond their capacity to afford them.

Money addicts experience degradation in almost every aspect of their lives. Interpersonal relationships disintegrate, physical and mental health decline, and the capacity to enjoy life becomes as truncated as the day-to-day existence of a heroin addict. In the same way that a drug user develops tolerance to the substance that he or she is taking and thus requires more and more to achieve the desired effect, a Money addict can develop tolerance toward the amount of Money he or she has.

The result is that addicts feel there is never enough Money. They may begin lying to family members and friends about how they are making or losing Money and the amount of time they are spending on Money-focused pursuits. Money addicts often experience distortions of identity and reality in their relationship to Money. They can feel that their lives are out of control, and they may even engage in illegal activities—like the business man turned cocaine dealer mentioned above—to keep the flow of Money coming at the rate needed to fuel their addiction. Some Money addicts engage in hoarding behaviors while others spend fluidly, far beyond their means. Both poles of this miser/spendthrift continuum can create a great deal of dysfunction and suffering.

Many people possessed by Money addictions had childhoods in which one or another parent was absent. In many cases, there is a history of addiction in parents or other adult caretakers. They are more likely to say family members have rejected them in the past. Usually at least one parent or a sibling has had serious Money issues. These issues can become generational. Grandparents who suffered a severe economic crisis can so traumatize their children that they in turn pass the legacy of this crisis down to the grandchildren. Many of us heard stories of the world wars, the Great Depression, the Vietnam era, or other sorts of calamities that befell earlier generations, and these can shape our worldview of Money today.

Money addicts order things or services they know they will not be able to pay for when the bills come due. Our growing national debt crisis may be an extension of this problem as entire nations now purchase goods and services they cannot afford. The real estate bust of 2007–12 uncovered many people who bought houses they knew they lacked enough Money to pay for. While some buyers were merely naïve, others acquired property through falsifying documents and other types of fraud. Unrealistic expectations of a real estate market that would just keep expanding forever seduced many buyers. Most knew that only a continued run-up in value would allow them to eventually pay off a debt they could not otherwise cover; they rolled the dice anyway. Some never intended to pay, planning to walk away if things did not work out. This is just bank robbery with a pen. Those who could have remained hidden in an up market, were suddenly exposed by the harsh light of investigations, forensic accountants and the simple reality of not being able to pay their bills. As Warren Buffet once said, "You find out who is swimming naked when the tide goes out."

The following list does not describe all the features of Money addiction. Some of us who are not addicts may periodically do a few things on this list. However, if you see yourself or someone you know in a number of the features below, chances are good that a Money addiction is at work.

- Having unreasonable expectations of success with risky investments, despite the known odds.
- Believing that one is unusually lucky or deserving of some sort of special treatment or advantage not available to others.
- Spending beyond one's income; using credit cards and loans to excess.
- Having many Money secrets: hiding purchases from others or lying to them, hiding or destroying bills, avoiding balancing checkbooks, refusing to discuss finances or getting very upset when asked about them, avoiding creditors.
- Choosing intimate relationships based on a partner's economic status to the exclusion of other qualities needed to assure long-term relationship fulfillment and success; the same factor can affect choice of friends.
- Having many emotional issues about Money. This can include excessive worry, anxiety, compulsively checking account balances, arguing with others, trying to borrow from others to cover debts (so-called borrowing from Peter to pay Paul), and lending or borrowing Money in risky ways to create excitement.
- Feeling that spending is some sort of secret, risky, or taboo act.
- Suffering loss of basic services, loss of a car, or even loss of a place to live through eviction or foreclosure.

- Having trouble enjoying the simple pleasures of life that do not involve Money, as if nothing that is free can really have value or worth.
- Not valuing one's own worth, manifested in undervaluing one's time and/or undermining capacity for success through the proper valuation of services and expecting fair payment or quid pro quos for what one provides.
- Experiencing the quality of one's life diminished—rather than enhanced—by a relationship to Money.

Possession by the Midas Complex also shows up in behaviors that are symptoms of more diagnostically recognized disorders. In bipolar disorder, for example, formerly depressed persons having manic episodes often feel invulnerable and in possession of limitless energy. One of the ways this feeling often express itself is though unrestrained spending. People suffering from bipolar disease will start new businesses, convinced they have some fantastic new Money-worthy ideas. They will buy things they do not need, contract for services they cannot afford, even purchase real estate on a whim. They will consume as much as they can, running their credit cards to the limit and draining their savings. Kleptomaniacs represent yet another facet of the Midas Complex. They will steal things they do not need, often things that have no real value but that appear as objects of irresistible charm. Why else would famous actresses with millions steal clothing or jewelry from a store? For the rush, it seems.

TREATMENT AND RECOVERY FROM MONEY ADDICTIONS

Most people will buy three times as much with credit cards as they will with cash. Money addicts will spend even more. Credit card companies know this and make billions of dollars off the Midas Complex every year. Because we do not actually see the Money we spend, we do not really touch the power and taboos of the god present in the substance of Money itself.

Addicts will buy things with credit that they never would with cash. An easy intervention is to simply cut up their credit cards; have them pay cash for everything. Even so, Money addicts will feel uneasy without their cards so substitutes must be provided—a precious stone or other transitional object to hold in the pocket or purse to make up for the seemingly magical property of the missing silver, gold, or platinum card. They may feel somewhat lost, disempowered, or disorientated without a credit card in their pocket or purse. Moreover,

- Money addicts need someone they trust to whom they are willing to make themselves accountable. That means someone who will agree to oversee all spending: cash purchases, credit card use, loans, gambling, or any other sort of monetary exchange.
- Money addicts should stay away from sales, promotions, or any environment that generates shopping excitement. They should stick to buying essentials only and ask their ally to accompany them when they must make any large purchase.
- Money addicts must never borrow Money or contract for any services unless there is a clear plan and means to repay the debts without great sacrifice.
- Money addicts must keep accurate records of all expenditures, purchases, borrowing, or lending.
- Money addicts simply should not gamble. If they do (addicts can slip) they can prevent damage by only having a set amount of cash with them and no means to acquire more after a loss.
- We can understand Money addiction much in the same way as substance addictions and treat them in a similar manner.

Interventions with the "fiscally ill" often call for approaches similar to the twelve-step procedures that have proven efficacy with many substance addictions. The goal is something we might call *Money sobriety* or *Money sanity*. What is enough? How does one go about living a fiscally healthy life? These are essential questions for Money addicts. They must first realize that they have lost control of their lives and then learn how to go about regaining (or claiming for the first time) a sane, stable, productive, and more fulfilling relationship to Money.

Those who are collaterally damaged by Money-addicted family members often need treatment as well, just as the family members of addicts and alcoholics can benefit from the twelve-step approaches of Al-Anon. Victims of Money-addicts are not simply naive. Even the best clinically trained professionals can be taken in because Money addiction is, in many ways, often socially sanctioned in our Money-centered culture. In a culture that says a person cannot be too thin or too rich, hundreds of thousands of girls suffer from eating disorders, and millions of women and men suffer emotional and physical distress in their pursuit of wealth.

When the Nazis took power in Germany, many wealthy people suddenly lost everything. In *Man's Search for Meaning*, holocaust survivor Viktor E. Frankl notes, "We who lived in the concentration camps can remember the men who walked through the huts comforting others, giving away their last piece of bread. They may have been few in number, but they offer sufficient proof that everything can be taken from a man, but one thing: The last of his freedoms—To choose one's attitude in any given set of circumstances, to choose one's own way." Many others throughout history have lost their life savings, their status, and all their precious belongings yet nevertheless manage to create abundant, meaningful, happy, and rich lives.

It must be obvious to many readers that I also suffer from a fear of poverty. This work, like others, has been a process of facing fears. Joseph Campbell used to advise students, "Follow your bliss." As a writer and a professor who today now helps many students find their own writing voice, I have modified his admonition somewhat. Many of us lack sufficient bliss to follow. So I tell my graduate students today, "Follow your affect." It is wonderful if one can manifest creativity by following the flow of one's bliss, and I really wish that process could have worked for me. It never has. Following your affect means being true to the emotional currents flowing through you. For many of us that means following our sadness, disappointment in life, anger, outrage, insight, and even our fears.

The list below notes a few of the questions we often ask as we face our Money hopes and fears together in my Midas workshops. I encourage you to take a little time to make your own Midas inventory by addressing some of the following:

- How has Money disappointed me?
- In what ways has Money surprised me or changed my world?
- How did Money influence my parents?
- What differences did my mother and father have around Money?
- What do I wish my parents had taught me about Money?
- What is my biggest and most shameful Money secret?
- What do I want from Money and what do I really need?
- How much Money do I need to really be happy? How much is enough?
- What are ten fulfilling or fun things I have done that did not require Money?
- What do I want to teach my children or other loved ones about Money?
- What would I do if I won the lottery?
- What would I do if I lost all my Money? Who would stand by me, who would leave?
- What can I do today to move toward a saner and more fulfilling relationship with Money?
- What does my real prosperous life look like and how can I achieve it?

Despite whatever fiscal discipline one can muster and whatever Money sanity one can achieve, as an individual or in personal relationships, there are many other factors that impact our financial lives. This chapter has examined some of the ways the Midas Complex affects our inner lives and relationships. Chapter 4 looks at ways the culture we inhabit often directly challenges us in whatever attempts we make to achieve a balanced relationship with Money.

CHAPTER 4

LIVING ON BORROWED TIME IN TAXING SITUATIONS: THE DEATHS BY A THOUSAND CUTS

Midas Myth #4: *We can have everything we want right now.*
Reality: *Life has limits (and this is not a bad thing).*

MONEY HAS LEFT THE BUILDING

As was detailed in chapter 1, human society evolved for hundreds of thousands of years without Money. Unlike fire making, tool making, hunting, and gathering, Money has only been with us for a few thousand years. Like many inventions, Money started out as large and cumbersome. Herds of domestic animals and silos full of grain were logistically challenging to transport. The shear physical mass of monetary forms impeded commerce. Money constantly evolved from actual biological necessities of life in the form of food, other basic needs, materials, and tools, to various symbols that represented those necessities. Initially those symbols—coins, in particular—had precious metal in them, so they also possessed some sort of intrinsic value.

As human society grew in complexity and size, monetary symbols also become more concentrated in value and easier to transport, thus steadily increasing the pace of commerce. Paper Money was a significant invention that, once the printing press came along, allowed for the value of hundreds of tons of grain and thousands head of cattle to be represented by a single piece of paper. The most remarkable thing was that a simple piece of printed paper (or linen with silk and metallic threads, in the case of our own currency) could be exchanged for the biological necessities of life that it represented. In most cases, that is. Because there were times throughout the history of Money when the collective faith in the realizable value of paper currency collapsed. One example of this was during the American Revolution.

As was mentioned in chapter 1's discussion on inflation, Benjamin Franklin went to the king of England in 1766 to request permission for the colonies to print their own currency. Commerce based on English currency had become cumbersome for the dynamic and thriving local economies of early America. It took a long time for the clipper ships to sail across the Atlantic and return. This slow pace of banking did not suit the energetic pace of the colonists and, more important, it did not represent their growing sense of independence from the mother country. King George's absolute refusal to allow this act of fiscal self-determination was one of the key issues that led to a declaration of complete independence from England ten years later. The Boston Tea Party was a mere coda that, because of its dramatic nature, seized the historical imagination as a precipitating act. Desire for unfettered commerce, with or without taxation on tea, was actually the main engine driving the more visible forces of revolution.

A dilemma about how to finance the war then faced the American colonists. The new dollars they then created, the continentals, were fully independent of the well-established, trustworthy English pound and the various silver pieces of eight and gold coins in wide usage at the time. What backed the continentals? It was nothing more than faith in the revolution and the future hope of an independent political nation with its own national economy. The new army would now offer a farmer a pile of printed paper for his hogs and grain with the promise to exchange those notes for equal value after the war. Any provider or producer of goods who refused the new dollars risked being branded as a Tory, an antirevolutionary. Therefore, most people went along with the new currency even though many had their suspicions. After the continental collapsed at the war's end, as feared, Americans remained wary of paper Money for more than a century, preferring instead to conduct most commerce in gold.

Early US dollars were so-called yellow backs because gold backed them; people could exchange them for gold. The gold standard ended in 1933 when President Franklin D. Roosevelt outlawed private gold ownership except that of jewelry. In 1934 the US Gold Reserve Act demanded private citizens turn in their gold. The government then promptly raised the official price of gold from $20.67 to $35 per ounce. This created a huge profit-by-seizure for the government and a substantial devaluation of the dollar. Silver-backed bills replaced gold-backed ones. Then, in 1968, the government withdrew silver from coins and dollars. At that time, the silver in a one-ounce silver dollar coin was worth one dollar. The Money itself possessed the intrinsic worth of the precious metal.

When President Richard Nixon ended the direct convertibility of the dollar to gold in 1971, his act severed major world currencies from any real commodity, for the first time in Money's history. Gold has not been used to back any major economy since. We then made the transition to a "fiat currency" system, which allowed the government to print more Money than actually existed in the form of gold reserves. However, some people began calling for gold's return in response to the government's rampant printing of new paper currency subsequent to the Great Recession.

Today, silver and gold coins are no longer in circulation but are instead traded for their numismatic value or simply for the worth of their precious metal. In 2012, a face-value $1 silver coin was worth about $35, the same as an ounce of gold when President Nixon took the US off the gold standard. In 2012 gold traded above $1,900 per ounce then crashed back down the following year to below $1,200 as silver sank below $20 an ounce. Despite daily fluctuations, however, gold has largely kept pace with infation in ways that paper Money has failed to do. That is, $35 in cash, put into a box in 1971, is still only worth $35 and will buy a lot less today then it would have then.

The evolution of Money from biological and material necessities for survival, to precious metals and notes backed by those things of value, was gradual. It was an evolution from heavy and large materials to increasingly compact and light symbols of value. The more compact the Money is the faster it can move from place to place, and the more of it people can hide or secure in vaults. Once government eliminated precious commodities from the monetary system, abstraction and transformation took off at a breathtakingly rapid pace.

After a short time, many began to see cash itself as cumbersome. Governments, banks, and large wealth holders had used letters of credit or checks for centuries. Now these came to the common person. With the advent of widespread checking, cash became increasingly unneeded. As long as there was currency stored somewhere to back it up, people could easily make purchases large and small with a mere signature on a piece of paper. Checking increasingly facilitated the ease of commerce and rapid exchanges of capital from one place to another. It also took Money to a new level of abstraction: checks were a symbol for currency, which was a symbol for precious commodities, which was a symbol for biologically relevant supplies. Checks removed Money one step further from being something people actually needed for sustenance of life. They also increased the speed at which commerce could proceed. When people could use checks they no longer needed to count, transport, or protect large quantities of cash.

Then Money took a dramatic step into the unknown, irrevocably changing the nature of commerce worldwide, and having a dramatic and still rippling impact on the psychology of consumers. Along with the new technologies of psychological manipulation mentioned in chapter 2 came the invention of entirely new forms of Money in order to make consumption of more products ever easier. Society failed to head conservative economist Adam Smith, who warned in *The Wealth of Nations* that an economic orientation focused on growth can lead to "the endless pursuit of unnecessary things." The biggest step toward transferring a larger share of consumer savings into the hands of product providers and the creation of unprecedented levels of personal debt was the invention of the credit card.

CREDIT: IT TAKES THE WAITING OUT OF WANTING

Credit cards allowed the ordinary consumer to purchase goods with a promise to pay in the future instead of having to use cash now. Credit was not new, of course; large institutions used it for centuries before plastic cards were introduced. The local bar or store might run someone a tab, and mortgages were already a well-established institution for the often larger-than-cash-available purchase of a home. Credit cards threw the centuries-long gradual transformation of Money into high gear. The entire consumer society sped up dramatically, as if a lead foot dropped onto the gas pedal of retail merchandising.

One of the earliest campaigns to advertise the benefits of credit cards used the slogan, "It Takes the Waiting out of Wanting." This marked a dramatic shift in the Money psychology of American culture. For our first two centuries as a nation, concepts of thrift and living within one's means were predominant values. Lenders generally only gave loans and mortgages for a term of five years. They often required as much as 50 percent down payment. Up until the 1930s, people bought most homes with cash. Later, mortgage burning parties were a source of pride for many Americans as a ritual assertion that they no longer had any debt on their homes. Today, however, there is greater pride around the length, amount, and terms of a loan acquired allowing a home purchase far beyond the purchaser's real means. This was one of many changes in the psychology of Money that led to the Great Recession. Too many Americans were exuberant about how much Money the banks would let them borrow. Then they spent it.

Somehow, the decades of rising expectations, which began in the postwar prosperity of the 1950s, created a large cohort of Americans who began to believe they somehow deserved a lifestyle beyond their economic means. A pervasive illusion took root that home prices would continue to go up forever, showering unearned wealth on whoever could acquire a home. Unrestrained lenders exploited that mass fantasy by making it possible for almost anyone who could pick up a pen to acquire a mortgage. When home prices came down and credit got tight, millions walked away from their homes. Banks pushed many more residents into the street as home values dropped below their mortgage amounts.

The ideal of living close to your true economic center of gravity, so intrinsic to American culture in the past, seems to have noticeably eroded in the last generation. (I will discuss the effect of the securitization of mortgages as another new, radical, and dangerous form of Money in chapter 6). The point here, however, is to simply note the profound effect that credit cards have had on our psychology. It is easy to see how a generation of people who learned that they no longer had to save up and wait for what they wanted could become psychologically primed to feel that there was nothing really wrong with having a house that they could not afford—or anything else, for that matter. Why wait if they can have a dream house now, believing that the growing value will eventually create more equity to justify a mortgage leveraged beyond their true means? The fantasy of instant gratification is seductive. Advertising is deliberately so. The credit needed to acquire the advertised goods provides the intoxication. Suddenly almost anyone can "buy now and pay later." Easy credit was like rocket fuel for a national Midas Complex to take off.

Advertising for easy credit became a powerful, insidious force in changing the purchasing attitudes and mores of Americans. A sign on a bank once paradoxically read, "We can loan you enough money to get you completely out of debt." With the advent of credit cards, many people purchased goods they could not afford and increasingly acquired more debt. Then credit card debt itself became a commodity. Banks charged interest on the debt and, as such, it was in their best business interests to encourage people to take on unprecedented levels of debt through selling them the Money to realize their material dreams.

Before the government outlawed such practices in 1970, credit cards, most notably the BankAmericard, were mass-produced and mailed unsolicited to millions of people. Betty Furness, a special assistant to President Lyndon Johnson, said this practice was like "giving sugar to diabetics." Widespread credit problems resulted in the wake of banks sending out over one hundred million cards nationwide without the requisite credit applications that we so often receive in the mail today.

A recent television commercial typifies the metamessage that credit companies have been working to propagate through the media for years. There are a few variations of this theme. In one, a shopper enters a toy store during the Christmas shopping season. Everyone is happy. The shopping is virtually choreographic, with one customer juggling toys in the air and everyone ecstatically moving through the checkout line with a quickened, almost manic pace. Each purchaser moves through the line, rapidly swipes a credit card, and then passes through to go home with their purchases, and to experience, we imagine, even more joy in giving them to loved ones.

Then, one person in line takes out cash. The cheerful holiday musical soundtrack slows to a mournful dirge. All the shoppers and workers slow their movements, bending over like cheerful, helpful robots whose batteries have suddenly run out. Everything grinds to a stop and everyone in the whole tableau is suddenly soooo sad. Then, an attractive, young, wise shopper pulls out her credit card for the purchase and everything springs back to life with the music, the toys juggling, and so much joy. The metamessage: Cash is a drag, but credit is joyful. This ad proliferated at the depth of the Great Recession when many Americans lacked cash for holiday purchases. The credit companies were clearly saying, "You don't have to wait for the economy to improve to afford this." Not surprisingly, some psychologists point to the third Monday in January as the most depressing day of the year—when the holidays are over and the credit card bills begin to arrive.

Over the five decades since credit cards began to see widespread usage, banks have touted them as the answer to frustrated desire. Steadily and subtly, they have also simultaneously promoted a message that there is something inherently wrong with cash. As the above scenario and similar ads of its genre blatantly display, cash is slow, as wagonloads of grain and cattle herds once were. The ads promote an ethos that the joy of satisfaction should happen quickly. Of course, the advent of credit cards has also placed millions of consumers in a state of virtually never-ending debt. Today, three out of four American families have at least one credit card. Half of American families carry a credit card balance with an average debt of more than $7,000.

There are now more than nine hundred million credit cards in circulation. They facilitate about $1.5 trillion of annual consumer spending. A handful of banks extract a fee from every transaction. Recently, some retailers have been tacking on their own card use fee—on top of the card company's percentage. The interest charged is unregulated, resulting in rates that far exceed biblical admonitions against usury. Such exorbitant rates were previously matched only by corner loan sharks with whom the safety of one's kneecaps was uncertain.

Economists have well documented the links between our credit-indebted culture and a soaring national debt with a stagnant economy. The focus here, however, is on how the psychology of Money and indebtedness, by whatever means people acquire it, plays a big role in the degree of stress each individual suffers. Various "stress" surveys list debt as one of the most heavily weighted items on lists of culprits that can affect a person's mental and physical health. According to the National Violent Death Reporting System, roughly one in six American suicides appear to be linked to economic stressors.

For many, the induction into the culture of debt is starting earlier and earlier. Concerted campaigns on campuses nationwide, with credit fairs and many free products, have created a new youth culture of credit consumers. On college campuses, 70 percent of students with credit cards carry over $2,000 in debt. According to a 2009 survey by Sally Mae, one-half of college students have four or more cards. Only about one in five make regular payments. College credit card debt is rising right along with tuition and student loans.

Easy access to credit card debt for students merely greases the rails to the much larger burden of easily accumulated student loan debt. Total student loan debt now exceeds a trillion dollars. This is more than the total auto or credit card debt and is exceeded only by mortgage debt. America's economic failures have created a new debtor-class generation. My generation is not much better off. Various estimates indicate that Americans over sixty years of age still owe some $36 billion in student loans.

In 2010, the *New York Daily News* printed a story about a twenty-three-year-old woman who was a recent graduate of Northeastern University. Her website was soliciting donations to help her start paying down her $200,000 student loan debt, borrowed just to finance her bachelor's degree education. She said, "Monthly payments just for the private loans are currently $891 until next year when they increase to $1,600 for the following 20 years." This young person is facing a great deal of psychological stress for years to come. I imagine graduate school is out of the question for her and millions like her.

One of the things driving health care costs so high today is the considerable debt many medical students accumulate before they can start earning a living. Their often staggering six-figure debts forces many new doctors to choose more lucrative ways of practicing and are a factor driving up the cost of health care nationwide. Out of necessity, more new doctors must regard medicine more as a business than did the family doctors of earlier generations. Likely, many other altruistically minded students face mercenary choices after leaving school in debt.

MONEY STINKS

Credit card companies and banks make billions of dollars skimming interest and fees off credit transactions. Previously, those billions remained in purchaser's pockets and the hardworking providers of products who now have to pay a percentage to the credit mob to stay in business. Prepaid credit cards are now intentionally enrolling millions of people without bank accounts or credit as fee generators as well.

When I was a child, in South Philadelphia, my grandpa had to give a little envelope to Uncle Benny. He came around the pharmacy once a week to pick up the protection Money for his boss who kept the bad elements out of his neighborhood. Except grandpa's payment to the local mob boss was less than most merchants pay out to the credit companies today. Too many of their customers are paying for purchases with credit for them to opt out and just require cash. Few businesses can pull off a cash-only business anymore, though many offer incentives for cash. They have come to realize what an astonishing coup the credit card companies have pulled off—forcing consumers and merchants alike to pay a tithe with every transaction. In grandpa's day, people called the recipients of such unearned largess *organized crime*; today they are major banks.

People rarely use cash for significant purchases anymore. Who pays for a car or a home with cash today? That's right—drug dealers and others in the underworld. Well, immigrants also use more cash, but only because they are (1) denied credit and (2) may not have yet developed the new American psychology of buy now with credit and worry about how to pay for it later. As Anatole France ironically observed a hundred years ago, "It is only the poor who pay cash, and that not from virtue, but because they are refused credit."

Cash is dirty. It smells. It is of the underworld. It is gauche. The news media delight in showing large stacks of cash piled high next to drug packets sized in raids on major drug dealers. Cash is suspicious. Credit is clean, bright, and shiny. Notably, as our economy has become more dependent on oil, our new Money is actually composed of petroleum—the primary ingredient in plastics.

Credit card manufacturers carefully design their new cards to mimic objects of past value. We have silver, gold, emerald, diamond, palladium, and platinum cards. They gleam as if made of precious materials. Recently, many have embedded holographic images in them, creating a shimmering, jewel-like quality. A few very exclusive cards have actually incorporated precious metals and gems into their manufacture.

Aurum non aulit, is an old Latin expression regarding gold, meaning, "gold has no scent." Not only does gold, unlike cash, carry no olfactory traces of those who held it previously, it also leaves no trace of information, like cash and unlike credit cards. The financial underworld often uses transfers of gold or cash. They are thus mistrusted forms of commerce by governments that wish to tax financial transactions.

I believe the transformation from *cash is king* to *cash is unclean* has been deliberate. It was accomplished through decades of media manipulation and symbolic representations acting on our deep psychologies—the symbolic forming aspect of the imagination and the unconscious. Financial institutions and governments make nothing off cash transactions. Credit card companies do not get their 3 or 4 percent transaction fee and cannot charge their 12–22 percent interest on the balances. Moreover, the government has no way of tracking cash purchase and payments whereas checks and credit cards leave a clear trail for taxation purposes. Therefore, powerful vested interests wish us to use credit instruments instead of cash.

Cash is more central to the underground economy. The underground is much larger than drug dealers. Millions of workers and providers take wages in cash and cash for products when they can to avoid onerous taxation and fees. They are not unlike the early colonists who no longer wished to be subjected to England's taxation. Even some therapists I know prefer cash or checks for their services because they regard credit card indebtedness as antitherapeutic. Chapter 8 will discuss more alternatives to conventional monetary transactions.

ELECTRONIC ALCHEMY TURNS MONEY INTO LIGHT

As Money continued its frantic pace of transformation in late twentieth and early twenty-first centuries, it evolved into forms never previously conceived. Commodities became coins, coins became bills, bills spawned paper checks, checks gave way to plastic cards and then Money simply disappeared. As Adlai E. Stevenson once said, "A fool and his money are soon parted, but now it happens to everyone."

The advent of computers has increasingly electronicized monetary exchanges. It is now no longer necessary to even mail pieces of paper—whether check, note, cash, or credit card receipt—from one place to another. Monetary transactions began to happen at the speed of light. Billions of dollars now move around the globe every moment as electronic impulses moving through fiber optic wires. The record of their transfer is recorded in silicon chips located in a server safely hidden somewhere in a deep basement. Do you know where the chip is that has the record of whatever cash you may have given to your bank? It is not in the vault. The Money has vanished. The cash, gold, silver, and other goods have all been converted into light.

Metaphorically, this move from material to light over the last few thousand years parallels a widespread Western religious belief about the conversion of our material bodies and the earth itself into light. This theology holds that this process of purification will eventually result in rapture. The sufficiently purified will be lifted into heaven in pure light bodies while the rest of humanity suffers, caught up in the sensory tangles of the material plane. It is curious that in the face of the widespread ecological and environmental destruction that has followed in the wake of humanity's overconsumption of material and energy, most theologians have seemed relatively unconcerned. Perhaps it is because this conversion of material to energy to light is actually seen as God's plan. Those of us who think that life on earth is heaven enough and can even be paradise if lovingly cared for, the evaporation of the stuff of life into abstract lines of code on computer discs is symbolic of an alarming global trend.

In the year 2000, a number of people started getting concerned about this. As various Y2K disaster rumors proliferated various people thought, Hey, what happens to my Money if the computers go haywire? How can I prove it was even in the bank if there is no electronic record? Some withdrew their cash, which is a little funny because that cash has no real intrinsic value either. But it feels more tangible than an invisible etching of numbers on a glass chip in some unknown location. Many people will hold onto worthless currencies and stock certificates for defunct companies because they still "feel" valuable. The next evolution of electronic commerce is the transfer by mobile device. Purchasers facilitate a transfer of funds to the provider's account, through simply waving their cell phone at their computer terminal. *Beep.* No cash or card required. And, of course, there will be a "little" fee.

Only a few thousand people in the world today, perhaps, really understand how Money works. Even the "gnomes" of Switzerland and wizards of Wall Street are not in full control. We continue in our daily lives, working and saving and pretending not to notice that for the most part the monetary system has left the building and entered a phase of life that most of us cannot fully understand.

Every two weeks, I get a paper check from my employer. Except it is not really a check. It looks like a check but in large letters printed diagonally across its face it says, "This Is Not a Check." It also says, in large bold letters, "Non-Negotiable." What sort of paycheck is that? When I show it to my students, it always gets a laugh (not about the amount, hopefully). They deposit their course fees with the institute and every two weeks I get "This is Not a Check" in my mailbox. Of course, the check is merely a record of an electronic transfer. My employer electronically transfers portions of those fees from their bank to my bank. My bank then electronically transfers those incoming molecules of light to another bank that holds the mortgage on my home and to the utility companies that provide me with power and water. The information light stream goes out to my credit card company, the bank that holds my car loan and to others to whom I owe light molecules for services they have rendered me. I never see any cash. I just get statements and, increasingly, even those statements are electronic on my computer.

Now, maybe this is a great thing. It saves trees and certainly is efficient. I have more time to write and enjoy my family. I no longer spread out on the kitchen table Saturday mornings with a stack of bills, checks, envelopes, stamps, and those helpful little return address stickers that the Salvation Army and other organizations send every year to make me feel guilty enough to send a check because they have already given me something of value without even being asked. (It works...sometimes).

I do wonder, however, what effect this is having on our children. Like many parents today, I work away from home. I spend days teaching at an institute, seventy-five miles away, where the ethos of an adult classroom does not allow for take your child to work days. When I work in my private therapy office in Santa Monica, my children do not see my clients. They do not see the Money. They do not see anyone paying me or me paying anyone else. They see no checks, cash, or bills. For them it must seem like magic. Everything just *exists*.

Of course, we have cash and credit cards for daily purchases, and the children get allowances. The large things, however—our home, cars, the utilities, and the rest—just persist as if from the largess of a beneficent universe. Time will tell what the electronicizing of Money means to the next generation. What is it doing to us? Does it trouble you at all that your savings and earnings are all converted into some invisible current of data or a light stream that you cannot locate and over which you have no physical control?

A multimillionaire friend of mine, who has committed a considerable portion of his personal fortune to environmental protection, told me once that he regards the accumulation of wealth for its own sake as "coagulated fear." Millions of people now hoard gold, other valuable metals, and precious stones against their fear of an impending unwinding of our current monetary system. If the dramatic increase in gold prices in the early years of the twenty-first century is any indicator, confidence in paper dollars and other notes worldwide is eroding. Thousands of people are spending sizable fortunes in preparation for an imminent monetary collapse. This phenomena, is not unlike the backyard bomb shelter movement of the 1950s, generated by widespread nuclear war fears during the Cold War. More recently, a 2012 reality show about so-called *preppers* shows many folks with elaborate underground bunkers stocked with stored food, precious metal coins, and weapons—lots of them—getting ready for the economic collapse of civilization as we know it. Many others, however, think gold and other commodities will collapse as stores of wealth, leaving only the dollar and US stocks standing as the preeminent forms of wealth. Only time will tell.

If all of us went to the bank tomorrow morning and said, "Gimme all my Money," the whole system would collapse. If just Bill Gates, Carlos Slim, and Warren Buffet asked for all their cash at the same time, the same thing would happen. The cash just does not exist in those quantities. The government allows banks to lend much more than they actually have in reserves. If they lend it to another lender, that lender, too, can lend more than it has on hand, and so on. In this way, the aggregate debt expands far beyond the cash reserves that actually exist and the apparent supply of Money keeps growing. This is another way that Money has disappeared through the magic of fractional-reserve banking, so called because the bank only keeps a fraction of customers' deposits in the vault.

The form and structure of Money itself is not the only thing undergoing rapid change in our time. Products and the way there are produced and promoted are also transforming at a historically unprecedented pace. Although we are an adaptable species, one of the most difficult things for human beings to cope with is uncertainty. Often we prefer a known, less satisfying situation to a novel one that may promise to bring more satisfaction if we are willing to abandon what we are already comfortable with. My worn-out jeans are no longer attractive to my wife. She urges me to get new ones, but I resist because the old ones, tattered and shapeless as they may be, are familiar, comfy—they *are me*, some part of me thinks. But, now I look great in the new ones. What was I thinking? I was thinking that change can be anxiety producing.

THE REAL PRICE OF CHANGE

One of the cultural issues fueling a consumer economy, which increasingly fails to well serve increasing numbers of people, is the pace of social and technological change. Once upon a time in American manufacturers took pride in the products they produced. A dominant business ethos was to make things well out of quality materials so they would last a long time. American consumers wanted value for their investments in consumer goods. My first telephone—a big, heavy, black rotary-dial phone—seemed to survive almost anything short of direct hit by a nuclear missile. Well, a house fire could take one out, but not much else. They were impervious to earthquakes and domestic fights. They lasted forever and never needed service. You could heave them at a wall, use the receiver for a hammer, drop them off the second-story deck or even into the bathtub and they still worked.

They built my old 1966 Dodge truck with thick steel and a slant-head six-cylinder engine that ran forever. When the body finally rusted through, thirty-five years later, it had well over 200,000 miles on it with only minor repairs along the way and one valve job. It worked in rutted oil fields and ran thousands of miles on pitted logging roads. It hauled twice its rated weight in chicken manure and firewood, pulled boats and trailers and more than a few cars out of ditches. It careened off a roadside cliff wall, a redwood tree, and a boulder along the way. It just bounced off everything it hit and rolled away with little to show for the numerous calamities to which I subjected it, other than a few dents. (I own no Dodge stock).

What about my 2002 Lexus SUV? I love it. But forget it if it ever hits anything. I have encountered a couple unmovable objects (the back-up view is not so clear and I have never fully mastered parallel parking). A tiny bump against the parking post and its lovely shiny, faux metal (plastic) bumper is shattered to the tune of a thousand dollars in the shop. Now, our cell phones last a few years at best, our computers the same. Manufacturers build planned obsolescence into most products. That is, they deliberately design components to fail in a shorter period than the time for which they could engineer them to last. Planned obsolescence in everything from light bulbs to automobiles assures that consumers have to continually replace many possessions that manufacturers could easily make to last much longer. In many cases, it is now as or even more expensive to repair something than it is to just purchase a new product.

In addition to wanting products that lasted, we also once valued things that we could repair. Many manufacturers kept replacement parts in inventory for decades. Today, we often cannot find replacement parts for things over a few years old. Labor costs are such that it is often not cost effective to repair things unless you can do it yourself. When we bought our new home, no one had lived in it for many years. The appliances were as if new. There was a well working, built-in electric range and microwave but the electric control panel did not work properly; the number buttons 1, 2, 4, 5, 7, and 8 no longer worked after the mice in the walls had nibbled on the wires. No one could find a replacement for this sixteen-year-old control and thus could only recommend that we replace the entire oven unit, which was virtually new. So, we just push combinations of 3, 6, or 9 to program the seconds and minutes we want and have gotten used to the fact that the other numbers do not respond. We can get 66 seconds instead of a minute, which is close enough to not pay more than a thousand dollars to replace the entire range.

Planned obsolescence has been with us for many years now. I think most of us are aware of it, so I will not belabor the issue here. However, another somewhat more insidious trend has crept into our consumer society, which is the pace of innovation.

THE UNNATURAL PACE OF CHANGE

The rapid transfer of our major systems to new technologies increasingly makes older technologies obsolete. This is different from the planned-for failure of specific items with a shorter life span then necessary built into them in order to speed the rate at which consumers are forced to replace televisions, phones, toasters, and even their ovens it seems. The pace of change also makes whole arenas of products undesirable and even unusable.

For decades, vinyl records brought the music of the world to our homes. Cassette tapes made that process cheaper and easier; they also brought pre-recorded music to our cars, and portable tape decks. Then digital sound technology took off like a rocket to Mars. Records and record players are now in antique stores. Eight-track tapes, cassettes, floppy discs, CDs and multitudes of their various players now litter the flea markets of America. Each new rendition is made to seem so much more wonderful, although some aficionados still believe digital sound is not as warm or pleasurable to hear as the old analog sound, replete with the little hums and clicks that made it seem more human. Now the devices are coming at a furious rate.

The Walkman gave way to iPods, shuffle pods, iPads, iTouch, and iPhones and other smart phones. We increasingly download media and even books electronically, to read them on the latest generation of digital devices. In 2012, electronic books exceeded sales of print books for the first time. As an ecology-minded consumer, I applaud the savings of packaging and manufactured materials. Downloads over the airways leave a small carbon footprint. I just listened to a book on my iPhone, and that was pretty cool. But all that other stuff we bought—those records and tapes and CDs and videotapes—are sitting in boxes in the garages and basements of America.

New technology made them obsolete before they were worn out, even to the limit of their preplanned shortened life. Kodak film recently produced and sold the very last rolls of its iconic Kodachrome color film. Development shops reportedly scrapped every machine in the nation but one capable of developing the film. Nevertheless, I love my digital camera, don't you? You make a mistake and you do not have to pay for developing. But wait! They just came out with one that has five million more pixels than the one I have now. Gotta run. Now it seems that the one I have, which was so wonderful just a few years ago, is already nearly worthless on eBay.

Manufacturers design things to break and so they have a huge new business in selling protection plans. The best protection plan, however, is a well-made or cheaply repairable product. Such items are getting harder to find. Retailers make a great deal of Money off warranty plans. To electronic stores, extended warranty plans are like alcohol sales for restaurants—the highest-profit item on the menu.

Young persons working in electronics or appliance stores today know their jobs will not last long if they do not sell their quota of warranty repair plans to customers. "Sir, do you know that the cost to replace just that screen on your new computer exceeds the cost of the warranty plan? They are pretty fragile and, honestly, just between you and me, they break all the time." One salesperson recently told my stepdaughter, who was shopping for her first notebook computer, "Just before the extended warranty ends you can just smash the computer, bring it in, and we will give you a new one for free." Well, it did give me an opportunity to give her a talk about civics and ecology. When Microsoft released its new Vista operating system, many were horrified to learn that their old printers and other accessories no longer worked with their computers. This forced people to upgrade all of their peripherals to work with the new computer.

HIDDEN FEES

One of the maddening aspects of modern life is the ways in which consumers have to be increasingly cautious of every service contract and financial arraignment into which they enter. I have the fortune of a good education; yet still find the myriad forms I have to go through each year wearying. The car rental application has an arcane calculation about gas: should I buy it there, look for a better deal on the street in whatever new city I find myself, or start with a full tank and try to come back with an empty one without running out of gas on the way to airport? I can balance a checkbook, but my math capacity does not include factor analysis or an intimate familiarity with algorithms. Yet, here I am like the rest of Americans, facing off against an army of accountants, statisticians, and MBAs who have already figured the odds, much the way the bosses at a Las Vegas casino have calculated the win/lose ratios on their various games.

Even though we think we have a choice, in reality the "house" always has an advantage over reasonably informed consumers—even those who aced high school math. They manipulate our choices—a degree of hassle and risk versus a comfortable but more expensive alternative—to guide us toward more costly options. We think we will not buy the expensive and unsatisfying airplane meal but in fact, that army of marketing consultants knows that when that rubber-chicken sandwich is waived under our noses four hours into the flight after a two-hour delay on the ground, many will pay.

My credit card frequently has little charges I have to catch through taking the time to look up the number, call, wait on hold, and then ask, "What's that one for?" Sometimes it really is for things I did not purchase. Recently, I received a new Visa Signature card without having requested it and my old card had not yet expired. When I called to inquire about this, someone said they had automatically upgraded me and raised my annual fee, and that I was now the recipient of a number of new services that I both did not need and did not want. I said, "I do not want this and do not want a higher fee."

The nice lady on the phone said, "I am sorry sir, you cannot go back to your old card. We sent you a letter telling you we would upgrade you and charge you more unless you 'opted out' and sent it back to us." This seems somewhat like the Mafia telling me that it is now protecting my business from the other bad guys and will be coming around to pick up its cash every month. I cannot opt out now because I did not read some small print on one of a hundred similar-looking solicitations for credit and services that fuel my fireplace each month. She said, "I can change it next year, but the computers will not allow me to make the change now." The computers won't allow it? I am hearing this more frequently—you have to pay the charges on X because the computer says so. My wife recently noticed that a "foreign transaction" fee of eighty-nine cents was reoccurring on her monthly credit card bill. Some research quickly revealed that her subscription to *Psychology Today* was from a company based in Cyprus, hence the currency exchange fee even though we had no way of initially knowing this was not an American company. She made them waive it.

The phone bill has half a dozen categories of charges so obscure, even when explained, that I cannot grasp their application. Retailers and other billing agents frequently make errors on charges. Oddly, the errors are more often favorable to the billing agent than the consumer. This whole conspiracy of back room marketers trying to figure out how to hide a charge, disguise a charge, manipulate a consumer into accepting a charge or service he or she did not initially want creates a hustler-type marketplace where we increasingly have to be on guard about almost every purchase. Which is the better deal, the three-for-the-price-of-two eight-ounce cans of black beans, or the discounted sixteen-ounce can? Where is that calculator? Whoops, I forgot that tonight is the night I make chili for the kids. I have to get home. There is just no time to do the math, better just buy some beans.

The complex psychology of consumer manipulation has reached new dimensions in recent years. Most of us know that supermarkets intentionally put milk and other daily necessities in the back of the store. This forces customers to walk through the entire store to pick up a quart of milk on the way home. They know this will make their customers see other things they may not need as much but will purchase anyway on impulse or convenience. This is why casino hotels always put the elevators to people's rooms at the back of the casino, to repeatedly force their guests to walk through the casino on the way to and from their rooms. The point is to seduce customers into more risk than they intended. Personally, I patronize markets that have the decency to post the per-ounce price for products so that a consumer can make an informed choice without having had a recent course in advanced mathematics.

Most people with full-time jobs or other full-time responsibilities have a hard time finding the time to get on the phone and get channeled though levels of automated phone trees to discover why there is an extra charge on their monthly credit card bills. Often it is just a few bucks here and there and hardly worth most of our time even if we do have it. Some companies count on that. In our hurried lives, we may question the mystery charge of seventy-six cents on a phone bill. But we just do not have the time to be put on hold and transferred around for half an hour only to be told the customer service representative is busy and will call us back if we leave our number—and then will not call. So, we pay. Some charges, however, are more substantial.

Consumers can get "slammed," which happens when they are transferred to a new long-distance provider with a different (usually higher) fee structure than the one they agreed to. They are "crammed" when the bill contains obscure charges by third parties for services they did not request and "rammed" when their provider adds charges for extra unrequested services or upgrades low introductory fees into higher charges without notice. The fact that there is a lexicon of slang for these sorts of practices is one indicator of how wide-spread they might be. Various estimates put the costs to consumers in the hundreds of millions of dollars. Not surprisingly, in recent years authorities have indicted organized crime members on fraud charges for being involved in such charge schemes. According to research conducted by David Rosen and Bruce Kushnick, published in *AlterNet*, New York landline customers now pay as much as 30 percent of their bill in various added on taxes and surcharges.

LOSING TRUST AND GAINING ANXIETY

For me the galaxy of daily cons, manipulations, and hidden or even false charges are merely annoying. For millions of consumers today, however, they are factors in destroyed credit and financial failures. When our major institutions take advantage of us, when their corporate model is based upon a Midas Complex, it can make us feel a little more helpless. Few of us can examine the minutiae of our utility bills sufficiently to fully understand all the charges. We rely on trust. When we cannot trust the major companies or governmental organizations with whom we must interact to keep our day-to-day lives on track, it can contribute to the generalized anxiety so many Americans feel today. In fact, general, nonspecific anxiety is one of the most frequent disorders that clients present to psychologists in our consulting rooms. This free-floating anxiety does not seem to emerge from a single source—that is, I am worried that my boss will fire me or my spouse might leave. Generalized anxiety disorder is more of a global feeling that something seems wrong in the atmosphere of my life but I just don't know what it is.

Dishonest businesses possessed by greed violate the social contract of mutual benefit and certainly contribute to that vague sense that some predator is watching us from over the horizon. Many of my clients come in just nervous about life. They are like gazelles, grazing on the warm savanna that can smell the lion's breath in the breeze but cannot see it hidden in the tall grass. So then, inevitably, they wonder what is the matter with them. But what if we all feel somewhat like prey in this era where very clever and unimaginably ruthless people are continually trying to figure new ways to take a little more from us without our being the wiser?

Verizon Wireless paid a $25 million fine because consumer advocates caught the company charging its customers millions of dollars in hidden charges for services or rates they did not understand. Some were for usage or over-the-limit use where there was just too much smoke and too many mirrors for customers to understand what they were actually paying for. They charged customers for data transfers without it first being clear that charges would incur for such activities and for visiting web links that they advertised as free, including their own site. They even charged for attempted web visits that failed to connect. A few dollars here and there quickly added up to millions in bogus charges.

This fine represented the largest in the history of the Federal Communications Commission. Even so, millions of complaints about other companies indicate many other organizations intentionally practice deception. They do so through hidden, obscure, abstract charges on difficult-to-read bills with poorly described fees for actual desired services, services never ordered, and even charges for nonexistent services. Recently, over thirty million cell phone customers told the Federal Communications Commission they found mysterious charges on their phone bills. This means approximately one out of every six US mobile phone users believe their essential service providers are ripping them off.

Even when they are caught, as in the case of Verizon, how much does a fine like that and the millions it repaid customers really effect the future behavior of a company that grossed over $100 billion in the last few years? In fact, after the fine they attempted adding a special two-dollar charge for people who paid their bills online, a service they advertised and encouraged. The good news is that a widespread consumer protest forced them to withdraw the charge soon after they announced it. Similarly, soon thereafter, a consumer revolt against the Bank of America caused them to remove a five-dollar fee the bank tacked on for anyone daring to use their debit card. United and focused, consumers have tremendous power to affect the practices of many corporations. One of the cures for the Midas Complex infecting many of our companies is for consumers to unite and speak out against greed and to demand transparency in all financial relations.

We also need, however, more governmental protection and oversight to protect us from unscrupulous business who have armies of attorneys and marketing MBAs to devise the cleverest of schemes to covertly take a little bit from us here and there. Like mosquitoes that take a little blood night after night without ever killing the host, they can create constant irritations that can lead to degradations of our mental health.

NOT-SO-FUNNY GAMES

Digital entertainment providers have also discovered myriad ways to sneak off with our Money when we are not looking. Seemingly, innocuous, free games for kids on our iPhones, like the *Bakery Story*, are riddled with depth charges designed to raid parents' pocketbooks. While the game truly is free, it seems that you need to earn digital "coins" to buy ingredients to keep the bakery going. While it is possible to earn coins in the game, it takes a lot of time. After the slow pace wears children down, they realize they can just buy what they need with real Money. The game, however, does little to warn them that they are actually making a real purchase with one click. If I were to put in my password for my stepdaughter to download a free application and she then switched back to the game, nothing but her honest relationship with me (and that civics lesson at the Apple Store) would stop her from ordering as much as ninety-nine dollars' worth of digital goods with a click. Games such as *The Smurfs' Village*, which was the third highest selling game on the iPhone and iPad at the time, have added a warning that virtual items such as "Smurfberries" cost real Money. Many others, however, like *Tap Zoo* and the aforementioned bakery game, do not.

Some Internet sites hide in fine print information alerting consumers to the fact that a click of their mouse could transfer credit card information from a merchant they are shopping with to automatically enroll them in different club or service. All of a sudden, there are new monthly charges on their credit card for a service they did not want and did not order. These are often for discount sorts of clubs. This genre of consumer cons count on the fact that many customers will not notice the four, six, or even ten dollars per month charge billed directly to their card. Look up the name of a lost friend for $1.99 on a national search site, click the wrong button, and you are suddenly enrolled in a $25 monthly subscription that you will not know about until your next credit card bill. It happens fast, and the bait (cheap service) to switch (more expensive fee) is subtle. For the less-experienced or simply unwary Net surfer, many predatory schemes are lurking in the wings. It can make us feel a bit paranoid and exhausted to expect that we have to scrutinize every transaction we make for hidden fees. And feeling wary or hypervigilant much of the time can actually have a cumulative and corrosive effect on mental health.

If this bothers you, you could contact the providers and ask for honest information and truth in billing—demand such regulation from government. Consumers do have power with their collective clout. We vote with our feet by leaving services that cheat us and support service providers that hold to principles of transparency and clear consumer information. One of the cures for Midas Complex–driven commerce is united consumers.

EMPTY PACKAGES FOR THE EMPTY SELF

Packaging is following the increasingly deceptive trends in marketing and advertising. Architectural geniuses and masters of graphic illusion design package shapes to create the deceptive appearance of containing a larger amount of product than actually inhabits the package. The product does not fill the container to the top; the bottom of the package is false, extending far into the container cavity, belying the outward appearance of a larger container. In addition, for an increasing number of packaged products, the container shape, size, and artwork combine to create an optical illusion of size. Even container sizing information has become increasingly misleading. Today's medium cup of coffee is yesterday's small, a large is yesterday's medium, and the giant, enormous helping is yesterday's large. The only real supersizes are for artificially flavored drinks whose manufacturing costs are little more than that of the container itself.

Manufacturers frequently adulterate core ingredients with inert fillers to make them occupy a larger volume. This gives consumers an illusion that they are purchasing more product than they actually receive. When I had to put wood preservative on my old fence, I noticed that the active ingredient was only 5 percent of the product. The rest was "petroleum distillates." So, I bought a gallon of the active ingredient, some rubber gloves and a mask, mixed it with twenty gallons of diesel fuel, and saved over $500. The point is not so much about my thriftiness or cleverness but that for a few minutes research I was easily able to create a similar product for about 15 percent of the cost. The same is true of other products. The active ingredient cost $25.00 per gallon. I purchased the filler at a gas station for about $3.00 per gallon. The fence is still standing.

In our household, we now buy active-ingredient-concentrated laundry soap and other products with the filler, which is often just water, removed. Not paying for filler saves us Money and saves the environment because there is much less packaging and transporting of filler from place to place to place. It saves significant space in our closet and helps the planet. We are fighting back in small but significant ways, and most consumers can do so. It is aggravating to be constantly tricked into consuming products we do not need, purchasing packages that hide the true amount of contents, and paying fees that are so deeply hidden one needs an electron microscope to find them. This entire science of consumer deception dedicates itself to taking more of our Money than the manufacturer or marketer requires in order to make a fair profit. These sorts of tricks create a needless tension between providers and consumers and add needless stress to the collective culture.

TAXES, FEES, TARIFFS, AND FINES, OH MY!

According to former US Supreme Court justice Oliver Wendell Holmes Jr., "Taxes are what we pay for civilized society." I think most of us understand that government requires revenues in order to provide needed services. Our willingness to pay taxes is part of our social contract—we contribute to the common good and enjoy a more stable society as a result. Sometimes, however, government can go beyond its need to secure borders and assure the quality of weights and measures. Just like individuals, governments, too, can become fiscally ill and out of balance with what they take for what they give. If we dig into the complexity of taxation, a number of relatively obscured assessments, which add to our overall burden, become visible. The aggregate may be much larger than most Americans imagine it to be. Anyone who has ever been backpacking knows there is a point at which the mere addition of one more pound makes a burden unmanageable.

Former US president James Madison once noted, "The power of taxing people and their property is essential to the very existence of government." Every level of government levies a tax on our income. Federal, state and, in some cases, city taxes as well are taken out of our paychecks. At the end of the year, some receive refunds of previously withheld funds, yet many others find they need to pay even more. The self-employed have to keep track of all they owe and make regular estimated tax payments. In addition to the taxes on income, we pay for Social Security, Medicare, and disability and unemployment insurance. Some may not think of these as taxes. However, if we die before drawing the amount we paid into Social Security, including the lost gain on that income were it drawing interest, then it was a tax. If we stay healthy or can afford private insurance, then the Medicare payments were also a tax. If we keep our jobs, then unemployment payments were a tax. The same is true if we never become disabled when working.

Local governments levy neighborhood, subdivision, street, and sewer bonds and taxes for other improvements on property owners. In addition, real property is taxed both when we purchase it and annually. Even though, in California, property taxes are limited to 1 percent of the homes' value, in actuality many homeowners annually pay an additional portion for special assessments. In other states, property taxes vary widely. For rural residents who are not part of a water or sewer district, there is a well permit fee and septic permit fee. If you want to build a house on that old empty lot on which you must pay annual property tax, there are a multitude of building fees and taxes that can add as much as 20 percent to the cost of construction. Inside those homes, whether rented or owned, we pay cable tax, phone usage taxes, electrical usage tax, water use taxes, sewage taxes, dump fees, or trash pickup fees to use the municipal dump that was built with our taxes.

Portions of college scholarships can be taxed—not the tuition, but grants for room, board, and other expenses are taxable. Any portion of a debt we owe, which the lender forgives, can be taxed, as can a mortgage reduction. Even mortgages reduced by foreclosure and so-called short sales, in which a bank sells a home to a new buyer for less than the amount owned by the seller could create tax obligations for the seller. In the Great Recession, millions of property owners were stunned to learn that they owed tax bills for mortgage relief after giving their property back to the bank and losing all their equity. In the dot-com run up of the 1990s, many who worked for stock options were similarly shocked to learn they owed millions in taxes for stocks that were worth less come tax time then when received. It seems that when the options to purchase matured, the IRS considered the full stock value at that time to be income whether or not the worker actually took possession of the stocks.

The government taxes the purchase of cars, boats, and mobile homes. It then charges annual fees and tax for continuing ownership. As municipalities struggle to keep basic services operating nationwide, initiatives to raise sales taxes are rampant. In Los Angeles, they have risen to 9 percent. For those fortunate enough to purchase a luxury vehicle or plane, the government tacks on an additional luxury tax. To operate those vehicles, we pay a driver's license fee, an annual vehicle registration fee, and a license tag fee. Vehicle parts like tires and batteries have an extra tax added on, as does oil when we purchase it and when we dispose of it.

When we use the roads and bridges that our previous taxes paid to build, we are often charged road usage and bridge tolls/taxes. Parking tickets and traffic tickets are another way that municipalities add a stealth use fee on driving. For many drivers, the parking rules are so complex it is hard to get through a year without a ticket. With cameras increasingly monitoring our passage at intersections, the slow "rolling stop" is now costing many hundreds and even thousands of dollars per year for some in (barely) moving violation fees.

Many cash-strapped local governments are raising increasingly larger revenues through such automated covert surveillances of the population. The prices of traffic violations are rapidly rising in many municipalities. They are also adding myriad fees to tickets for everything from building additional courtrooms to hiring more traffic officers to write more tickets. We can fairly label much of this as a stealth tax on citizens.

When on the road, we pay fees to use our parks, to enter beaches, to launch and gas up boats, or to enter municipally owned marinas. There are taxes on landing airplanes and additional taxes on airplane tickets. In the United States, airplane travelers pay a 7.5 percent tax on a domestic ticket, a $3.60 tax and $2.50 security charge for each segment of a flight, $16.00 in international arrival/departure taxes, and a $4.00 passenger-facility charge. Anyone transported by boat on a US waterway pays a $3.60 tax for the privilege. In California we pay property taxes for local fire protection and some of the highest state income taxes in the nation. Nevertheless, in 2012 the State of California sent out bills for "backup" fire protection in rural areas. The state was broke and trying to balance its budget by creating new categories of extra fees, mostly paid for by the middle class.

Renting does not liberate us from taxes on residences and automobiles, since there are also hotel occupancy taxes, bed taxes, and car rental taxes that hit everyone when we travel. Even when we die, our heirs must pay estate taxes if the estate's worth is over a certain amount. If we try to give them assets before passing on, then there are gift taxes.

Shop owners and other businesspeople have to pay inventory taxes on goods in stock hence their annual "clearance sales," trying to reduce inventories before the annual audit. If you serve food to the public, there is a food license fee. All business pay both an initial and then an annual business tax. In 1975, President Ronald Reagan reportedly commented that the price of a loaf of bread included 151 taxes that, all totaled, created more than half of the total cost.

Importers pay additional taxes on the products they bring us from elsewhere. Domestic manufacturers pay taxes at various stages of purchasing and selling raw materials that others turn into taxable commodities—all passed along to the end consumer. For example, as many fans of the *Hunger Games* learned when they took on a new hobby, there is an 11 percent excise tax on the manufacturer of arrows. Bicycles, too, are hit with 11 percent. Eighteen percent is added on to flashlights; 24 percent to girdles, 32 percent to brooms, and a whopping 143 percent to peanut butter—an important staple for many low-income families. When we purchase these and hundreds of other items we pay sales taxes on the included excise, manufacturing, and importation taxes included in the purchase price—double tax, even triple.

Buyers of handguns and ammunition pay an extra 10 percent of the sales price to the federal government. Anglers pay a similar added tax on their equipment. Additionally, they pay taxes on fishing itself in the form of annual licensing, with increasingly larger fees for different kinds of fish caught; locations of ocean, river, or lake; number of poles used; and other criteria. Similarly, hunters pay varying animal, place, and season-specific fees for their rights to hunt. Many of these license and use fees for public lands and transportation are on infrastructures and national assets already paid for and maintained by income taxes—again, one of many forms of double taxation.

The government uses tariffs and subsidies to manipulate the market price of various goods in order to favor or hinder various businesses. With a similar effect as tariffs and subsidies, the government also levies so-called sin taxes, such as the extra sales taxes on liquor, cigarettes, marijuana, and even taxes on accepted bribes or stolen Money (unless you return it before the end of the tax year). These sorts of taxes have the dual purpose of (1) trying to slow down or discourage certain behaviors and (2) raising additional revenue. Thus, there is a $13.50-per-gallon tax on hard liquor and a 33¢ tax on every six-pack of beer.

In 2009, the federal government increased tax on cigarettes to $1.01 per pack. Before that, at 39¢ per pack, the US Treasury raised about $8 billion every year. Currently, even with many people quitting, it must be billions more. In addition to federal tax, state taxes range from 17¢ in Missouri to $4.35 in New York. In some places, city taxes pile on top of that. New York City tacks on an extra $1.50 per pack. Criminal organizations have embraced a lucrative new trade to supplement their more traditional arenas of drugs, gambling, and prostitution. Criminals sell cigarettes without tax stamps at a deep discount. Some are going so far as to counterfeit brand name cigarettes in China. They then smuggle them into the United States to avoid taxes, plus the labor and material costs of making such products domestically.

The United States collects about $8 billion yearly in taxes from alcohol, Money that during prohibition all stayed in the hands of criminals, as do nonmedical marijauna revenues today. Beyond its obvious humanism, one of the driving forces for full legalization of marijuana is to facilitate government taxation of the huge underground economy of domestic pot production. Now the nation's largest cash crop, by various estimates marijuana production currently generates more than $35 billion annually in untaxed revenues. By comparison, the annual revenues generated by corn and soybeans, the second- and third-largest cash crops, are $23 billion and $17 billion, respectively.

The need for Money can dramatically change the moral tone of a society. For example, prostitution is no longer universally criminalized in the United States. In Nevada, patrons of prostitution now pay a $5.00 tax on top of the service price for each visit, which the government then also taxes as income to the service providers. Like alcohol, postprohibition, a huge formerly underground economy is now a significant tax revenue provider. In California, sales tax alone on medical marijuana dispensaries is already creating about $100 million per year for the state. Taxing luxuries and sin is very good business for the government.

Legalization of marijuana could raise billions in tax revenues to cash-starved state governments across the nation. The states and the federal government could also save additional billions through ending the surveillance, arrests, adjudication, incarceration, and parole and probation services for millions of marijuana consumers. While states like California enacted three-strike laws to get violent career criminals off the street, more convicts are currently serving life sentences in prison for marijuana under these statutes then are there for murder. Since prisons tend to be more expensive per capita than universities, governmental hunger for additional revenues is beginning to erode almost a century of bias against marijuana users.

Gas taxes are a form of flat tax—that is, they are the same for rich or poor across the board. Many think this is how income tax should be calculated. A flat tax would reduce the considerable energy both government and citizens must spend tracking intricate complexities of the tax code, which is now some 75,000 pages long. There is no way to avoid gas tax, shelter our way around it, or get a discount or consideration for our income levels. Four-dollar-a-gallon gas is an extreme hardship to someone making minimum wage, but matters little to someone with an upper-middle-class income. Anyone who must travel to work or to gather other necessities of life has to buy gas, regardless of its price.

In my area of the country, there simply is no viable public transportation system as an alternative to driving. Even though our nearest major road connects millions of valley dwellers with millions of West Side dwellers, not a single bus travels along it except for a little beach shuttle in the summer months. Average state plus federal gas tax is 47¢ per gallon, which now far exceeds the entire price for a gallon of gas when I first started driving. Before these taxes are even assessed, however, gas companies must pay a variety of preliminary-to-the-pump taxes as the gasoline is processed along the way.

Oil companies pay a royalty of 12.5 percent on all the oil that they pump out beneath onshore federal lands before it is refined into the gas, which the government further taxes at the pump. States also charge taxes for oil pumped from their lands, as do many municipalities. They then add property taxes on the pipelines through which the companies transport their oil or natural gas. The government charges excise taxes at different stages of refining and transporting the many different finished products from oil. There are transport taxes on the rail lines or trucks that transport petro-products, bridge and road tolls, as well as business and use taxes on the stations that pump gas. How much tax does the government actually build into one gallon of gas? It is a good question. Probably only Ronald Regan really knows, and he is not talking. Could it be as much as for a loaf of bread—half?

When filing his own tax returns Albert Einstein once said, "This is too difficult for a mathematician. It takes a philosopher." He further commented, on another occasion, "The most difficult thing to understand is the tax code." It has not gotten any simpler today. As I go through this complex yet only partial list, adding the taxes we pay throughout the year to federal, state, and local taxes, our real tax rate clearly exceeds the government's tax bracket schedule by far. Some tax critiques estimate that all stealth taxes combined with the more visible ones can aggregate to over 50 percent of taxpayer's income. If you found the above litany somewhat exhausting, I have achieved part of my goal. I believe these ubiquitous taxes are part of the middle class's death from a thousand cuts. While few cuts bleed very much, the cumulative effect can be demoralizing. Most middle-class Americans today are assailed by a complex tax system that both consumes a large portion of their income and adds a great deal to the cost of almost everything they consume.

GOVERNMENTAL SHAKEDOWNS

Like some of the manufacturers and service providers mentioned above, governments are not immune to sneaky practices. It just so happens that while I was writing this, the pet police showed up at my front door. We live way up a small mountain, at the end of a dirt driveway off a dead-end road. People do not just drop by. In fact, we have never even seen a Jehovah's Witness at our door. But the county pet police, strapped for cash as they must be today, found us just the same. In the middle of a work-at-home day, I came to the gate to find a humorless man in a uniform demanding to know if we had a cat or dog in the house.

Once we admitted to having a spayed house cat that never went out-doors due to the numerous coyotes drooling in the bushes, he fined us. He demanded $40 for having to come to our house instead of us driving to their office, over an hour away. He then added $15 for an annual cat license fee, a $5 tag fee, asked for proof of my age (to get a senior discount since my gray hair was not sufficient proof), proof of the cat's shots, and proof that we had had the cat spayed. When I said I was too busy to produce all that on the spot and suggested he should have made an appointment if he wanted to assail us for unlicensed indoor cat ownership, he immediately wrote me a summons. He said that if I did not produce everything in five days I would have to appear in court. In ten minutes, the county had converted me from peaceful writer in his study to a criminal scofflaw five days away from being subject to arrest for felony pet ownership.

Though the whole incident was comical, it added a bit to my stress level that day. People with unmanageable stress levels fill my psychotherapy practice. Much more serious issues with government can quickly balloon out of control. Misfiled or unfiled federal taxes generate fees and penalties, which, over a few years, can even take down otherwise well-off people with good accountants and attorneys. As a therapist I regularly see people who have had breakdowns and cannot keep up with the complexities of their lives, including their tax bills, until they get well. The penalties for error, however, are often severe.

The IRS, like the pet police, has no sense of humor. It also has an extremely high rate of sentencing for the tax cases it decides to prosecute. A conviction for tax evasion or filing a misleading tax return is a felony, which can generate a five-year prison sentence and/or fines up to $100,000. Merely failing to file can generate a one-year prison sentence and/or fines up to $25,000 for each missed year.

WHAT WE GET FOR WHAT WE GIVE

Most of us value the various services government provides with our tax revenues. Even though I cannot currently pave my long, dirt driveway, which becomes a sea of mud in the winter, I am happy to have paved roads elsewhere, public sanitation, public education, a military to protect us from aggression, police to protect us from lawlessness, and many other services that government can provide. The question for many of us—and one of the ongoing purviews of this book—is more about *how much stress and trauma the government creates in our lives in order to raise the revenues it thinks it needs.* As the comedian Arthur Godfrey once put it, "I am proud to be paying taxes in the United States. The only thing is–I could be just as proud for half the money."

I find myself asking if the services that I receive are worth the cost we pay through hundreds of different taxes and fees. We want fairness in our dealings with government just as we do with service and product providers. When our arraignments are so complex we cannot follow them, it creates anxiety and resentment. The obscurity of so many financial arraignments today drives many into a low-grade constancy of aggravation. The aggregate of these minor irritants can actually have a corrosive effect on national mental health. Certainly, as was discussed in chapter 2, we display a lower quality of collective mental health than do the citizens of most industrial nations in the world. With one in five Americans now in possession of a psychiatric drug prescription, our consumption of mental health medications far exceeds that for most nations.

If the government practiced the same fiscal responsibility we do in our own home—avoiding waste, balancing the budget, living within our means, and being accountable to each other for what we spend—then I would feel more a part of a larger family working for the common good. If the government was making a significantly better world for us all with my Money, I would feel much better about paying so much tax. The United States pays only about 45 percent of citizens' health-related expenses. Most European nations, however, pay an average of 73 percent of their citizens' health care needs. If, once all hidden taxes are added to the bill, we are paying taxes similar to what most Europeans pay, shouldn't we then receive a similar level of social services?

Waste, corruption, tax-breaks for elites, ceaseless warfare, and neo-Darwinist politicians who think the weak or disadvantaged should just die off, leaving the majority of resources for the privileged or the most ruthless, all combine to create a tax system that takes more from the working and middle classes than it gives back. Even though most of us do not know the exact details of how the system works, we *feel* that something is wrong, something is unfair, and something is just not right with how much we pay compared to what we take from government. For some the response to that awareness is a feeling of helplessness and despair—others are angry about it.

Our government appears to be violating the admonition of Jean Baptiste Colbert, who was the controller general of finances for King Louis XIV. He noted, "The art of taxation consists in so plucking the goose as to get the most feathers with the least hissing." One of the ways many Americans hiss today is through tax evasion. The IRS estimates that Americans owe over $300 billion more than they pay in taxes. This amount is about 14 percent of the total federal revenues that the government would receive if everyone reported honestly. Thus, the government suffers from shortfalls and many citizens live with increased anxiety about their exposure to possible consequences. Few people, of course, ever talk about this, even in the privacy of my consulting room. Nevertheless, in the estimation of the *New York Times* journalist, Ron Lieber, who writes the *Your Money* column, more than 80 percent of Americans cheat on their taxes to some degree. As humorist Will Rogers used to quip, "Income tax has made more liars out of the American people than golf."

TAX FREEDOM DAY

Tax freedom day starts on April 28 for the average citizen. That is the day we actually start working for ourselves, having earned enough to pay our taxes for the year. The following chart, showing the average percentage of working time we must dedicate to paying taxes, also shows how that date has moved ahead through the last century.

1910	January 19	5%
1920	February 13	12%
1930	February 12	12%

1940	March 7	18%
1950	March 31	24.5%
2010	April 9	27%
2011	April 12	28%
2012	April 17	29.5%
2013	April 28	32%

The trend line over a century is alarming. This translates to most of us working two or three hours of every day for tax revenue production. Our payday starts long after breakfast and, for some, after lunch. State income taxes move the date even farther ahead. Some states have none. In my state, however, it goes as high as 10.3 percent. In reality, given my rough calculations around the hidden or obscured taxes most of us pay, tax freedom for many Americans actually starts some summer day. No wonder we are so ready for a vacation by July.

According to the Tax Foundation in Washington, DC, middle-class Americans now pay more in taxes than they spend on groceries, clothing, and shelter combined. So, if you are feeling like there is not enough left over at the end of the month no matter how hard you work or how frugally you live, the problem may not solely be with your family budget. Perhaps you are being overtly and covertly taxed into distress. The larger issue, however, is not so much about how much we pay compared with other nations. The issue that causes the most distress, in my experience, is the growing perception that not all Americans contribute in equal ways. From the top of the economy, many feel the poor do not give enough for what they receive. Ironically, however, the view from the bottom of the economy looking up at the top is very similar.

Internal Revenue Service data show that two years after the onset of the Great Recession, the four hundred individual income tax returns with the highest adjusted gross income averaged over $200 million apiece. The total income for this group was $81 billion, over 1 percent of all income in the United States. This was more than double its take in 1992. Thirty-three of them paid zero to 10 percent federal income tax; 89 paid between 10 percent and 15 percent, and the rest paid tax rates from 15 percent to 35 percent. Twenty-five of the highest earning hedge fund managers made an average of $1 billion each but paid only an average of 17 percent in taxes. The four hundred top earners made over 6 percent of the nation's total dividends, averaging $26 million apiece. Their net capital gains averaged $93 million, 16 percent of all capital gains and the highest percentage since the data was first released for 1992, when it was less than 6 percent.

Capital gains and dividends were both taxed at a maximum rate of 15 percent in 2012. This was distinct from the 35 percent maximum rate on earned income, which is how most of us make our Money—by working for wages, not by manipulating capital. While the tax rate is ostensibly progressive for most of us, some of the top earners in the United States benefit from a regressive tax system. They have used their considerable political influence to create government-subsidized welfare for the ultrarich.

For decades now, some extremely wealthy Americans have paid a considerably smaller percentage of their income for taxes then the rest of us. For them, every day is tax freedom day. Many economists feel that this group has gutted the US Treasury through withholding billions from government, significantly contributing to rampant budget deficits at local, state, and national levels. The upper 1 percent of taxpayers now have more wealth than ever before in our history. There is little evidence to prove the theory that these tax advantages have trickled down to the rest of the population. Conversely, there is considerable evidence that the majority of Americans have suffered quality-of-life losses, as this minority gained considerably more gold on top of their existing heaps. Politicians, who advocate for the 1 percent and are often members of that club themselves, consistently advocate for more tax benefits for their class while supporting proposals to balance the budget by eliminating opportunities for the lower, working, and middle classes.

Our current taxation policy points to what happens when a Midas Complex takes hold of an entire nation's economic policy. Chapter 6 discusses this in greater detail as it examines Midas Complex effects in some of our larger financial institutions. At first the kings and queens celebrate their rapidly increasing shares of gold. Servants at the party get some goodies that fall off the table. Eventually, however, as the social and physical infrastructure begins to crumble, quality of life begins to erode. In a global economy and global environment, it is increasingly evident to many elites that they, too, are running out of places to hide from the degradation of the environment occurring largely because of recent decades of unrestrained greed.

Generative capitalism grants many benefits to creative and industrious people who want to get ahead. But economic policy driven by people who have become fiscally ill, who suffer from possession by greed, becomes a danger to the majority. For old King Midas, everything he valued in life was lost as it turned to gold from his touch. We can no longer afford to allow today's kings and queens to harden everything that is lovely in our collective garden into inedible, silent, scentless, and relatively useless gold.

Recent surveys of Americans reveal that the majority of them no longer believe in the American dream. That is, increasingly fewer numbers of people think that it is possible to get ahead monetarily in the United States today. Many no longer believe they will own a home—particularly those who lost their homes because of our national economic crisis and through no real negligence of their own. Increasingly, as unprecedentedly large financial scandal after scandal is uncovered, feelings are growing that some elites have rigged the economic game in a way to benefit the few and exploit the many. This is the shadow of a collective Midas Complex: the gradual diminishment of the quality of life through the pursuit of abstract wealth at the expense of real wealth—the quality of our health and enjoyment of life. History is replete with two very different kinds of kings. Those who bless are the well-remembered leaders who used their power to assure the well-being of their entire nation. Then there are those who taxed severely, taking from the many for the benefit of their small class. A lot more turmoil generally surrounded them.

Many now feel we must reinstate fair tax policy and begin to let those who benefit most from the system pay the most as well. We also need to restore a fundamental foundation of the American dream that appears to have crumbled: the opportunity for anyone to change his or her economic fortune through hard work and participation in a system that has fair rules that apply to everyone—in other words, a true democracy for every economic class. Chapter 5 examines the often-differing effects of the Midas Complex according to one's class affiliation.

141

CHAPTER 5

GOOD-BYE HORATIO ALGER: THE INJURIES OF CLASS

*There's class warfare, all right, but it's my class,
the rich class that's making war, and we're winning.*
—Warren Buffett

Midas Myth #5: Hard work and frugality are the royal roads to riches in America.
Reality: *Inheritance, capital manipulation, stocks, tax breaks, resource exploitation, and profit from others' labor create most American wealth today.*

THE NEW AMERICAN ARISTOCRACY

For hundreds of thousands of years of human evolution, class did not exist—at least not in any way we can readily detect from the archeological record. People lived in small groups and needed every person's effort for the survival of the whole. Everyone hunted, gathered, cared for children, or made useful things. No one lived in a manner of luxury that far exceeded the means of the rest of the group. Perhaps there is some sort of racial memory embedded in our bones that makes us feel umbrage toward our fellows who seem to live on another planet of privilege. The schadenfreude some feel when elites are brought down by scandal or gross miscalculation reflects that longing for greater equality and a more even distribution of resources.

One of the founding principles of American society was the belief that we are all created equal. Two and a half centuries ago, this was a fresh and radical idea in the world. For centuries, European and other aristocratic societies around the world believed that some people, by virtue of their birth, were entitled to privilege. Others, by the same circumstance, were understood as destined to serve the privileged minority born to so-called noble families.

The American Revolution did away with kings and queens, princes and princesses, barons and baroness, dukes and duchesses, counts and countesses, lords and ladies, and all the rest. Unlike the image on the crests of European families and nations, our American eagle wears no crown. For its first two hundred years, a powerful fantasy persisted in America: any people from any origins could apply their talents and succeed in equal measure to their hard work and ingenuity. There were many holes in that romantic vision. Nevertheless, there was at least an ideal of inclusion and equal opportunity in the collective imagination that had not existed widely in previous societies.

In 1813, John Adams wrote to Tomas Jefferson, "The five Pillars of Aristocracy are Beauty, Wealth, Birth, Genius and Virtue. Any one of the three first can, at any time, overbear any one or both of the two last." Many early Americans were completely sincere in their advocacy for liberty and an egalitarian society. At first, however, the founders only extended the benefits of democracy to a minority of the population—white men with property. Nevertheless, the idea took hold, and through the significant efforts of all the other previously excluded classes, great steps toward the goal of equality occurred.

First, in the nineteenth century, the Thirteenth Amendment granted former slaves freedom. This led to the Fourteenth Amendment, in 1868, which gave freed slaves the rights of citizenship and conferred birthright citizenship to all. In 1870, the Fifteenth Amendment removed race as a barrier to the right to vote. Women followed suit with the suffrage movement, which culminated in 1920 with the Nineteenth Amendment allowing them to vote. In 1971, the Twenty-Sixth Amendment removed age as a barrier, extending the vote to eighteen-year-olds. Group by group, those previously excluded from participation in our democracy have fought for and won inclusion in the American dream. In the twenty-first century, realizing that we are one of the only democracies in the world that still disenfranchises former lawbreakers, we are finally beginning to reenfranchise millions of citizens who were stripped of their voting rights because they were once convicted of a crime.

We can now foresee a day when any American citizen, regardless of his or her race, gender, economic class, sexual orientation, or past mistakes, will have the inalienable right to vote, marry, receive equal pay for work, live where he or she wishes, and have equal access to work and education. Nevertheless, some politicians, dedicated to the elites, are still working hard to deny the poor easy access to the ballot box through regressive voter exclusion rules to prevent mail-in ballots for those who lack transportation and to halt early, late, or weekend voting hours that benefit working people. Not unlike poll taxes and literacy tests in our Jim Crow past, these attempts clearly intend to limit voting opportunities for groups who tend to vote for representatives who are more sensitive to the needs of the working and middle classes.

A federal court blocked Texas from enforcing a new voter identification law in 2012, writing, "That law will almost certainly have retrogressive effect: it imposes strict, unforgiving burdens on the poor, and racial minorities in Texas who are disproportionately likely to live in poverty." The centuries-long battle for real equality in America continues on its rugged, twisting pathway. Nevertheless, many of us carry the vision of a greater, all-inclusive nation. This makes us distinct from many other societies who do not even aspire to this ideal.

Regardless of our high ideals and our steady, albeit uneven, progress toward them, our nation largely descended from an aristocratic society. The resonance of that aristocracy is still with us today, as an echo passing through the generations long after it was trumpeted in Europe's Middle Ages. Political pundits occasionally note that former president George W. Bush, senator John Kerry, and other American notables, starting with George Washington, were descendants of English royalty. It is no longer a widespread belief, however, that people are born with "blue blood," thought to be superior members of elite society by virtue of their genetic heritage. In fact, many more ordinary than notable Americans can trace their ancestry back to some royal family. This somewhat belies the fantasy that some sort of "conquering" gene exists that "great" families can pass along. Nevertheless, America is yet to achieve its ideal of becoming a classless society. The lines of class are merely drawn more vaguely now than in seventeenth-century Europe.

In European aristocratic society, even if a family lost its great wealth it could remain upper class in name. Relationship to a royal family was often sufficient to elevate one's status, as was extraordinary distinction in battle, colonial acquisitions or other notable service to the crown. In America, it is not so much breeding or closeness to a particular family that designates one's class, even though that can help some. It is instead almost exclusively determined by the degree of wealth one possesses. Money is the most egalitarian force in our society today, perhaps in all of history. Money immediately transfers power and status to whomever possesses it. In this way, as John Adams lamented, it is often more influential than education, talent, morality, and character.

For some people, Money is a way to keep score as evidence of their achieved class status. One expression succinctly demonstrates this theme: Fuck you, Money. That is, the certain amount of Money that can allow people to abandon manners, social compromise, and collaboration with others yet retain social inclusion because they have something else others want. This expression has a sociopathic theme embedded within it: the fantasy that with enough Money one no longer has to work with the often difficult but soul-making challenge of reciprocal human relations. One can just order room service and proudly display a T-shirt emblazoned RICH BITCH. This perceived power of Money to buy freedom from social constraints is a Midas

Complex fantasy. In truth, many wealthy people suffer the loneliness and depression that often arises for those who fail to nurture their relationships with others.

One of the greatest and prevailing fantasies of the American dream is one of class migration. Since our founding, most Americans have believed that through hard work and carefully acquiring sufficient capital, people could advance themselves from the lower, working, middle, and upper middle classes to upper-class status. The upper class today is reminiscent of noble status in European societies. Actually, middle-class people today live better in most ways than did the royalty of ages past. This bit of historical understanding should give most of us some comfort. Even so, the upper classes of income and wealth do enjoy privileges today that most others lack.

A multitude of Midas Complex–driven media creations such as *Lifestyles of the Rich and Famous* revel in spotlighting the rare social and material privileges of the superrich. Class migration is a feverish desire in the American psyche. It is a driving ambition that often sacrifices health and relationships, provoking ceaseless work for many and billions spent on lotteries and other get-rich schemes. Multitudes of game shows offer a chance to marry a millionaire or somehow become one through winning that much Money or having one's talent discovered on national television. When I was a child, a TV show, *The Millionaire*, captured my fantasy of a stranger coming to our door with a seven-figure check and changing our lives forever.

We may take some solace from the wealthy entertainer Johnny Carson, whose Malibu home had its own exterior climate control, among other luxuries (a series of mist generators could cool the whole complex on a sunny day). As someone with a net worth of around $300 million at the time, Carson admonished, "The only thing money gives you is the freedom of not worrying about money." In other words, as I have come to learn from others in his class, the rich deal with all the same human issues the rest of us do, just not as much the worry about Money. However, even that is not true for many.

Although economic downturns differently affect people according to their economic rank, the Midas Complex is not confined to any single class. Plato

147

noted that both wealth and poverty cause discontent. Like the flu or cancer, the Midas Complex is an equal-opportunity illness. As a therapist, I bare witness to serious financial wounds at every point of the economic spectrum. While everyone faces some sort of psychological challenge around Money, the shape of the wound often differs according to one's status on the economic hierarchy scale—one's class.

AMERICA'S DIRTY SECRET

Despite our rhetoric of equality, class remains America's dirty secret. We are actually a very class-bound society, with more rigid class divisions and harder lines between the classes than most people believe we posses. Many people are concerned about their ranks on the monetary scale and subsequently what places they hold on the social hierarchy. The many ways in which we internalize social concepts like rich, poor, working class, or middle class can profoundly affect our self-image, behavior, and mental health. The manipulation of class status fears and longings fuels much of the advertising psychology discussed in chapter 2. Even though elite Americans lack aristocratic titles, the demarcations are relatively clear to most of us. We know that the people in *People* magazine are not really "The People." We know the streets, boulevards, neighborhood names, compass directions, and zip codes that mark the transitions from lower- to middle- to upper-class neighborhoods.

In our form of taxation, the government ostensibly taxes people according to their place on the socioeconomic scale—their ability to pay. In his 1776 book *An Inquiry into The Nature and Causes of the Wealth of Nations*, Adam Smith wrote, "The subjects of every state ought to contribute toward the support of the government, as nearly as possible, in proportion to their respective abilities; that is, in proportion to the revenue which they respectively enjoy under the protection of the state." Smith, often cited as the father of modern capitalist thought, further stated that "a goal of taxation should be to remedy inequality of riches as much as possible, by relieving the poor and burdening the rich.'"

Generally, under this so-called progressive system, the more people make, the more the government expects them to pay in income taxes. Of course, people who make more also can afford attorneys, accountants, and tax consultants to help them find ways to avoid taxation. Even more so, wealthy citizens increasingly have disproportionate power in elections and tend to support candidates who advocate tax laws in their favor. Since the 1970s, so-called supply-side economists have supported policies that lowered taxes on the rich. The rationale for this has been to provide the "job creators" with incentives to grow their wealth. As chapter 4 discussed, many think this upper-class-driven retooling of the tax code deprived the government of revenue, drove up the deficit, and contributed to the Great Recession. Nevertheless, the historical intent of progressive tax was to raise greater revenues from those who were most able to pay and also demonstrably benefiting the most from a stable society protected and supported by tax revenues.

In the midterm elections of 2010 and the national elections of 2012, there was a great deal of impassioned discourse concerning class warfare, taxation, and income inequality. The struggle for power and privilege by the have-nots against the haves is becoming ever more heated and vocal in American discourse. I imagine it will continue to be an increasingly prominent feature of national politics in the years ahead. As a herald to the current debate, during the 2000 presidential race, President George W. Bush looked around a room full of tuxedoed and evening-gowned attendees gathered for a fund-raiser and unabashedly announced, "This is an impressive crowd...the haves and the have-mores. Some people call you the elite...I call you my base." He was apparently joking in response to the class war rhetoric already stirred up in the public dialogue at the time; or was he? He did not seem to perceive America as divided merely into haves and have-nots. In fact, he accurately referred to his people as the *have-mores*—a class beyond mere haves. The have-mores are a numerically small but increasingly powerful group in the upper reaches of the economy—the American aristocracy.

During the presidential campaign of 2008, Republican senator John McCain created a national uproar when he offered his view that, for taxation, people should not be considered rich unless they made more than $5 million per year. This made many feel that, as someone who owned at least seven homes, he was out of touch with the economic realities of most Americans. The middle class did not follow him into the national election, throwing their support to a candidate they felt was more connected to the economic concerns of the nation's largest economic group—the middle class.

In the 2010 tax reform debates about whether the tax cuts Bush awarded his have-mores should persist, Democratic leaders in Congress and President Barack Obama proposed that $200,000 for individuals and $250,000 for families become the new line between middle- and upper-class tax rates. A University of Chicago professor protested on his blog that if the government drew the line at $250,000, his family would suffer significant cutbacks in its lifestyle. The responses around the country to his statement, from people struggling to live on considerably less, were so vituperative that he feared for his family's safety and quickly took his Internet posting down.

Discussions about just how much income qualifies someone as rich remain pointed. People on the East and West Coasts and some urban centers, where an average home costs over half a million, claim that a $250,000 cutoff makes people who think they belong to the middle class feel that they are being taxed at the same rate as billionaires. Many high earners do not consider themselves rich because they compare themselves to the small group of people who earn more, rather than the larger group who make less than they do. As H. L. Mencken once quipped, in America "a wealthy man is one who earns $100 a year more than his wife's sister's husband." To some degree, economic class is relative to the local economy. Regardless, there are some generally recognized income ranges. Drawing from a range of national surveys and governmental data, the Pew Research Center defines the middle class as households with incomes from $39,000 to $118,000. Most people in America call themselves middle-class if they earn $70,000. In New York City, however, that figure is $165,000. The 2012 "fiscal cliff" debates finally settled on $400,000 for the new upper-class tax bracket. No one, it seems, could credibly argue that anyone with an annual income of that magnitude is still middle-class.

The irony of the class-based, progressive-tax battle is that, relatively speaking, the vast majority of Americans are closer to one another in wealth and income than they imagine. The superrich are in an entirely different league today. This group is targeted for increased taxation because of the blatant inequality demonstrated by the dramatic disproportions of wealth in America today. These disproportions generally have little to do with hard work or creativity. They are mostly about the few with the capacity to make the system work for them in ways that the rest of society cannot. Rather than the most successful Americans creating a flood of wealth that lifts all boats, however, it increasingly appears that due to the Midas Complex extreme personal wealth aggregation is happening at the expense of the infrastructure needed to support the basic needs of the majority.

Patriotic Millionaires and the 1 Percent Class War

A group of millionaires has advanced a countertrend in tax policy debates. They urge the government *not* to cut taxes for the rich. When asked why he was advocating that the top earners pay more in taxes Morris Pearl, the managing director of BlackRock, said, "I don't want to pay more than my fair share, but I don't want to pay less either.... It's not like some huge sacrifice that's going to change my lifestyle, so I don't even feel like it's anything to be particularly proud of." He is a member of a group calling itself, Patriotic Millionaires for Fiscal Strength. They called on Congress to restore higher rates on their cohort after President Bush cut them in the years preceding the Great Recession.

Their website notes the following statistics as argument for their position—taken against their personal financial interest but on behalf of the nation's interest—that millionaires should pay more as an act of patriotism because:

- only 375,000 Americans have incomes of over $1,000,000
- between 1979 and 2007, incomes for the wealthiest 1 percent of Americans rose 281 percent
- during the Great Depression, millionaires had a top marginal tax rate of 68 percent
- in 1963, millionaires had a top marginal tax rate of 91 percent
- in 1976, millionaires had a top marginal tax rate of 70 percent

- today [2012], millionaires have a top marginal tax rate of 35 percent [which was raised to 39.6 percent in 2013]
- reducing the income tax on top earners is one of the most inefficient ways to grow the economy according to the nonpartisan Congressional Budget Office
- letting tax cuts for the top 2 percent expire as scheduled would pay down the debt by $700 billion over the next ten years.

Only about one hundred of the over one million earners in this class have joined this group. It is a start toward the reversal of a national Midas Complex. Billionaires are also chiming in. Warren Buffet announced in the *New York Times* that that it was unfair that he and billionaires like him are taxed at a lower rate than the secretaries who work for them. He said, "Some of us are investment managers who earn billions from our daily labors but are allowed to classify our income as 'carried interest,' thereby getting a bargain 15% tax rate. Others own stock index futures for 10 minutes and have 60% of their gain taxed at 15%, as if they had been long-term investors. These and other blessings are showered upon us by legislators in Washington who feel compelled to protect us, much as if we were spotted owls or some other endangered species."

"It's nice to have friends in high places," Buffet continued. "I paid only 17.4% of my taxable income — and that's actually a lower percentage than was paid by any of the other 20 people in our office. Their tax burdens ranged from 33% to 41% and averaged 36%. If you make money with money, as some of my superrich friends do, your percentage may be a bit lower than mine. But if you earn money from a job, your percentage will surely exceed mine — most likely by a lot."

Mitt Romney reported a tax rate of 13.9 percent on some $22 million in earnings for 2010 and even less in some years before his presidential run. With a net worth of around $250 million, one of the richest men ever to run for president admitted that he was not very concerned about the poor, imagining that the government was already taking good care of them. His wife Ann reportedly drives several different Cadillacs. She said she also has a "horse in every port," including one that competed in the 2012 Olympics. Nevertheless, Mrs. Romney incredulously told *Boston*

Globe reporter Michael Levenson, "I don't even consider myself wealthy." In fact, it was the Romneys' class that was being well cared for by the government through a preferential tax rate—not the poor. Most of the poor cannot afford the basic necessities of life. Government assistance for jobs and education, which would allow them to get ahead, have been constantly cut to advantage members of the have more class to have more.

In 2012, Facebook's cofounder Eduardo Saverin renounced his US citizenship just before the company's initial public offering. His move to Singapore, which has no capital gains taxes, saved him hundreds of millions of dollars in US taxes. Under current laws it is unlikely he will ever be readmitted to the US should he ever wish to return. While not all financial elites are willing to surrender their citizenship to avoid paying their fair share, dozens of other ways exist for moving Money offshore and avoiding US taxation while using US taxpayer–created infrastructure and freedoms to generate billions in income.

A 2012 hearing by the Senate Subcommittee on Investigations found that US multinational corporations had more than $1.7 trillion in untaxed profits designated as "undistributed foreign earnings." In the 1950s, corporate tax generated 32 percent of all federal tax revenue while payroll tax on workers created about 10 percent. Today, corporate tax only accounts for about 9 percent of federal tax revenue while payroll taxes now generate 40 percent. Yet, corporate profits were up over 400 percent in the "greed decade" between 2000 and 2010. The average CEO made 231 times what his or her average worker made in 2013. In 1970, the ratio between pay at the top and the bottom was only twenty to one.

The subcommittee found that the Microsoft Corporation, to take just one example, used "aggressive transfer pricing transactions" in places like Singapore to avoid US taxes, saving up to $4.5 billion on goods sold in the United States. Microsoft competitor Apple also saved billions in taxes by also using legal, multinational tax avoidance strategies that were more complex than anything most experts have ever seen. Subcommittee hearing chair Carl Levin said, "The share of federal tax revenue contributed by corporations has plummeted in recent decades. That places an additional burden on other taxpayers. The massive offshore profit shifting that is taking place today is doubly problematic in an era of dire fiscal crisis."

THE 99 PERCENT SOLUTION

When wage earners cry out for tax fairness, the elites often label their assertions as class warfare. There is a class war in America, but it is in the other direction—the elites are making war on the majority of the working people. As President Obama said in 2013, "The wealthiest individuals and the biggest corporations shouldn't be able to take advantage of loopholes and deductions that aren't available to most Americans." When the have-mores keep more at the expense of the nation, then a Midas Complex is at play. When Midas turned his garden's flowers to gold, no one could enjoy their scent any longer, including the king himself. When the have-mores build vast estates but the local schools lack sufficient tax revenues to properly educate the workers who maintain them, a similar paradox of extraordinary wealth making us poor is in action. Many teachers, police officers, and firefighters today can no longer afford to live in the neighborhoods they serve.

Aspirations for wealth are not merely driven by the desire for a better life. Most of us have such longings, regardless of where we are in the economic spectrum. The longing for more is a fundamental aspect of human nature. Even my friends and clients with a great deal of Money long for better health, the academic achievement of a child, the success of particular projects, or the interest of another with whom they wish to associate or be loved. Having Money also does not make them immune from illness, accidents, or old age. We are all common in our human frailties and mortality. Many wealthy people, however, do long for more Money even though their needs are well covered. More Money brings more power, social and political influence, or even inclusion in a new class beyond the upper class—the have-mores. It also allows greater opportunity for good works. Not all who accumulate are selfish. Many do so in order to gain greater influence to improve the world and the quality of life in it, as chapter 8 will discuss.

The Patriotic Millionaires clearly make up such a group—one that has its Midas Complex well in hand.

In the latter decades of the twentieth century, some conservative politicians told the American people that a system of trickle-down economics was best to ensure the highest level of prosperity for the largest number of people. The theory behind trickle-down economics, in essence, is: if the government gives the rich generous tax breaks and other incentives, they will make more Money. This Money will overflow and drift down to the rest of us in the form of new jobs and other opportunities that the rich will create. This theory, however, did not account for the influence of the Midas Complex on the psychology of the primary wealth holders favored by these policies. Comedian and social critic Bill Maher comments that trickle-down is when those at the top grab all the Money in sight and anything they accidentally drop the rest get to keep. In another commentary, he said that *trickle-down* just meant that those at the top were simply urinating on the rest of the nation.

During the last few decades in the United States, instead of trickling down, the direction of the flow reversed. Then a massive siphoning up of wealth into cisterns controlled by the nation's most powerful families and individuals occurred. Chapter 6 documents how many wealthy investors squandered this wealth on speculative and unregulated financial activities that had little or nothing to do with the best interests of the majority of Americans. Real trickle-down economics happens when the government taxes extreme wealth and then invests in programs that allow people to readily gain education, health care, and job-skills training so they can make a better living and then pay more taxes themselves. More jobs for workers on the huge estates of hedge fund managers has done little to promote better lives for the lower classes or to improve the American economy.

In the big stock market run-up before 2007, two thirds of the equity increase went to the upper 1 percent. From 2007 to 2013, Wall Street profits were also up dramatically for this group while unemployment increased over 100 percent and the average homeowner lost more than a third of his or her equity. The bottom 60 percent of Americans had two thirds of their net worth tied up in their homes. The top 1 percent, in contrast, had just 10 percent. These facts alone clearly demostrate who bore the brunt of the Great Recession. Unlike during the Great Depression, the elites in America hardly seemed to notice the flood of equity pouring out of middle-class homes and the rampent job loss among the working poor, who had no equity to lose but their daily wages.

The recent so-called 99 percent movement is the result of the middle classes suddenly coming to realize that they have more in common with the bottom of the economy than the top. This nascent movement and national dialogue may mark a radical departure from the middle class's history of looking upward with longing and politically aligning with the elites. If the lower and middle classes become more aligned, their power to change the economic policies of the nation could become unassailable. The growing ranks of economically disenfranchised Americans are a huge potential political force that could guide the course of this nation back toward its founding ideals.

GROWING POOR

At both ends of the economic spectrum lies a minority. Regardless of how the lines are actually drawn, the minority at the top has a disproportionate amount of political power and the minority at the bottom has a disproportionate amount of political disenfranchisement. This obvious fact flies in the face of our fantasy that our nation is a true democracy that is "indivisible, with liberty and justice for all," as our Pledge of Allegiance emphatically states. As his book title conveys, my friend Mark Gerzon notes that America today is more accurately portrayed as *A House Divided*. The growing number of citizens who are most divided from America's promise are the poor.

In America, poverty is legally defined as describing individuals who annually make less than $10,830 in pretax cash income or families of four whose combined income is less than $22,050. Poor people rarely own stocks, and few own homes. Middle-class households tend to have $25,000 to $100,000 in assets with home ownership as a central feature of their class values. The 2009 census revealed forty-five million Americans live below the poverty line, the highest number of poor Americans since the government started keeping such records. Every indicator shows their numbers have been steadily growing since. If we include factors such as medical expenses, transportation costs, and such, it pushes the official poverty rate to more than forty-nine million, or roughly one in six Americans in 2013, including one out of every five children.

In 2009, the number of US households receiving food stamps increased by two million. By 2012, twelve million, or one in ten families, were receiving this basic survival aid, the highest level of food assistance in American history. According to an analysis by Isabel Sawmill and Emily Monea of the Brookings Institution, about ten million more Americans will likely descend into poverty over the decade from 2010 to 2020. The majority of them will be children.

An annual survey by the Kaiser Family Foundation reports that in 2012, the total number of people in the Medicaid program was almost fifty million people. The ranks of the poor continue to grow at faster rates than ever previously recorded. As their numbers increase, they steadily reduce the ranks of the middle class. Very few in the upper class are ever hit hard enough to migrate all the way down to the lower 20 percent.

Historic economic disparities between the races are also continuing to widen. The poverty rate for whites is around 9 percent, yet it is over 25 percent for blacks and Hispanics. Over fifty-one million people in America lack health insurance, a number roughly double the population of Texas. Moreover, young people in the lower ranks of the economy are increasingly finding it harder to gain an education that could lift them out of generational poverty—the one thing that decidedly helps people change their class distinction.

Higher education was once the primary means to class migration. Nevertheless, the World Economic Forum now ranks the US thirty-fourth in primary education. The worst scores tend to be in the most under-funded schools. Thus, the dimming of the American dream starts in high school for many who increasingly find themselves unprepared for college once they graduate. Almost every other wealthy nation heavily subsidizes higher education, but in America, social Darwinist politics (only the strong will survive) increasingly leave more low-income students behind. As economist Tyler Cowen notes, "Thirty years ago, college graduates made 40% more than high school graduates, but now [in 2012] the gap is about 83%."

The gap between equally qualified and capable poor versus affluent students who can complete their bachelor's degree has also grown dramatically in recent years. Professor Sean Reardon, a sociologist at Stanford University, says, "The racial gaps are quite big, but the income gaps are bigger...it's becoming increasingly unlikely that a low-income student, no matter how intrinsically bright, moves up the socioeconomic ladder. What we're talking about is a threat to the American dream." In recent years, affluent families have tripled the amount by which they outspend low-income families on enrichment activities like sports, music lessons, and summer camps. Moreover, many affluent students need not work during school, freeing them to focus on their studies. They can also afford private tutors, editors, SAT prep courses, coaches, psychological help, and other support. This is the result of a Midas Complex being allowed to take hold of many facets of government.

So many of the opportunities I had as an impoverished high school dropout who then received a college education are not available to today's generation of economically disadvantaged students. Few grants are available any longer, and tuitions have skyrocketed along with the interest rates charged for loans. Lack of public support for poor students to gain a good education is one of the major things contributing to a seemingly permanent underclass of undereducated and underemployed citizens. When the dreams of better life are crushed, widespread despair often results. Today our prisons are full of people who never had the chance to get a good education. Ironically, prisons cost a lot more than schools to run. Even more shortsighted, "tough on crime" advocates have successfully removed educational programs from most prisons, practically assuring an endless cycle of crime and poverty for those who wind up there. Most wardens agree, however, that only a minority is there to protect public safety. The rest just have no legitimate means to earn a living and/or suffer substance abuse and other mental health problems, often as the direct cause of economic stressors in their lives and families of origin.

As a psychologist, I sometimes find it useful to look at a grouping of the words that describe a specific phenomenon. A sense of the underlying complex can then sometimes come through. It is an impressionistic, subjective process that touches on the feeling or tone surrounding phenomena rather than an analytic one. Consider the following list of adjectives and epitaphs often used to describe the poor. Multitudes of feelings hitchhike on the word *poverty*. Like the ghosts in Disneyland's Haunted House who, through a trick of holography, enter your ride's vehicle to accompany you home after your visit, most of us feel some undesirable response when this word arises in our minds.

A lexicon of poverty

Aimless
Bad
Bad investment
Bankrupt
Broke
Bum
Busted
Cheapskate
Common
Crapped out
Debt
Deficit
Depression
Destitute
Dirty

Failure
Freeloader
Garbage
Homeless
Impoverished
Illegal alien
Needy
Inferior
Lacking
Lazy
Loser
Low-class
Low-quality
Money-grubber
Moneyless
Needy
Okie
Of little worth
Parasite
Pauper
Penniless
Poor
Ruined
Shabby
Shiftless
Smelly
Tasteless
Tacky
Tired
Trailer trash
Trashed
Wasted
Welfare mother
Without means
Worn-out
Worthless

This partial listing of words associated with poverty and the poor may leave us thinking we do not want to have those sorts of appellations attached to us. Few of us can outwardly change our race, but most of us imagine that in America we can change our class. The sad truth, however, is that the myth of Horatio Alger is practically dead today.

Horatio Alger wrote a number of books in the late nineteenth century. Most, like his best selling *Ragged Dick*, embodied a rags-to-riches story line in which the protagonist was a young, impoverished boy. Through hard work, staying power, courage, and honesty he manages to pull himself up by his bootstraps and escape poverty. Many Americans felt that Alger's writings espoused the quintessential American dream: upward mobility available to all who really try. Alger's name became synonymous with this myth, which stubbornly persists in the American psyche even though statistics increasingly show this to actually be a more rare than common experience. In fact, only about one person in one hundred, born into the lower 20th percentile of the economic hierarchy, will migrate to the upper 5 percent in his or her lifetime. Those born into the ranks of the upper classes, however, are significantly less likely to migrate downward. In other words, it is almost as if aristocracy still exists, fixing most Americans into the class in which they are born.

In the twenty-first century, downward mobility has become much more common than the reverse. Contrary to our iconic poverty images of urban despair, roughly one out of three Americans below the poverty line now lives in the suburbs. Ironically, many originally fled there to gain greater quality of family-oriented life and escape the dangers and poverty of the cities. Scott Allard, a University of Chicago professor, cowrote a 2010 Brookings Institution report that noted that since 2000, the number of poor people in the suburbs jumped over 37 percent to almost fourteen million—more than double the poverty rate in cities. He said, "As a result, Americans who never imagined becoming poor are now asking for assistance and many are not getting the help they need." This is largely because so many of our social services and philanthropic aid groups are in the habit of turning their attention to the inner cities and rural outliers where the poor have traditionally congregated.

FALLING INTO THE GAP

In 2012, the top-earning 20 percent of Americans—households making more than $100,000 each year—received almost 50 percent of all income generated in the United States. The bottom 20 percent of wage earners—those below the poverty line—earned only about 3 percent of all income. That ratio, between the top and the bottom, is nearly double what it was in 1968. The international Gini coefficient finds US income inequality at its highest level since the Census Bureau began tracking household income. The United States also has the greatest disparity of wealth between its upper and lower classes among all Western industrialized nations.

Most Americans, however, do not believe the gaps are really as large as they are, according to a survey done by Michael Norton at the Harvard Business School and Dan Ariely at Duke University. Most people, from all demographic groups, "believe that the wealthiest 20% held about 59% of the wealth when the actual number is closer to 84%." The 25 percent gap between perceived and actual inequalities is huge. Even with its more skewed appraisal, however, the vast majority thinks even that is unfair and that it should be more balanced. The authors note that with the top 1 percent of Americans possessing around 50 percent of the nation's wealth and the lower 40 percent holding virtually none, the current gap exceeds the wealth inequities of US society just before the Great Depression.

One of the reasons for the wide spread illusory perception of a lesser gap is the success of Alger-like propaganda that makes millions of people still believe they have more opportunity to advance in life than actually exists. Second, it may feel unpatriotic to many to look at America's shadow as directly as we are doing in the present book. I do this, however, because I love America and want it to become as great as it imagines it could be.

America has never really been an equal society. Part of our greatness is that we at least hold a common vision of that possibility. Among true aristocracies, the lower classes have no hope of upward migration. At America's beginnings, its wealth was similarly unequal. In other words, despite our national fantasy of creating a new, free nation with equal opportunity, at the outset we were more a democratic variation of European aristocracy.

In 1760, 1 percent of Boston's population held 44 percent of the wealth, while the upper 10 percent controlled about two-thirds. Servants coming from Europe were indentured and although they were white and ostensibly had the same rights as their wealthier employers, they were frequently treated almost as badly as black slaves from Africa. Today, with the American Revolution and two and a half centuries of reform behind us, the economic gaps are chillingly similar. Now, unlike then, however, we allow most of the masses without property to vote and more have access to education. So, some things have changed and more is now possible.

In the hopes of quelling class rebellions, the rich have propagated the myth of upward mobility and equal opportunity for America's poor for over two centuries. The psychological outcome is not only the widespread disparity of perception versus reality. More insidiously, it creates the feeling in many that if they are not prospering there must be something wrong with them. In many cases, the system is stacked against people becoming financially prosperous. Those who beat the system are a small, highly touted minority. Many hard-working Americans, however, suffer in silent shame imagining they *should* be doing better. They struggle with the painful knowledge that no matter how hard they work they can never achieve significant financial gains.

If we converted our incomes to stacks of hundred dollar bills, the working class's stack would be a few inches high, the middle class's share would be about half a foot, and most of the upper class pile would stack a foot or two high. The top tier's stack, the pile of the .01 percent, however, would reach beyond the peaks of the Himalayas! Another way to conceive this is to cut a pie into thirds and give each group its share. One piece would go to the upper 1 percent, the upper 90–99 percent would share another and the lower 90 percent of Americans would divide the rest between their multitudes with most of that third piece going to the upper 10 percent of their huge group. If you are not getting enough pie right now, you know who is eating it.

DREAM OVER

In 2012, nearly half of the people in the US were not living what they would call the American dream." StrategyOne, part of the Daniel J. Edelman public relations firm, found that about half of American's answered "no" when asked: "Are you living the American Dream today?" In households earning between $40,000 and $50,000 per year, only about 40 percent answered yes, in contrast to over 70 percent of those making $75,000. More strikingly, about half of those who said they were not living the American dream thought they never would. Upward mobility as a foundational myth of American society seems to be crumbling. The idea that we can improve our lot through hard work and application of our gifts has been common to our dreams of an America that was a land of equal opportunity. This dream led millions of citizens from other countries to our shores.

However, many of the early American colonists were caught in their own Midas Complexes. Possessed by a fantasy of manifest destiny, they imagined America as a virgin land just waiting for them to exploit and gain "her" wealth, even though other people had lived here for thousands of years and already called this land home. As the wealth distribution of colonial-era Boston reveals, however, many in the early years did not fare so well. Then as now an aristocratic minority seized much of the newly won wealth for its own families and reduced the rest of the colonists to servitude. Later generations also found serious obstacles to upward mobility despite our fantasy of having thrown off the shackles of class, though more did make their way up the scale than was possible in aristocratic Europe. A report from the Economic Policy Institute, however, shows that in the twenty-first century, economic mobility in the United States slipped to thirteenth out of the seventeen most developed nations.

Many people feel demoralized by the belief that it should be easier here; that our government and other institutions should aggressively support mobility as evidence of their commitment to democracy and freedom. So, many people tend to blame themselves, not the system, if they do not succeed. Downward mobility is not merely uncomfortable or imbued with the sorrow of lost dreams; it is dangerous. A disproportionate number of impoverished Americans are losing their freedom, which, even more than prosperity, has been the central hallmark of the American dream since the inception of our nation.

OUR TWO-TIERED JUSTICE SYSTEM

Wealthy people are significantly less likely to be arrested for the same crimes as poor people. When arrested they often get lighter sentences and go to less severe prisons. My father was in prison in the Watergate era during which the government incarcerated several presidential aids. Reporters wrote a great deal, at the time, about the comfortable circumstances of their incarceration. Because of our family's well-written pleadings to the court, we were able to get my father transferred from the more severe Terminal Island Federal Prison to the West Coast version of "Club Fed," a minimum-security federal prison camp in Lompoc, California. A large minority of inmates there were millionaires caught on tax charges, fraud, other white-collar crimes, and federal drug charges. I often recognized the names of my father's new friends. Some were plucked straight out of recent headlines of the time, like Augustus Owsley Stanley III, "The Bear," who manufactured massive quantities of LSD, and reputed mob bosses whose names prudence dictates I should still decline to mention.

During my Sunday visits I regularly witnessed catering trucks pull up to the outdoor picnic tables and watched as uniformed waiters brought out feasts on silver platters replete with lobster, prime rib, and other nontraditional prison fare. The guards allowed everything but alcohol. Limousines parked in the visitors area held prostitutes who serviced the high-end prisoners while guards, whom prisoners had paid to look the other way, did as their prisoner employers required. After all, one told my father, what was the harm? It kept the prisoners happy, which in turn made life for everyone more pleasant. According to my father, drugs of every sort flowed through the facility. Almost anything could be acquired for a price.

Certainly, these wealthy prisoners lost their freedom, which, as anyone who has done time can attest, is punishment enough for most crimes. Nevertheless, in every other way they enjoyed privileges denied to similar prisoners who lacked the funds for bribery and various catering and commissary services. Notably, even though there were no armed guards or towers or walls surrounding the prison, few prisoners ever attempted to escape. Those who did were mostly those held on immigration charges—they tended to be both poor and filled with a longing to return to their home countries.

To a large degree, we have a two-tiered justice system in America. One is for those who can afford the best attorneys, expert witnesses, and psychologists who can recommend that defendants get psychotherapy, drug treatment, and sentences to residential recovery sites instead of incarceration. There is another tier of justice for the poor: they are served by public defenders who often must carry huge caseloads. Poor defendants often experience greater antipathy from jurors who are likely to believe that the rich are somehow intrinsically more moral and have merely become the victim of circumstances for whatever crime they have been charged with. Anatole France once wryly summed up this aberration in justice by saying: "The law, in its majestic equality, forbids the rich as well as the poor to sleep under bridges, to beg in the streets, and to steal bread." The law, it seems, may be possesed in part by its own Midas Complex, riddled with bias favoring those who have the gold and against those who lack it.

The inherent class bias in our justice system is most dramatically evidenced by the fact that wealthy murderers are rarely executed. The NAACP notes, "The death penalty is the most lethal form of social injustice in the United States. The race and class bias which permeates the American justice system result in this most extreme punishment being handed out almost exclusively to the poor.... Nearly all of the 3,500 Americans awaiting execution on death row today have low-income backgrounds." Moreover, they are disproportionally men of color.

Nevertheless, even though the justice system frequently treats black men unfairly, O. J. Simpson's multimillion-dollar "dream team" was able to overcome the widespread cultural bias against black men who kill white women. (White men who kill black women are rarely if ever subjected to similar prejudices.) They were also able to overwhelm the resources of the district attorney's office and to win an acquittal even when most people believed Simpson was guilty, as do the prosecutors to this day. If in fact he

166

was, then this exemplifies how the power of class in America can actually trump the disadvantages of race.

A Prison Diary, written in 2001 by a former member of the British Parliament, Jeffrey Archer, is the poignant journal of a man of privilege whom the courts strip of his rights and force to spend time locked up with commoners in Belmarsh Prison. It is written in a very different voice from that of gritty prison narratives like Eldridge Cleaver's *Soul on Ice* or Leonard Peltier's *Prison Writings*. Nevertheless, this born-to-the-purple English lord is sensitive to the suffering of the less fortunate around him and thus a sympathetic character. Because of a political scandal, he endures real losses of his vocation and the comfort of friends, family, home, and familiar food (which he goes on about a great deal at times).

This otherwise serious book, however, is unintentionally comic much of the time. Archer's complaints about the indignities and deprivations of prison life reveal much about how accustomed he is to treatment and privileges that the majority of society never receives—much less when they are prisoners. It is as if he cannot see the irony in many of his statements because the things he misses about life "outside" are often features that his fellow prisoners have never encountered in their entire lives, even as free men.

Like the justice system outside, because of Archer's wealth and status, the guards and even the warden inside often treat him deferentially. Like Charles Colson of Watergate fame, Archer's short prison experience converts him to a prisoners' rights advocate. It seems it almost takes a direct experience of prison to create a sense of advocacy in most members of the privileged classes for those who, often merely by virtue of being poor, have lost their freedom and their safety.

The Buddha reportedly left a life of privilege, and once outside the gates of the palace he discovered illness, old age, and death are inevitable in life. This experience bred compassion in a man who was formerly an idle prince. It became the foundational mythos of one of the world's great religions. As I have written about the unmitigated savagery of American prisons and the grave inequalities of our justice system in *Angry Young Men* and elsewhere,

I will not belabor this issue beyond the economics of prisons, since that problem is germane to this book.

If we look at the rise and fall of crime rates and incarceration over the last hundred years, only one significant social factor positively correlates with the ebb and flow of criminalization rates: the employment rates of young men. Crime chases poverty like a coyote after a rabbit; they are intimately linked. As poverty becomes increasingly rampant in America, we must brace for more crime ahead. However, we already possess the largest prison system on earth. Prisons are bankrupting many states today as spending on cellblocks increasingly outstrips spending on classrooms. While the United States has less than 5 percent of the world's population, our 2.4 million incarcerated citizens represent about 25 percent of the world's total prisoners. These bleak facts bear mute testimony to a nation possessed by its Midas Complex.

The majority of US inmates are there due to our nation's protracted war on drugs—predominantly a war against the poor. Current estimates of correction's aggregate national costs exceed a staggering $70 billion per year. This does not include the grave, incalculable costs to families and communities from the mental and physical health damages that accompany released prisoners. Many traumatized former prisoners, without receiving any viable job skills training or education in prison, have no hope but to become permanent members of the underclass.

We could change all this by decriminalizing drugs, which were the precipitating cause of more than half our prisoners losing their freedom. Poverty, lack of education, and lack of job training are the reasons most others wind up in prison. Prisons are a poor investment in our future. Education is much cheaper. But quality education is increasingly becoming more of a privilege then a right in our increasingly class-bound society. The poor represent a cautionary tale to the middle class. We tell our children, do this, don't do that, so you do not wind up like them. Once believing themselves to be immune from the vagaries of economic disenfranchisement, increasing numbers of middle-class Americans are now facing limitations previous reserved for the class below them. Increasingly wider swaths of America's middle class are becoming the *nouveau poor*.

THE MIDDLE-CLASS BLUES

Most Americans fall into the category of the middle class. The gutting of America's middle class is an economic phenomena generated, to a large degree, by late twentieth and early twenty-first century Midas Complex-driven economic policy that favored the elite and disadvantaged the working poor and middle classes. When people believe that they have the opportunity to do well but fail anyway, it can be psychologically devastating. Anxiety, depression, low self-esteem, addictions, and other dysfunctions often have such dysfunctional belief systems at their core.

We may think others who appear to be doing better are cleverer, harder working, more skilled, more blessed, or simply luckier than we are. But what if no matter how closely we watch the pea under the walnut shell or the ace in the three-card monte player's hand we never win because the game is rigged? I often find such discussions with my clients and students sobering. As we unpack the reality that cultural and political issues induce much of their suffering, however, some sense of relief often arises. Then we start thinking more about how to change the system instead of just trying to change ourselves. The largest obstacles to upward mobility often have little to do with how assiduously people have applied themselves.

Although my clients come from the full range of the economic spectrum, most of them are middle-class. As we consider some of the words associated with this class, think about what they are really saying. What values, mores and philosophy of life do they represent? What is the felt sense of being middle-class?

A Lexicon of the Middle Class

Comfortable
Credit-worthy
Deferred gratification
Homemaker
Educated

Family man
Disciplined
Frugal
Gainfully employed
Homeowner (or mortgagee)
Insured
Law-abiding
Sober
Stable
Taxpayer
Upwardly mobile
Working woman/working mom
The worried well

While none of this class lexicon has the derogatory, self-esteem busting tone of the verbiage attached to poverty, there is little in it that captures the imagination. It is a short list. The middle-class imagery is not romantic, soulful, exciting, or deeply motivating. Few contemporary songwriters focus on middle-class issues. No middle-class blues singers lament, "I woke up this morning and found a new scratch on my Volvo." The hip-hop artists are not protesting, "Our kid's school had to have a bake sale for new gym equipment." For me, as someone who grew up in poverty where I often lacked shelter and it was a challenge to get enough to eat at times, the middle class still feels palatial.

Undercover journalist and academic Barbara Ehrenreich wrote, *Nickel and Dimed: On (Not) Getting By in America,* about her two-year-long experiment intentionally trying to live on the minimum wage. In it she notes that it was a shock for her at one point to realize that after sleeping in the back of her car and staying in cheap motels, "trailer trash had become a demographic category to aspire to." In other words, she had been poor so long that what looked down scale to most middle-class people looked like up to her. When you are poor, the middle class is very desirable. However, our collective imagination regarding the large middle of America is often imbued with the critique that it is devoid of soul. The French word for it is *bourgeoisie.*

We rarely hear young people today saying that what they really aspire to be when they grow up is middle-class. More often they exhort, "I want to be rich!" or engage in an occupation likely to bring riches. Some, however, express a willingness to answer some call of the soul with the possible specter of near poverty as its admission price in the arts, education, religion, philosophy, public service, environmental protection, and social action. In these and similar vocations the quest is for more of a qualitative, psychological, or spiritual reward over a quantitative, monetary one. I sometimes joke with my students that one of the purposes of their liberal education is to make them philosophical about the fact that they will never make a lot of Money. It always gets a nervous laugh.

"Safe" middle-class occupations often have low allure. However, they also carry less anxiety than occupations, which may be seem more personally rewarding but less financially sure. My stepson is a prodigy drummer in an excellent high school music program. While we are very supportive of his talent, we are also pragmatic. There are so many drummers (and now smart digital drum machines) but so few openings for rock stars or studio musicians. Then you need luck and other things to go your way. One of the discouraging jokes a relative told him recently at dinner was, "What do you call a drummer without a girlfriend? Homeless." Therefore, we are also working on a plan B. We talk about music teacher, public advocacy attorney, chef, and other middle-class occupations that do not seem quite as exciting but for which he also possesses talent that could help shape a good life, would pay his bills and still allow him to play music.

"SECURE" NO LONGER DEFINES THE MIDDLE CLASS

As is well documented in Howard Zinn's *A People's History of the United States*, the middle class originally emerged in the early Americas. On one side of the economic pole were the very rich: mostly Eastern landholders, robber barons, and industry monopolists—almost exclusively white men. On the other side were the Indians, black slaves, and white (often indentured) servants. In between were merchants, tradespeople, and small farmers whom the elites allowed to prosper—to a degree. The large land-holders and other significant wealth holders gave some rewards and benefits to the middle class in exchange for joining with them to keep the lower classes and Indians in place, and assisting the rich in their larger ambitions.

The war with England was one such early example where there were just not enough wealthy men to mount such an enterprise. In fact, in most American wars, the sons of the rich could buy their way out of battle. In the 1770s, however, the ideal of freedom intoxicated many in the "merchant" class with a deep enough fervor to risk their lives and property even though, in large, it was the wealthy then (as now) who prosper most from almost every war. The English instituted a scuttage tax under the feudal system in the Middle Ages, which allowed the rich to pay a tax instead of having their sons inducted into the army. The tradition continued in more subtle ways in America. As many people noted in the 1960s, not a single senator's son went off to fight the Vietnam War. Although we currently have no military draft in the United States, the vast majority of new soldiers come from poor families.

One can legitimately advance the proposition that high unemployment and unequal access to higher education are covert forms of conscription, a virtual draft on the poor who often see military service as the only opportunity they have to escape intractable poverty. If so, we can see that the government reaps a significant benefit from keeping a large pool of young men undereducated and unemployed. In the American Revolution, they fought for an ideal—freedom. Today, one way for many young people without means to economic advancement is to join the military and then get an education through the GI Bill if they survive. The children of affluent families, however, need not put their lives or limbs at risk to gain an education, though some enter military service for purely patriotic reasons.

One of the primary middle-class dreams, after home ownership and educating children well, is to save enough to retire. Many desires become deferred in service to that "someday" when people will feel they can take it easy and do what they wish with their time. Many middle-class Americans regard their home equity as a sizable portion of their retirement fund. However, one out of every seven mortgages in the United States were either delinquent or in foreclosure in 2012. Many more had zero or even negative equity though people were still making their payments. According to a survey by Wells Fargo, the average American today has saved less than 7 percent of what he or she needs for retirement. Most middle-class Americans think they need about $300,000 to fund their retirement. But that figure does not cover the $200,000 most will need for medical care alone. On average, most have only saved $20,000. Even those aged fifty to fifty-nine have an average of only $29,000.

Laurie Nordquist, director of the Wells Fargo Institutional Retirement Trust, notes, "Barring a miracle, a winning lottery ticket or a big inheritance, they're going to be forced to dramatically cut back their lifestyles after retirement." Another survey, conducted for the Consumer Federation of America, found that 21 percent of the people they contacted actually said that playing the lottery was "the most practical strategy for accumulating several hundred thousand dollars" for retirement. Roughly, half of all retired people leave behind $10,000 or less in savings when they die. Most people, in the current middle class and below, will have to keep working long past the previous generation's retirement age.

A study by the Center for Retirement Research at Boston College found that Americans are now $6.6 trillion short of what they need for retirement. We too have pushed back retirement beyond the visible horizon. My family and I have stopped making plans for the "someday" when the need to work for others will cease. Nevertheless, I am grateful for my employment. What of this book? In truth, only a few hundred American authors per year make a good living writing books. Nevertheless, it is a real privilege to have the opportunity to write. For most of us, however, there is not a large check at the end of the process. The rewards come from the satisfaction of contributing to the dialogue, consulting work, expanding our world of relationships, and the sheer need some of us possess to speak our minds. It is rarely a road to riches. Most middle-class enterprises, however, are not dedicated to acquiring riches as their primary goal.

We reserve the real "wow" in our language of class for the wealthy. If we allow the words to linger on our emotional pallet for a while, even the common terms *wealth* or *rich* provoke a different emotional resonance from *poor*, *poverty*, or *middle* of the road. Such is the psychology of Money. If we think about lemons long enough, our mouths will pucker. These words are loaded. They tap into complexes in our unconscious. They have an impact on both our self-image and the way we perceive others.

A Lexicon of the Rich

A-list
Affluent
Alluring
Bankable
Beautiful people
Blue blood
Capitalized
Connected
Hedge fund manager
Escape velocity
Elite
Entitled
Estate holders
Filthy rich
Flush
Have-mores
Heirs and heiresses
In the clover
In the Money
Insider
Investor
Investment banker
Jet set

Leisure
Loaded
Lords and ladies
Lucrative
Made bank
Mogul
Moneybags
Moneyed
Moneymaker/rain maker
Mover
Nest egg
Nobility
Opulent
Powerful
Profitable
Prosperous
Remunerative
Rich
Riches
Royalty
Ruling class
Set for life
Stockbroker
The 1 percent
Thriving
Upper class
Valued
Winner
Well-heeled
Well-off
Well-to-do
Wherewithal
Worthwhile
Worthy

In the language of class, there is a notable directionality—upper and lower. Up is good. Down is not so good. What is up? Heaven. What is down? The other place. Up are: sky, spaciousness, no limits, light, freedom, and good air. Down are: soil, hard pack, rocks, swamps, mud, dirt, decay, and limits. *Top-drawer* derives its directionality from the old cash registers that kept the larger bills in an upper drawer. The rich are on *top of the heap* and *kings of the hill*. They live and work on top of tall buildings and build estates on hilltops and ridgelines. The poor reside in the cold and flood-prone canyons, on the other side of the tracks, in the inner city, and in basements. The middle classes live and work between the executive suites above and the worker's quarters below, or in suburbs situated between the urban elite's country estates and the rural poor outside the commute range to the city.

On the RMS *Titanic*, a much larger percentage of the wealthy clients from the upper decks survived the sinking as compared to the second- and third-class passengers. The first-class passengers, many of whom continued to dance and dine for almost an hour after the ship hit an iceberg, had first access to the lifeboats. Third-class amenities were below decks (steerage) in an area that locked them off from access to the life-saving boat decks above. Consequently, a much higher percentage of them drowned.

Today, as on the *Titanic*, upper-class people live significantly longer than members of the lower classes due to their access to better health care, better nutrition, less environmental stress, and protection from violence. As noted in chapter 2, white women live an average of eighty years, compared to about sixty-seven years for black men. Ironically, in public opinion polls these women are much more worried about violence than are black men, who are much more likely to die from or be injured by it. Race and gender have little to do structurally with this profound mortality gap. It is not biological. Most of it is cultural, stemming from either class privilege or privation respectively.

White women have been at the forefront of the last few decades' demand for wage equality. This is a just battle for the elimination of a wage gap based on gender. However, there has not been anywhere near as large an outcry for the mortality gap based on race and poverty. Thirteen years' difference in life expectancy is a serious inequity. Most citizens at the bottom, however, feel they lack access to the levers of social transformation and instead focus their energies more on surviving day to day. Are the upper classes still dancing, feeling assured of access to lifeboats, while the ship of the nation flounders with the lower classes locked down, out of sight, below decks? Today one of the largest police forces on earth—most of whom are middle-class—regulate a restive and growing population of citizens who feel excluded from the promise of America. As the heavily policed gatherings of the 99 percent have shown, the police are increasingly in the role of guardians for the elite whose financial crimes, in turn, are under-regulated or even unenforced.

THE BEST GOVERNMENT MONEY CAN BUY

Throughout the history of the United States and in the European nations from where most early American colonists immigrated, wealth holders have enjoyed greater rights than citizens with fewer assets. Royals generally granted titles of nobility to those with great wealth, or conversely to those who gave great service to the crown and were thus rewarded with the great wealth such titles often facilitate. The Queen of England gave the Beatles knighthoods. This was not because of the great service they had provided to women in distress or on the battlefield in some war with France, but largely because of the extreme revenues their record sales brought to the national treasury. They wrote a song complaining about it: "Tax Man."

The English still call their major ruling body of Parliament the House of Lords. If we follow our political taproots all the way back to ancient Greece and Rome, we find the leaders of those governments also tended to be disproportionately wealthy people, as were the signers of the Declaration of Independence, along with our first president and Congress.

In 1994, Arianna Huffington's former husband Michael spent over $30 million, which included $20 million of his own Money, to try to win a

177

senate seat. He lost that election—and his wife in the process, it seems. At the time, it was the most ever spent outside a presidential election. It seems that even in this era of big Money, however, politicians cannot always buy elections, which lends some hope for the future of our nation. This sort of megaspending for public office was just getting started, however.

A few elections later, in 2010, billionaire Meg Whitman spent over $160 million of her own Money in a failed bid to become California's governor. If one were to spread out $160 million in $100 bills, it would cover about 178,060 square feet, slightly more than three football fields. In a stack 664 feet high, the bills would reach over half way up the Empire State Building. Most of us can imagine what we could purchase for one million dollars. When asked, many say "a really nice home." Take that and multiply it 160 times—you get a nice little *town*. Meg Whitman surpassed the previous record for spending on an elected office set by billionaire Michael Bloomberg, who successfully purchased the mayorship of New York City a year prior for $85 million. Not too many people can drop that kind of Money on an aspiration to become the people's representative.

The record for a statewide race stands with Jon S. Corzine of New Jersey, who spent over $63 million, of which all but about $1 million was his own Money. After this successful 2000 bid for the US Senate, he went on to become governor of that state. In 1999, according to estimates, he earned over $400 million during the initial public offering of Goldman Sachs, of which he was CEO at the time. So, purchasing a Senate seat for only a few months' worth of his previous year's income was relatively inexpensive for him.

Given the cost of media-driven campaigning today, if candidates lack the personal fortunes of someone like Mayor Bloomberg of New York, who was the tenth richest person in the United States at the time of his election, few can run without some way to attract large backers to whom they inevitably become accountable. In 2013, 237 members of Congress were millionaires. That works out to 44 percent of the House of Representatives, with seven of them having a net worth in excess of

$100 million. What is the percentage of millionaires among the people they represent? About 1 percent.

Many Americans today note that we now have "the best government Money can buy." Hoover Institute fellow Peter Schweizer published an expose graphically titled, *Throw Them All Out: How Politicians and Their Friends Get Rich off Insider Stock Tips, Land Deals, and Cronyism That Would Send the Rest of Us to Prison.* In it he details how elected officials frequently use their legislative positions to make Money through insider trading on stocks and real estate transactions. He notes that members of Congress do not have to disclose land deals from which they profit. They are often in a position to know exactly when and where federal projects will affect real estate values. But, as lawmakers, they have exempted themselves from the same insider trading laws that govern the rest of us. So, not only do the majority arrive in Washington wealthier than the people they represent but their wealth tends to increase while they are there and after they leave by virtue of their special access to lucrative information that the "people" do not have. The median net worth of the American family is $65,000; for Congress members' families it is $912,000.

An even higher percentage of millionaires populate the US Senate. With about half gaining entree to its 2012 millionaires club, their average net worth is roughly $9 million and their combined assets exceed $1.3 billion. As former Republican senator Everett Dirksen once said, "A billion here, a billion there, and pretty soon you're talking about real money." Speaking of billions, the combined spending by President Obama and Mitt Romney for the 2012 election exceeded $2 billion, surpassing all previous financial records for a presidential campaign. According to various estimates, total spending for all the national seats in 2012 exceeded $8 billion. More than ever, our government is now of, by, and for the elites—government by Midas.

During the Bush administration, the richest members of Congress consistently voted in favor of tax breaks for the rich, even though they were already at their lowest rate since the era following the Great Depression. This is hardly a representative government of and by the people, as the forefathers once hoped for us to be.

THE MORE COMFORTABLE CLASS

I am invited periodically to speak on television shows, provide consultations for organizations and to keynote conferences. On some of those trips, my sponsors provide me with a first-class ticket. It also occasionally happens that the airline upgrades me by some circumstance of overbooking or as a benefit of my frequent flyer miles. Before becoming a rent-a-mouth, I always traveled by coach. Otherwise, my only experience of first-class travel would have been the walk-through we all make as we board the plane. We pick up the discarded copies of the *New York Times* while admiring the fluffy blankets crumpled on the wide seats with individual entertainment centers. We notice the remnants of first-class snacks and meals in the flight attendants' area, replete with empty wine and champagne bottles. The walk-through is designed to awaken a lust for class elevation in the rest of us toward the next ticket purchase. Then we are crowded into coach into almost unbearably small seats with no newspaper, poor meals or none, and the other depravities of flying long distances in a herd.

One of the things I realized traveling in second- and third-class trains and buses in India and Mexico was that as long as all travelers equally shared the discomfort, there was often a semblance of solidarity and community among the commonly discomfited. People would share food with neighbors, pass babies overhead to help mothers get on and off the crowded convenience, and demonstrate other sorts of courtesies that I have rarely experienced on a domestic conveyance in the US. I do not want to overly romanticize travel with the third world's poor since there was also a good share of unusual discomforts. There is the unique experience of having goat yogurt slopped all over one's shoes from large unsealed containers in the aisles, the troubling air filled with an odd brew replete with mixed scents of beetle juice, tobacco, garlic and mystery spice, and sweat, and the babble of many languages.

The point is that as long as we did not see those fortunate few traveling in other classes we were all more or less content with our lot. We were getting where we wanted to go and everyone tried to make the best of it. In air coach, many travelers seethe with petty resentments. It is obvious when we are feeling urgent in the long line to the bathroom that there is no line next to the thin curtain that divides the classes next to the sign that admonishes all passengers "down plane" not to use the first-class bathrooms. When the upper class rubs its privileges in the lesser class's face, a great deal of bitterness can result.

I attended mixed-race Los Angeles middle and high schools. I had an African American girlfriend and often took the bus after school to hang out with her and her brothers and friends in Watts. It seemed normal. My father had also dated an African-American woman. I found their lives and community to be very interesting and engaging, particularly in comparison to my own mostly white neighborhood in West L.A.

Some of my black friends told me that one of the things driving so much resentment in South Central Los Angeles at the time was that if one went only a few miles north, it was obvious that many in the same city were living so much better. Luxury cars cruised the edges of their neighborhoods with wealthier whites in search of drugs or sex. In fact, the evolution of the slang word *honky*, now widely used by blacks to describe white people, derives from the practice of white men honking their horns at black prostitutes in the neighborhood.

The close divide of West Side wealth and South Side poverty in Los Angeles bred a great deal of class resentment that might not otherwise exist were it not broadcast so visibly in the faces of the have-nots. Conversely, my friends reported that they were always at risk for police pulling them over for DWB—driving while black—if they went into the "better" neighborhoods to the north. After the 1965 riots, my own racial blindness no longer granted me safe passage in Watts. My adolescent relationship and friendships there sadly ended as a casualty of that class war.

Marie Antoinette's infamous commentary about the starving masses that had no bread was, "Let them eat cake." Even though this comment is merely attributed to her and may be a fiction of the popular press, her enemies' perceptions of her as frivolous, extravagant, and out of touch with the masses, did not go over well in France at the time. Eventually, poor Marie's head wound up in a basket. Imelda Marcos's 5,400 pair of designer shoes, discovered after the fall of her husband's regime in the Philippines, enraged that impoverished nation, as did Saddam Hussein's dozens of opulent palaces and gold-plated machine guns among many Iraqis who lacked even basic utilities. Visitors to the Vatican's wonders often feel a troubled concern about how many faithful around the world suffer in poverty while some church walls are virtually covered in gold and countless galleries display rare arts of the ages.

During the later years of the Great Recession, sales of luxury cars went up along with many luxury brands like Tiffany, Louis Vuitton, Givenchy, Gucci, and Yves Saint Laurent. This occurred as roughly one in seven American households struggled to put adequate food on the table each day. Newscasts kept reporting that the steadily improving stock market was evidence that the economy was recovering. However, that was just for the upper classes with the majority of stock. Everyone else continued suffering, long after the government said the recession was technically over, and it bred enormous class resentment across the nation. Resentment is different from envy. Envy can occur when someone has something you think that you could acquire, too, given a chance. Resentment occurs when people realize that no matter what they do they cannot have what the other person has because they are not insiders and never will be.

When I commute from my Los Angeles home to teach at the Pacifica Graduate Institute in Santa Barbara, I drive up US Highway 1 with the shimmering Pacific Ocean and fabled Malibu mansions on my left. Surfers dot the coastline's coves, just past dawn, already in the water before most truckers hit the highway. I often sigh with a tinge of envy. How did they make their lives so free as to be in the glorious sea while I have to lecture for eight hours today in between my four-hour round-trip commute? Ah, poor me, wonderful them. Despite whatever poverty or indolence they may actually possess, they seem to be indulging in lives of pure pleasure. They are the privileged members of some fantastic aristocracy, like the Hawaiian kings of old who were the only ones allowed to surf. Of course, many of them then strip out of their glistening wet suits, put on their work clothes, and arrive for labors somewhere else, too. But the sight activates my longing for leisure. Then as the morning mists give way to the full sun of another hot Southern California day I turn into the 101 and pass through miles of the open fertile fields of Ventura and Carpinteria on my right. There I often notice hundreds of agricultural fieldworkers bent over rows of crops.

Like a bottle discarded out the car widow, any sense of deprivation I possess quickly shatters on the highway below. I am relieved that my back is not bent this day and that my work actually provides enough compensation to support my family. My labor tires me, but the fieldworkers' labor exhausts them. I am safe at work; they are damaged by stooped labor, exposure to toxic chemicals, machines, and injuries that accompany stepped-up piece-work—wages based not on hours but on how much product they pick each day. My work provides a desirable lifestyle. Their work barely assures day-to-day survival for their families.

Many of these workers along the road are Mextec Indians. A few decades ago, they lived in Mexico on lands that their families had inhabited for over seven hundred years. Whether by misguided compassion or Machiavellian design, some people convinced them that if they used superfertilizers from the United States on their fields they could increase their production. Their land was poor; small plots tacked onto steep mountainsides. Nevertheless, they had produced small but steadily sufficient crops for hundreds of years. With their indigenous methods they had sustained the lives of their culture and their community.

The chemicals did indeed produce bigger crops. Word spread, and most everyone embraced this so-called green revolution. Within a few years, however, the chemically induced overproduction burned out the thin soil. Production then declined. Farmers became indebted to the chemical companies. Rains washed away the depleted soil until only rocks remained. In less than one generation, this gift from the north destroyed their fragile existence in mountain settlements. Without crops, and facing debt, they left in droves. Many moved north to settle in the agricultural communities of Santa Barbara and surrounding counties. Some live as many as twenty people to a small home in order to afford the exorbitant rents in our region.

I really love those strawberries. They are cheap and abundant. The kids go wild when I come home with baskets of them as a small return on my time away. However, I know the story and it weighs on me. Honestly, I would rather pay triple the price for those luscious, red sweets if I knew those workers had health care, disability, some sort of retirement, and education for their children, who are now increasingly joining gangs. They do not long to join the ranks of their bent-backed parents in the fields but have little opportunity to gain new skills.

So, there I am like so many of my peers, stretched between aristocratic freedom and virtual serfdom. This is a psychology of the middle class: we long to move up and fear sliding down. Caught as we are in our anxieties, most of us stay where we are with an uneasy gratitude, whistling through the economic graveyards of American life.

One of the many people I interviewed for this book is a Catholic Nun named Sister Mary Lobo. She has worked for many years in the poorest part of central India where this interview took place. There, she facilitates microcredit lending to groups of women who, individually, try to support their families on about one dollar per day. She expresses concerns about the real dangers that can occur when increasingly fewer people control the resources of the many saying,

> Perhaps the West could examine or explore the consumer values that are being promoted through this global market, you know, this could be questioned. People in the West could simplify life perhaps and see in which way they can save their resources, volunteer, build bridges, show solidarity, welcome communities of people from these countries, come together in transforming human consciousness in whatever way we can feel around, whichever way can be worked out reasonably, you know? So, I think much needs to be done.

> See, the whole situation I feel is becoming quite explosive. Either we support each other, we work together, or the system will collapse

with its own weight. The whole power of the global economy, and the few elites who are controlling the resources, controlling the electronic media, controlling the market, the corporate world that holds the market, you know, how long can they do it? It's a false system. It doesn't really understand. It's not in tune with the ground reality, the big populations that we have in the third world. Is that the only way, that we all get as rich as possible? Or is there another aspect to human life? I think we should explore this.

We will hear more from Sister Mary in chapter 8.

Political scientists Jacob Hacker of Yale University and Paul Pierson of the University of California–Berkeley make a very compelling argument that a multitude of governmental policy changes that overwhelmingly favored the very rich have caused the recent declines of the lower classes. Their book *Winner-Take-All Politics: How Washington Made the Rich Richer—and Turned Its Back on the Middle Class* debunks many popular explanations, such as globalization and new technology, advanced by those who attempt to occlude the view of class war as a real issue causing class declines in the United States.

Many statistics support their view. The wealth of people making $50 million or more per year increased more than 500 percent during the same years the rest of the population was suffering though the Great Recession. Hacker and Pierson believe that this "massive change in the distribution of wealth and income in the U.S.... has happened largely through changes in industrial relations policies affecting labor unions, through corporate governance policies that have allowed CEOs to basically set their own pay, and so on." The terrible polarization of wealth and power in this country means we can no longer claim equal opportunity for a majority of Americans.

The statistical evidence is massive. It could fill many a book. We have other things to consider, however, and I think the point is clear. It is as if the engines that pull the economy along became uncoupled from the rest of the train somewhere along the way. The superrich were in the few first-class cars connected to the engines and kept on going while the other ninety-five passenger cars were left behind to sit idle on the tracks or slide down hill. Most of us do not have stocks and bonds. So, when financial experts broadcast that the market is improving, what does that mean to millions who are out of work or losing their homes and dreams?

The net result of all these above policies is that wealth distribution in America today looks much like the European aristocracies that so inflamed John Adams and other American patriots during our nation's origins. What remains different is that here, at least, some people have a chance to migrate upward, despite their status at birth. So, what can we do to make it more democratic so that all can have that chance? Low-cost, quality education for all, for example, would go a long way toward achieving that. As discussed above, the more elite education becomes, the more our democracy is in peril. We can do much, however, to remake our nation as a more egalitarian and free country, as chapter 8 will detail. To understand more deeply the problem that the Midas Complex's hold on our nation represents, however, we need to better examine the psychology of the players who brought on the Great Recession.

CHAPTER 6

THE PREDATOR'S BALL: WHEN MIDAS RULES CORPORATIONS

Banking establishments are more dangerous than standing armies.
—Thomas Jefferson

Midas Myth #6: *Money managers always have our best interests at heart.*
Reality: *Some people who want our Money just want our Money.*

THE SHADOW OF MONEY

In chapter 5's lexicon of the lower class, a number of the words appeared more associated with the shadowy side of Money than the neutral language of the middle class and the more idealized terms reserved for the upper class. *The shadow* is a concept from analytic psychology developed by Carl Jung. The shadow represents the hidden, repressed, dark aspects of any phenomenon or aspect of the self that is not in accord with our idealized image. In the shadow, we feel most awkward, inferior, sinister, and ashamed. In many ways, as the lexicon of the upper class reveals, Money has a great allure—a glittering, golden promise of freedom and pleasure. Every phenomenon, however, has its opposite pole, like the dark side of the moon. Money is no different in this respect. The myth of Midas is all about this polarity of opposites: King Midas's gift turns into a curse. Consider some of the language from the other side of the coin: the dark side of Money:

Black market
Blackmail
Blood Money
Bribe
Carpetbagger
Con game
Con man
Criminal
Dealer
Deadbeat
Enforcer
Extortion
Fraud
Gangster
Gold digger
Graft
Hush Money
Loan shark
Miser
Mobster
Money-grubber
Mugger
Payoff
Payola
Ponzi scheme
Protection racket
Ransom
Robber
Robber baron

Selling your soul
Social climber
Shadow economy
Tax dodger
Thief
Underworld economy

Today, we might also add a few investment bankers, Wall Street traders, mortgage brokers, CEO's, and hedge fund administrators to this list.

These words and others like them can provoke emotional reactions from us. They are muggers waiting in the dark alley of our psyches. Most of us, as the secrets exercise in chapter 3 revealed, have had encounters with the shadow side of Money. Many of us have had to struggle with seductions from the dark side when given the opportunity to do something that would bring us more Money at the expense of our moral principles. As a concern of the soul, Money carries with it many potential hazards to our full development as human beings. It is no coincidence that Moneta, the Roman goddess from whom the word *Money* descends, was actually the goddess of warning.

In Mark 8:36 the Bible asks, "For what shall it profit a man, if he shall gain the whole world, and lose his own soul?" One of the more revered teachers in the lineage of my meditation practice, Swami Bramanada Saraswati, said that if we neglected our practice in order to pursue gifts in the marketplace it was like "selling a diamond for the price of spinach."

Many of us periodically feel forced to consider some sort of "devil's bargain" around Money. For me it is something like, "If I take this extra work—course, seminar, consultation, or client—our family will have more Money." That is good. This year we need more over last year for: braces, writing camp, and a new car. They raised our health and home insurance. Food and fuel costs are up. School transportation is way up since the high school canceled the free bus. The driveway needs repair after hard winter storms. And more. The draw toward earning more is great. However, more work means less quality time with the kids, who are growing up fast; less time with my lovely wife; less time in the garden; less time for hiking, kayaking, having long lunches with friends, or doing any of the other things I love. Selling time for Money is a dangerous calculation. I could sell all my time and make twice as much but have a significantly lowered quality of life.

My difficult choices at this time of life are very privileged ones. Many people pray for problems like these. For others the bargain is much more intense. Should I commit this crime, risk my health, my reputation, my freedom, or even my life for this Money? Or, how can I get any Money at all? In my adolescence, however, my choices were much harder. The poverty of my childhood fueled a lifelong commitment to creating a life in which the choices would be more palatable.

DAD'S PAST-POST CON GAME

My father, Kip, was a gambler on horse races. Even though he was an excellent judge of horses, gambling did not work out much of the time, as our rapid rides up and down the economic scale attested. In order to even the odds somewhat, Kip employed various con games around the horse racing business. One of his most lucrative, elaborate, and dangerous cons was the *past-post scam*. In those days, before cell phones and other electronic devices, the racetracks would shut down all their pay phones at the start of a race and allowed no information out until the horses had finished their run.

On certain days when it was raining and the track was muddy, conditions could slow the entire day's proceedings. Then officials might run some races a little before the official post time to gain some time. That meant the results could be known to anyone inside the track before the race had been scheduled to finish, but not to anyone outside. Occasionally a race could actually finish before its post time—its published start time. It was the policy of bookies, outside the track, to keep taking bets from their customers until the posted start of the race. Then, like everyone else around the country, they would wait for the official results to be announced before paying out or collecting on their bets. However, if the race had already run, the knowledge held inside the track was tantamount to insider knowledge of a stock move before it happened. It was illegal and highly profitable to those willing to take the risk of trying to trick bookies, many of whom were connected with the criminal underworld.

Kip spent many years at the track and got to know the whole system well. One of the smaller cons he ran when I was a child was the *parking lot tip sheet scam*. He was ostensibly a "tout." At least, that is what he told people he did for a living. A tout is like a stockbroker of horse racing. A tout has insider knowledge of the horses, just as a broker supposedly knows stocks better than the average investor does. Kip published a daily tip sheet called *The California Wire.* He had a small booth right outside the racetrack entrance where every morning he sold these tip sheets that we printed up at home on a small printing press the night before. There were various prices—$20, $50, and $100 sheets, each one on a different color of paper: Green, pink and gold. The implication was that the more expensive the sheet, the better the information. This parallels stockbrokers' range of preferred services over their more pedestrian portfolio management.

Every morning before the first race or two, a few bettors who believed that Kip had some sort of inside take on the day would purchase his tip sheets in the hopes of gaining an edge on that day's winners. We were at the track all day, every summer, whenever the horses were running at Del Mar, California, or Agua Caliente in Tijuana, Mexico. During the school year, whenever I was staying with him, we were at Golden Gate Fields in San Francisco and other tracks. Every so often, when the sales of the *Wire* lagged, he would have me run out with him after the fifth race to the parking lot to help run a scam that could boost sales the next day.

In the back of his station wagon was a hand-cranked, portable printing press with movable rubber type. We would know, of course, which horses were the actual winners, and which would place and show (take second and third place) for the first five races. We would then make up new $100 sheets on the spot with that day's date on it. They were exactly like that morning's sheet except with a few more winners on them. He often got at least one pick right on his own. He was not a total fraud, and actually could pick a winner now and then. The new sheet would still have whatever good picks he made the day before, but for the first five races there would be a few substitutions with the known winners. He would also throw in a few place or show horses. This was just to make it appear that even when he did not get the winner he was close. In other words, even though he knew the results of the first five races, he tried not to overdo it and to create something that still looked believable. That is, if you believed that some guy in a little plywood booth wearing a worn wool newsboy's cap could really have the inside track on the road to sudden fortune. One thing I learned by the time I was nine years old was that most gamblers were naive and were caught up in what my clinical colleagues today call *infantile magical belief systems*.

I fanned each page in the sun, quickly drying the ink. Then I carefully folded the sheets and applied the same seal that the real sheets had that morning. Then we put them all in a canvas bag slung over my shoulder. After the last race—or earlier, if we finished in time—I would stand outside the gate and hand out gold sheets to the departing gamblers, yelling, "*California Wire* had four winners today!" Bettors rarely bought the $100 gold sheet, so it was a gamble that someone who actually bought one that morning would compare his legitimate sheet to the counterfeit one we were giving away at the end of the day. Anyway, "What could he do about it?" my Dad would say, telling me not to worry about it. The average bettor who took home only the counterfeit sheet at the end of the day would think, "Wow, this guy is a great tout. If I had bought his sheet this morning I would have made a killing." So the next day he would be back at Kip's stand, anxious to fork over $100 for the top sheet.

All he got, of course, was Dad's best guess for that day. Maybe one winner or two at his best, but if he bet the whole sheet he would be a loser like most bettors at every other racetrack around the world. We only did this once every few weeks. Maybe some guys caught on, but Dad would take the heat. The after-the-races counterfeit *Wire* was a small con that might have pissed off the occasional small-time gambler who caught on to what he was doing. But, just like Bernie Madoff, my father felt that if a sucker took the bait it was his own fault for being a fool. The past-post scam, however, was a big-time score that pissed off bookies—and they had guns, or at the least had associates with them. It was a real high-risk, high-reward game.

Here is how he got the information out once the results were known, the post time had not yet passed and off-track bookies were still taking bets: He had one guy who would stand in the very upper tier of the racetrack. On the top floor of a building, about half a mile away, was another guy with a powerful telescope. The angle was such that he could see the man in the top of the stand who had a series of simple hand signals to telegraph the number of the winner. The man with the telescope had a phone that was on the line to my dad. Kip had a backroom office with fourteen more phones in it and every one of them had a bettor on the line. Each of those bettors had at least two phones and was on the other line to his bookie. The message passed like electricity through a wire, hand-to-hand, in seconds. The man in the racetrack signaled that it was number 3. The man with the telescope saw it was number 3. "Number 3," he said to Kip. "Number 3," Kip said into the fourteen other phones with bettors on the line, hanging up each one in turn. "Number 3," they said into their second phones with a bookie on each line. Bang, bang, bang it went and everybody scored at the end of the day. Except the bookies, of course, who all lost Money.

Dad's confederates made solid, but not huge, bets spread out to bookies all over the country. They had to be cagey; it was a sure thing. However, he could not control the greed of so many friends. It was risky because even in those days without computers, bookies had a sharp nose for statistically anomalous outcomes. More than one larger-than-usual bet coming in on a past-post day could alert them to something going on. But, no one could figure out how he did it.

More than once in my childhood I had to go meet strange, tough-looking guys with bulges in their jackets at the front door and tell them that my dad had not been home for several weeks. "He's in Miami," I said. Miami was the linen closet in the bathroom. In any case, he was never caught and the past-post scam bailed him out of a few cash-poor times. I learned, however, that cons can rig any game and that the riggers, not the suckers, are the ones who make the Money. Dad was a small-time grifter compared to the corporate con men of our era. The crooks that brought on the Great Recession far surpassed any of the con men that I spent my childhood around, both in the scale of their cons and the viciousness with which they went after their suckers.

The code in my father's little mob was to bleed people a little, here and there, such that they could live to be subject of another small con another day. The Wall Street gangs rampaging through the Great Recession had no such "honor among thieves." They were so far from the ravages of the street that their identification with the upper classes and a psychology of inherent privilege and superiority seemed to breed an attitude of utter contempt for their clients. That sense of privilege also appeared to make them heedless of retribution. They apparently did not believe they would ever be held accountable for their wrong actions, and this has actually proved true in the majority of large-scale financial crimes. The architects of the Great Recession apparently possessed a willingness to utterly destroy the economic vitality of clients, whole institutions, and even the entire nation—simply to profit a few. Possibly, more than for the simple gain of a few more billions, they did so just because they could, the same reason serial killers murder strangers—for the thrill. Their code was cold-blooded and ghoulish, like the one that said, "Rip the client's face off" and then, apparently, have a good laugh about it.

THE PSYCHOLOGICAL POWER OF GREED

In 1987, the movie *Wall Street* made its debut. Gordon Gecko, the ruthless stock trader played by Michael Douglas, coined the now famous catch phrase "greed is good." What he meant was that greed is the energy that fuels the stock market and, by implication, the capitalist economy. The actual lines from the film are: "The point is, ladies and gentleman, that greed, for lack of a better word, is good. Greed is right, greed works. Greed clarifies, cuts through, and captures the essence of the evolutionary spirit. Greed, in all of its forms; greed for life, for money, for love, knowledge has marked the upward surge of mankind."

Over twenty years later in the sequel—*Money Never Sleeps*—the banks were the villains, not just one trader. The producer of both films, Oliver Stone, says, "I think the banks became what Gecko was in the 1980s. Greed became greed plus envy [which] gave us more and more and more. As

Gecko in the new film says, 'greed is now legal' in the sense that the banks were doing what he was doing back then and he went to jail.... The idea that the entire system was dependent on a credit bubble that could pop overnight was really hard to convey on-screen." Another film, *Margin Call*, made in 2011 with Jeremy Irons as the ruthless CEO of a fictional investment firm, conveys in simple dramatic terms the callous self-interest and deliberate deception that led directly to the Great Recession.

Wall Street trader Ivan Boesky reportedly made the original "greed is good" speech. Like the fictional Gecko, Boesky actually did go to jail for insider trading. Michael Milken is another infamous trader who went to jail for insider trading. He was enamored of hostile takeovers, gutting businesses for their salvageable parts like a butcher with an MBA. He used to host an annual conference known as the Predators' Ball.

The events that took place on Wall Street from the summer of 2007 to the fall of 2008 gave new meaning to the word *greed* and shook many of us to our core concerning our capacity to trust the leaders of our economy. Young men coming out of the best business schools, armed with MBAs, discovered that they could steal more with securitizations and leverage then any mobster ever could with a machine gun. Many people were left wondering, "What happened to civics, morals, ethics, belief in the common good, and a collaborative American society?" How did young men from "respectable" families that had handed them a multitude of class privileges turn into ruthless predators, willing to savage entire institutions and even whole nations for their personal gain? Criminals, many may think, mostly come from poverty and hunger, not from advantage and ease; my father's partners were all undereducated and lacked good job prospects. But the financial crimes of a few members of the upper classes now outstrip all other forms of financial crime.

As mentioned in passing in chapter 2, when Barings Bank in England went bankrupt in 1995 it was Britain's oldest and one of its most prestigious banks, having been founded in 1762. What happened? One young, rogue trader named Nick Leeson simply could not bear to tell his friends at work the truth: he was losing tons of Money in the stock market. He was a golden boy with a record for more successful trades than others. His record of accomplishment gave him greater latitude and trust, which he abused, ultimately committing massive fraud to cover the tracks of his growing losses. He lied to everyone, too embarrassed to reveal his errors and get out while the bank could still recover. Like a drunken gambler, he kept doubling his bets. When a huge earthquake hit Kobe, Japan, the Nikkei (Japanese stock market) took a dive and Leeson was on the wrong side of highly leveraged bets in that market. In a few months of trading, he wiped out a firm that had been in business for over two hundred years. This was just a preview of what was to come to other financial institutions around the world a little over a decade later.

By various reports, JPMorgan Chase and Goldman Sachs—two of the largest investment banks in America—ruthlessly took advantage of competitors in questionable ways in the early years of the twenty-first century. They took piles of insecure subprime home mortgages and packaged them into mortgage backed-securities called "collateralized debt obligations." These new securities hid the inherent toxicity of individual mortgages issued to borrowers without the means to repay them. Brokers then sold these packages of mortgages to unsuspecting investors who thought that people who knew more about finance then they did had vetted the contents. Most investors at this time never imagined the rampant greed and outright contempt these huge bankers and traders had for their clients and the stability of American economy. Few investors who purchased these new breeds of investment had any way to become aware of their poisoned nature. Buoyed by degrees, certificates, and the governmental regulations that many of us rely upon to help make credible the people we trust, investment advisers intentionally deceived them.

Despite the Great Recession, which it helped bring on, JPMorgan Chase's profits were way up by 2011. The firm handed out million-dollar-plus bonuses to many top-earning employees. This occurred while millions of Americans were still reeling from the unexpected, sudden loss of their homes, retirement funds, and other savings. In 2012, former employee Greg Smith publically exposed their widespread callous treatment of clients in the *New York Times*. He wrote about why he quit the firm after twelve years, noting,

Not one single minute is spent asking questions about how we can help clients. It's purely about how we can make the most possible money off of them. If you were an alien from Mars and sat in on one of these meetings, you would believe that a client's success or progress was not part of the thought process at all. It makes me ill how callously people talk about ripping their clients off. Over the last 12 months I have seen five different managing directors refer to their own clients as "muppets," [stupid people; puppets who can be manipulated] sometimes over internal e-mail.

He quoted the traders as also gloating about "ripping out client's eyeballs."

In other news, in 2012 Chase CEO Jamie Dimon admitted losing $2 billion of clients' Money on a bad trade. Most experts believe the loss was closer to $6 billion. After the news broke, the bank lost over $2 billion of its market value in just three days. Nevertheless, Chase's shareholders approved $23 million in compensation for Dimon for 2012, after he dismissed the widespread outcry about the trading loss as a "tempest in a teapot." Even though he admitted his acts were "stupid," he unabashedly continued lobbying for lawmakers to not further regulate the very activities that led to this spectacular loss. Under current rules he broke no laws; he only betrayed the faith and trust of the investors in the bank he led. Another trader, however, operated far outside existing laws, accumulating investor losses that far outstrip the high-risk bad bets made by big Money men at the helm of our major financial institutions.

THE INCREDIBLY CHARMING MR. MADOFF

There are many new books about the precipitating causes of the Great Recession. Sorting out all the details is outside the purview of this book. Beyond metafinancial analysis, however, there is one prominent psychological feature that stands out boldly—greed. The face of the Midas Complex is everywhere while the complex itself often remains well hidden. More than any other element, rampant avarice was the reason that the economy crashed.

Echoing Gordon Gecko, greed was the primary force that took so many of Bernie Madoff's clients to the cleaners. Most of them believed that their favored status and closeness to insider information entitled them to greater investment returns than less fortunate others exiled to investing outside the borders of country clubs. There, insiders passed information with a wink, a nod, and envelopes full of cash to gain admission to the inner, in-the-know, circle. Investigators have well-documented Mr. Madoff's insane insatiability. He is languishing in prison for the rest of his life. Others of his cohort are facing charges, and numerous lawsuits are pending against investors who withdrew fictional profits from his accounts over the years—the largest such financial fraud in US history. Wall Street fraud now exceeds, by far, that of any practiced by the underworld, organized criminal class.

Greed, it seems, is a somewhat contagious element of the Midas Complex. When greed becomes part of the sanctioned mores for any social group, then it becomes increasingly easy for individuals to become less questioning of that value. Many people periodically look to others around them for the mirroring of their moral codes and values. We ask our parents, teachers, mentors, spouses, friends and associates, "I am thinking of this or that—what do you think?" When they answer, "Lie, cheat, take the Money and run" above all other choices, it sets a moral tone. It helps create a community of confederates organized around greed. It takes a whole village to steal a nation's wealth.

In his first prison interview with Brian Ross and Kate McCarthy, Madoff said he could not believe he got away with his massive Ponzi scheme for so long, even after the Securities and Exchange Commission investigated him. He felt his scheme was so transparent that any investigator could have unraveled it with a few phone calls. Nevertheless, he fooled them all with the unabashed charisma and guiltless countenance that is a common feature in criminals who do not care about the consequences of their self-indulgence on others lives.

According to Steve Fishman of *New York* magazine, when a prison consultant asked Madoff how he got into the whole mess he said, "People just kept throwing money at me.... Some guy wanted to invest, and if I said no, the guy said, 'What, I'm not good enough?'" A drug dealer in his unit reported that Madoff told him that he "took money off of people who were rich and greedy and wanted more." When asked about how he felt about his victims, he reportedly said in a voice loud enough for other prisoners to hear, "Fuck my victims, I carried them for 20 years, and now I'm doing 150 years."

In truth, his swindle also destroyed the economic lives of thousands of innocent people and numerous charitable organizations as well. Likely there were a few greedy fools, but Madoff's callousness and grandiosity in the face of the extensive harm he did is more characteristic of a deeply etched criminal personality than a financial wizard gone wrong. His response to learning that two of his investors had committed suicide over their losses lends further evidence to his unconscionable attitude. He reportedly merely commented that they were "weak." The Midas Complex can be fatal. The greater degree to which Money represents a person's identity, the more destructive power Money has to distort and even destroy their sense of self.

In a tragic footnote to this grotesque folly, on the second anniversary of Bernie Madoff's arrest, his forty-six-year-old son Mark was found dead of an apparent suicide, in his six-million-dollar New York City apartment. This happened just two days after a bankruptcy trustee filed a lawsuit seeking assets his father may have hidden with his family members. The suit included Mark Madoff's children, who allegedly had assets hidden in their trust funds. Mark Madoff's death, however, did not stop the lawsuits against his family and his brother Andrew remained under investigation for complicity in their father's scheme.

Past investors sued other members of both the immediate and extended Madoff family, staff, and other close associates. The theory was that they were all in positions of control in the family business and had the means to know what was going on. Others, it is alleged, received a great amount of illegally gained cash from Bernie Madoff, and the victims wanted it back. Mark Madoff reportedly earned about $30 million from the firm over its last eight years and took $17 million more from the family's accounts. The lawsuit sought $67 million, and there were at least half a dozen other suits against him.

The bankruptcy trustee's suits also named various banks and other large financial institutions. He alleged that they had aided and abetted Mr. Madoff and continued to profit from his schemes long after they should have stopped since they had their own questions about his accounting sheets, which were made up from thin air. The suits alleged that there was sufficient information to suggest something was not right but that they failed in their diligence because they were blinded by profits as great as their losses would be if they were to discover that it was all a swindle.

Untold numbers of well-trained financial experts seemed to turn a blind eye as rivers of cash flowed from Bernie Madoff into their investment coffers. Senior executives at JPMorgan Chase reportedly voiced significant concerns about Madoff's business more than eighteen months before his house of cards collapsed. Nevertheless, according to bank documents, they continued doing business with him. David J. Sheehan, the trustees' lawyer, could not have been more to the point when he said that Mr. Madoff "would not have been able to commit this massive Ponzi scheme without this bank." One man's greed ruined an uncountable number of lives, which in turn infected hundreds of others with his promises of easy Money.

In late 2012, Peter Madoff became the sixth person to plead guilty—for his part in his older brother's scam. He received a ten-year prison sentence. His wife and daughter had to forfeit millions of dollars of their assets. The US Attorney continues to explore criminal charges against many others involved in the whole affair.

In retrospect, it is apparent that any straight-ahead investigation into these dealings would have reveled their transparently fraudulent nature. Huge flows of cash were moving in and out of Bernie Madoff's accounts, with no evidence that it was ever invested in securities. This is the fundamental red flag for a Ponzi investment: returns to older investors are paid with cash from new investors, with no investment profits ever created. In a *New York Times* interview with Diana B. Henriques, Mr. Madoff discussed financial institutions, "willful blindness." He felt they deliberately failed to note discrepancies in his documentation. "They had to know," he said. "But the attitude was sort of, 'If you're doing something wrong, we don't want to know.'" And, of course, the gutting of America's economy runs much deeper than this. As we will see, there were many other pirates operating with apparent impunity on our financial high seas.

THE ROBBER'S PAY GRADE

The average bank robber in America takes away about $4,000 from a crime. From 1990 to 2010, the annual number of attempted bank robberies in the United States ranged from a high of 11,876 to a low of 8,193. Taking a rough average of 10,000 such robberies each year, the total annual proceeds of bank robberies are roughly $40 million. Over twenty years, in one of the most prosperous nations on the planet, the total bank theft haul would be about $800 million. A billion is 1,000 million. By some estimates, Bernie Madoff stole $65 billion. Elie Wiesel called him a "god." In fact, it is not for certain that even God has that much Money, coming as he does from a small Middle Eastern country with no oil. It would take an army of bank robbers committing decades of bank thefts to equal the loot carted out of the savings of Mr. Madoff's investors.

Most bank robbers are arrested for their crimes. Once charged, the courts tend to sentence them to long prison sentences. It is a very high-risk, low-reward activity. Some may think, why risk prison or being shot when it is easier and more lucrative to steal with a pen, some paper, a great smile, and the ability to gain other people's confidence?

Another way to understand the magnitude of recent large scale, so-called white-collar crime is to compare it to all crime in America. According to FBI statistics, every year over ten million property crimes are reported in America. Collectively, victims of property crimes lose over $17 billion per year. Of that, about $7.5 billion is in motor vehicle thefts, $5 billion is the result of larceny thefts, and $4 billion is in burglaries. So, Madoff's crime alone exceeded, by far, the entire annual property crime activity for the rest of the nation. These crimes annually cost the government billions of dollars in police services, adjudication, and incarceration expense.

Perhaps some of our public safety and justice funds would be better dedicated to policing the large wolves in our major financial institutions over the intensive focus on small time street-level crime, which never comes near the economic damages wrought by professional thieves at the top of our economy. As film director Charles Ferguson noted when accepting his 2011 Academy Award for best documentary, *Inside Job* (about the 2008 financial crisis), "Forgive me, I must start by pointing out that three years after our horrific financial crisis caused by financial fraud, not a single financial executive has gone to jail, and that's wrong." In his later years, the famous gangster Lucky Luciano is said to have told a reporter (who had asked him, if given the chance would he do it all again?), "I'd do it legal. I learned too late that you need just as good a brain to make a crooked million as an honest million."

Greed took down the stock and bond markets, many banks, and the real estate markets. The stockbrokers who figured out how to turn residential real estate mortgages into a security allowed the mortgages on millions of real people's homes to be sold like hog futures, thus ruining countless lives. Many of these same brokers were still reaping huge profits and bonuses as the stock market slowly recovered into 2013, far ahead of the rest of the economy that was still floundering.

RIPPING OFF THEIR FACES

The book *13 Bankers: The Wall Street Takeover and the Next Financial Meltdown*, by Simon Johnson and James Kwak, documents how some ruthless banks operated in the 1990s. It notes, "Traders and salesmen would boast about 'ripping the face off' their clients—structuring and selling complicated deals that clients did not understand but that generated huge profits for the bank that was brokering the trade." Although this was all well known a decade before the crash of 2008, the banks and Wall Street traders of the early twenty-first century were even more corrupt, learning nothing from the past except how to create even more sophisticated rip-offs of their unsuspecting clients. Now they surgically removed their client's faces with anesthesia, so skillfully that no one even noticed until all of their investment capital was irretrievably gone.

In his book *The Greatest Trade Ever*, *Wall Street Journal* reporter Greg Zuckerman explains how a hedge fund manager named John Paulson reportedly paid Goldman Sachs $15 million in 2007 to create an investment for which he allegedly was allowed to cherry-pick the investments that they layered into packages of mortgage-backed securities called *tranches*. Traders rated these packaged obligations into different categories of risk and then sold them to investors. This is an exotic but legal way to turn mortgages into securities that can be bought or sold by investors. It seems, however, that in this case Mr. Paulson reportedly selected underperforming securities to hide inside these packages for Goldman to sell to its clients. If true, why would he stick rotten apples at the bottom of the barrel? According to David Fiderer, a writer for the Huffington Post who analyzed the Zuckerman book, he did so in order to then bet against these same securities' success by taking out insurance against their poor performance, knowing more than anyone that they were destined to fail.

This is like betting against a fighter who was otherwise favored to win because you are the only one in the room who knew someone had paid him to throw the fight, or betting against a favorite horse in a race because you had drugged it. In gambling events, they call this knowing that "the fix is in." In other words, inside players have rigged the outcome and the bet is a sure thing. Just as in my father's past-post scam, everyone made Money but the bookies. In the case of these financial institutional swindles, the brokers made Money while the investors who trusted their certified, institutionally vetted, and governmentally licensed investment advisers to guide them through the complexities of this new breed of investment all lost.

When the Security and Exchange Commission's investigation of Goldman's deal ultimately resulted in fraud charges, it noted that within a year of the deal closing, 99 percent of the portfolio had been downgraded. This created losses of over $1 billion for Goldman investors. Coincidently, that is just about the same amount John Paulson and Goldman Sachs made through taking positions against their clients. However, Goldman stock plummeted more than $14 billion at that time—so these fellows wound up ripping the face off their own company, too, it seems. Ultimately, by some estimates, beyond the billions he made for his fund, Paulson made as much as $4 billion for his personal profit off the "subprime" crisis. Goldman Sachs eventually agreed to pay $550 million to settle the fraud suit brought by the Securities and Exchange Commission, but no one went to jail. Yet millions of people lost their homes and countless investors lost their life savings.

BANKERS WITHOUT CONSCIENCE

In the 1970s, a Goldman senior partner created a list of principles to guide banks. They are still part of the firm's business mantra today. Among them are the beliefs that their clients' interests always come first and that they base their success on serving their clients well. These guidelines caution that their prime assets are people, capital, and reputation and that if any of these are ever lost their reputation will be the most difficult of all to regain. But among today's ruthless crew of financial predators, concerned only about their individual gain at any expense, the traditions of mutual benefit through time have been jettisoned by some amoral financial geniuses with no thought for anyone else's future. Greed by a few amid the long-held trust of many brought our national economy to its knees.

This is not finance as we have known it. This is more like psychopathology. We have a word in psychology that we reserve for people with no conscious who take advantage of others with no remorse or limit: *psychopath*. Psychopaths, as chapter 7 discusses, are people characterized by a general lack of empathy for other people. One of the foremost psychological researchers on psychopaths, Robert Hare, titled his book about them *Without Conscience*. When psychopaths are born into the lower socioeconomic sector, they tend to become street-level criminals who hurt a few people and wind up in jail. When they get Harvard Business School educations, however, they tend to become master criminals who hurt thousands, even millions of people and then, at worst, wind up in county-club "soft" prisons for a short term followed by a long, well-paid tour on the lecture circuit.

In the 1990s, allegations against Bankers Trust's derivatives business brought a number of audiotapes to the surface. These tapes reveled aspects of how the traders there did business. One trader, who sold Procter & Gamble some dubious derivatives contracts for which they later sued the bank, was recorded saying, "It's like Russian roulette and I keep putting another bullet in the revolver every time I do one of these [deals]." In a video-taped training session for new employees, a bank instructor discribes a hypothetical transaction among Sony, IBM, and the bank saying, "What Bankers Trust can do...is get in the middle and rip them off—take a little money." After an employee asks another trader about how to go about winning a client's confidence, he replies, "Funny business, you know? Lure people into that calm and then just totally fuck 'em." That particular recording was instrumental in destroying the reputation of the bank. It never fully recovered. In an unprecedented response to the rampant financial fraud of the early twenty-first century, Great Britain now requires *all* work-related cell phone conversations by traders to be audio taped in order to combat fraud.

Predators prey on confidence. Confidence can make us naive and cause us to fail to do our due diligence, trust our own instincts, and require proof. If someone asks, "Don't you trust me?" when offering a deal we can say, "Yes I do, but I do not trust human nature, which includes getting possessed by the Midas Complex." Every con man knows that he cannot cheat an honest person. Greed blinds us. Predators lack the morality that guides the majority of us. They use trickery and illusions to create and then play on the unreasonable expectations of their prey. When the Midas Complex takes hold of people, their moral playbook bursts into flames and all they want is the gold you are holding, which they already perceive as rightfully theirs.

Now we are seeing that this sort of criminal conspiratorial mentality is not isolated to a few institutions. Like a whole new breed of mobsters that has never had to draw a gun, a new league of psychopathic men (mostly) with great educations are robbing people for amounts that would make any organized crime boss want to send his own children to an Ivy League business school over any other investment.

One curious bit of information from British researchers that may shed some light on how young men, in particular, get caught up in ruthless financial games is a study that shows that futures traders get a testosterone spike on days when they make an above-average profit. On mornings when men's testosterone levels are higher than average, their average afternoon profits are higher than on their low-testosterone days, suggesting a possible cause-and-effect relationship. Traders who display physical characteristics of having been exposed to higher levels of testosterone as fetuses (lower index-to-ring-finger ratios) tend to make more Money and stay in business for the longest time. More experienced traders show a stronger tie between testosterone and profits than younger traders. Higher testosterone is associated with aggression, even violent aggression; the so-called roid rage that some athletes and others who inject testosterone display at times.

When the Great Recession began, Bear Stearns was the first massive financial firm to crash. At that time it was the fifth-largest securities firm in the United States. This firm, too, it appears, took full advantage of its investors' faith, built up by former generations of ethical wealth stewards. Here too advisers sold investors packages of toxic subprime mortgages that they knew were likely to fail because the people who took them out lacked the means to repay them. Jimmy Cayne was chief executive of Bear Stearns at the time. He was then one of the four hundred richest people in America. He lost around a billion dollars when the company collapsed under the weight of worthless mortgages. While numerous employees lost pensions and investors lost savings, he was widely criticized for frequently being out of the office, playing golf or bridge, leading to comparisons with Emperor Nero, who watched Rome burn while playing the fiddle. Of course, many investors are happy to take large risks for large gains. That is capitalism. There is no harm in playing a game for which we know the real odds.

WHAT ARE THE ODDS?

Las Vegas posts odds for almost any imaginable bet, from hoops and horses to picking the date that Skylab will fall to earth. People will place bets on who will be the next pope, when our government will admit that UFOs are real, when scientists will find the Loch Ness monster, and when Jesus will return to earth. While some of these unlikely odds are as high as five thousand to one, Bear Stearns said the instruments they sold were low-risk secure investments that would give a modest, steady return over time. Investors did not think that they were gambling or playing with Money to burn just for the fun of it. People sank their life savings into these sorts of investments, which were touted as the answer to otherwise uncertain retirements. Moreover, just like Goldman Sachs's deal, the instruments were so complex and convoluted that even a perceptive investor could not unwind it and fully assess the value. Here, too, they relied on their advisers. Their fortunes were as decimated as those of the families who put their trust in Bernie Madoff. At every level of society a con is only a con, no matter how expensive his suit or how pedigreed his education or institution.

Former securities broker Frank Partnoy wrote an expose of his former employer Morgan Stanley in which he details the same sorts of predatory practices against some clients. In his book *F.I.A.S.C.O.: Blood in the Water on Wall Street*, he revealed that brokers would target unsophisticated or simply trusting clients to sell them products that would fail. And they would create positions on the other side of the deal to profit from their losses. I imagine these boys celebrating their victories over the rest of society, in private enclaves, like the buccaneers of old in their secret island coves, drinking from three-hundred-dollar bottles of scotch while singing, "Yo ho, yo ho, a pirate's life for me."

Few investors at this time could imagine the naked greed and sheer contempt that some huge bankers and traders had for them. This sacking of the American economy is akin to Chinese manufactures that hid poisonous ingredients in baby food or filled wallboard destined for the interiors of people's homes with sulfurous toxins. They did this just to make a profit, regardless of the harm or even death that could befall the purchaser. *Caveat emptor*, "let the buyer beware," is the watchword of contemporary commerce. However, most of the investors who purchased these investments had no way to beware. Traders deceived them with layers upon layers of sophisticated and complex fraud.

The financial collapse of 2008 has not put an end to such practices. Massive financial fraud appears to continue unabated in some large institutions. In 2012, Barclay's Bank admitted to rigging the London InterBank Offered Rate (LIBOR). It agreed to pay US and British regulators $450 million dollars in penalties. No one went to jail. In response to one of Barclay's traders indicating he might be willing to rig the rate, which sets the interest for trillions of dollars in bank transactions, another trader reportedly said, "Dude. I owe you big time! Come over one day after work and I'm opening a bottle of Bollinger." UBS paid $1.5 billion to settle allegations of its own wrongdoing with LIBOR, while many other banks remain under investigation for their role in this international conspiracy to benefit a few at the expense of many though rigging a financial fundament that was supposed to be as tamper-proof as race results before post time.

HSBC paid a record $1.9 billion to settle charges that it facilitated moving billions in Mexican drug Money and Iranian terrorist Money into the US financial system. Standard Chartered, another British bank, paid $327 million to US regulators concerning alleged illegal transactions with Iran, Sudan, Libya, and Burma after having paid $340 million to a New York state regulator over similar allegations. These are just some of the headliners of 2012.

Few of us expect our banker to run out the back door with our Money yelling "Yippee!" and to then throw a big party with cocaine and call girls at our expense. Here we are though, with a growing rogue's gallery of corrupt and deceptive corporations joining those from the recent past such as WorldCom, Enron, Anderson Consulting, Galleon Groups, and—well, just too many others to list. It is starting to look like a pattern instead of a few anomalous scandals. Now that so many people without apparent conscience have risen to the top of our financial institutions we have to reconsider how we do things. If the Midas Complex is contagious, society must learn how to better inoculate those in positions of trust and influence. If we cannot cure the Midas epidemic, however, then we may need to do a better job of quarantining it.

The consequences of loss of trust now go much further than the gutting of a few big companies and a broken economy. The United States has dropped off the list of the top twenty least corrupt nations in the world, according to a comprehensive assessment by Transparency International. This places us now closer to Qatar, Chile, Uruguay, Estonia, Slovenia, and the United Arab Emirates than it does the mostly European nations that dominate the top twenty. As the American people lose faith in the integrity of their financial and political leaders, we are witnessing increasing levels of depression, addiction, and anxiety. These are symptoms of a collective Midas Complex and decaying national mental health.

Of the world's one hundred largest economies today, more than half are corporations. This means that less than half of the major wealth holders remaining in the world are still sovereign nations. Bill Gates, Warren Buffett, and Carlos Slim—the three wealthiest men in the world—have greater net worths than the combined wealth of forty-eight nations at the bottom of the global wealth hierarchy. Mitsubishi's economy is bigger than Indonesia's, even though the latter ranks fourth in the world population. Even though they only employ about .03 percent of the world's population, the combined revenues of the world's top two hundred corporations exceed 30 percent of the world's gross domestic product. Thus, corruption in any institutions like these should be a concern to all and be subject to much greater regulation by the government.

MONEY'S PATHWAY TO MEMBERSHIP

Evolution has deeply etched the desire to belong into the human psyche. Most of us long for membership in something—a family; a tribe or kinship system; a community; a religious, social, political or cultural organization; a nation; or even a bowling league. In social situations, we are often curious about one another's memberships. What is your religious affiliation? Are you a Democrat, Republican, or Independent? Members often regard those who do not belong to a group with suspicion as outsiders, rejects, loners, and the unaffiliated. Money is one of the ways that many demonstrate their membership in one class or another or in a segment within a class. Upper-, middle-, and working-class registries often have very different cultural experiences and values.

Status and a sense of membership or belonging often link to Money. Changes or intractability around economic status often have a profound impact on personal identity and concomitant well-being. The movie *Fight Club* made a pointed commentary on class affiliation and inclusion. In it the main character Chuck Palahniuk says, "Another new fight club rule is that fight club will always be free. It will never cost to get in. We want you, not your money. As long as you're in fight club, you're not how much money you've got in the bank. You're not your job. We are all going to die, someday."

A real community of shared labor toward the shared good is possible—or was at one time in this country. Isolated as that life was at times, there was community. Neighbors banded together to make lard and butter, put up feed corn, mash grapes for wine and gather hops for beer, raise a barn, bale hay, thresh wheat, pick apples, and plow snow off roads. One neighbor cut hair, another mended shoes. From the cradle to the grave, you needed neighbors and they needed you. Money, for all the good it can do, has also undercut the fabric of community. Increasing numbers of people seem to feel that a sufficient amount of Money can allow them to default on the social contract that has kept humanity growing for millennia.

How is it possible that so many people who hold key positions in our economic culture have been able to work solely in their own interest, against the common good? Chapter 7 attempts to address this concern from a psychological point of view.

CHAPTER 7

PSYCHOPATH NATION:
THE MIDAS TAKEOVER

It is said that for money you can have everything; but you cannot. You can buy food, but not appetite; medicine, but not health; knowledge but not wisdom; glitter, but not beauty; fun, but not joy; acquaintances, but not friends; servants, but not faithfulness; leisure, but not peace. You can have the husk of everything for money, but not the kernel.
—Arne Garborg

Midas Myth #7: *Charm is evidence of a person's goodness.*
Reality: *Trust your deeper instincts. Some charismatic people are simply dangerous.*

Mohandas K. Gandhi considered these seven traits to be most perilous to human society:

1. Wealth without work
2. Pleasure without conscience
3. Science without humanity
4. Knowledge without character

5. Religion without sacrifice
6. Commerce without morality
7. Politics without principle

He could just as well have been laying foundations for this book. His summary is also a succinct description of psychopathic thinking and behavior in a range of key fields of human endeavor.

WHAT IS A PSYCHOPATH?

The word *psychopath* is quite loaded. All kinds of psychological traits and behavioral theories hitchhike on this human condition. A few quick terms may help orient the reader since understanding psychopathy is quite germane to gaining a better understanding of the Midas Complex. At its core, the Midas Complex is a psychopathic condition.

Narcissistic person: Self-involved, yet needs to be seen by others; rarely harmful but usually annoying.
Asocial person: Self-involved to the exclusion of others; rarely harmful but usually perceived as odd.
Antisocial Person: Harmful to others' welfare; potentially dangerous.
Psychopath/sociopath: Aggressively antisocial, the most dangerous predator on earth; lacking in empathy and incapable of imagining the common good.

Narcissitc traits fall along a spectrum. In its milder form a person is just more self absorbed than most. At its worst, narcissim becomes malignant and the individual's chronic emptyness can become a danger to all. What follows is not about the deranged criminals or cinema psychos many may think of when they hear the word psychopath or sociopath. This is not another attempt to document the lives and motivations of serial killers and other superpredators, even though research on these most obvious of deviants informs us about their nature. The majority of psychopaths, however, do not actually rape, slash, or murder anyone, yet they are extremely dangerous. Highly adapted psychopaths are like human chameleons. They can fake being normal well enough to mix among more ethical people whose moral contracts induce them to work for the common good alongside their own success and survival. Criminal justice institutions capture and then study very few of these socially well-adapted predators, so we know less about them.

In corporate life, for example, people do not generally come at others with guns, knives, or clubs—although that does happen periodically. Socially advantaged, highly adapted psychopaths, however, are more likely to direct their psychological weapons against the emotional and economic well-being of others. Many know them as the source of knives in their backs at work and other collegial unpleasantness. Millions of investors know them as some of the cunning thieves in chapter 6 who drained their life savings, gutted their pensions, manipulated the stock market, destroyed the housing market, created rampant unemployment, undermined the economy, and even raided the national treasury for personal gain. When King Midas received the golden touch, everything in his environment subsequently became lifeless as his riches grew. His greed transformed him from a kind, compassionate lover of life into the killer of his own beloved daughter. When the Midas Complex takes hold of people, they may use their power to suck the life out of everyone and everything around them in their insatiable quest for more and more. Under its influence, people can appear truly psychopathic.

COLD CASH: PSYCHOECONOMICS

American (now global) capitalism is the most dynamic economic system the world has ever seen. It is also the most virulent. It transforms most other cultures it contacts and often goes to war with those that resist conversion to its economic values. As with other potent forces of human invention, like nuclear power, our economic system benefits many people in significant ways. This is not, however, without significant cost to others.

A common feature of Midas Complex-driven nations is a dramatic divide between the *haves* and *have-nots*. When only one-third of fourth graders can read at proper grade level in the wealthiest nation in the world, and our child poverty rate is five times that of any other industrial nation, citizens must begin to question whether the compassionate heart of American capitalism has turned cold. As discussed in chapter 5, many features of the social discourse concerning wealth and entitlement in America today reveal a growing divide between the economically enfranchised and those who feel they have no leverage in what was once imagined as the bastion of equal opportunity. The outcome of the nationwide reimagining of the American economic system and its core values is still under way. This book merely articulates some of details of a class battle in progress.

When someone held in high regard betrays a person, it can create a particularly acute wound in the survivor's psyche. We may not actually have an intimate personal relationship with our banker, a governmental official, our employer, our retirement fund manager, or others with whom we hold a fiduciary relationship, but we see them as standing between economic chaos and us. When a trusted adviser betrays us, it is as if he or she has personally wounded us or at best simply failed to protect us.

In the Great Recession, as millions of hardworking Americans lost their homes and their life savings, they could not help but sickeningly note those who waltzed away from the disaster with bags of ill-gained loot. A corporate mentality of all for me and nothing for the rest negatively affects the psychology of an entire nation. A Money-sane culture, however, would unflinchingly question naked emperors and other charlatans, demanding accountability, transparency, maturity, and responsibility from individuals and institutions charged with projecting economic interests in the name of the common good.

We can find symptoms of psychopathy throughout societies, particularly during periods of accelerated transition and socioeconomic strain. At certain junctures in history, the psychopathy of a single charismatic leader seizes entire nations. Psychopathic tyrants stay in power because they deter all others from speaking the truth. Psychopathic epidemics can flare up in that silence. It is important for us to have a greater understanding than the social sciences have thus far provided about the power of psychopathy to move economic institutions and whole nations. Some psychopathic nations gained infamy for their aggression toward other states, others for the treatment of people inside their own borders. When psychopathic aggression breaks out on a national scale, the seizing of others' wealth (gold) is often evidence of the Midas Complex at work. In most places, morally sane people knew what was happening but could or would not try to stop their nation's tyranny.

There appears to have been a steady cultural drift away from core American values of equality and justice in recent years. Roughly, seven stages describe the steps any nation takes in its descent from an economically sane and civil society to a Money-mad and psychopathic nation. A collective Midas Complex, which provides rationales for dominant groups to oppress vulnerable others, often grips such nations. Other ideological constructs such as religion, imagined racial or cultural superiority, and political ideology can evoke similar declines.

CULTURAL DRIFT: SEVEN STEPS FROM CIVIL SOCIETIES TO PSYCHOPATH NATIONS

1) Tolerance for others and inclusion of all.
2) Creation of an *other*—people who are perceived as not being on the majority's playbook.
3) Disparagement of the other and exclusion from the dream.
4) Demonization and pathologizing of the other along with restriction of rights.
5) Gathering the other into restricted zones and contained environments—the creation of ghettos, reservations, prisons and gulags.
6) Confinement of the other and destruction of bridges back into the majority.

7)   Penetration of the restricted zones, violations of the citizens' human rights and destruction of their lives.

Based on this seven-step scale, where do you think America is today? Most of my graduate students think we are somewhere between steps 5 and 6. Step 7 is where civil war and acts of genocide occur. From Adolf Hitler's Germany to Saddam Hussein's Iraq, a psychopathic society portrays psychopathic acts as normal behavior. Psychopathic subcultures can become the dominant note in any national voice. It is imperative, then, for the morally sane majority to push back against the attempts of any psychopathic minority to control a nation. Usually such persons and groups gain power by preying on people's innate fears of change. The founding, maintenance and continued expansion of the largest prison system in the world most dramatically evidences the disenfranchisement and repression of the lower socioeconomic sectors in America today. It is a stage 6 phenomenon.

POPULAR PSYCHOPATHIC CULTURE

Friedrich Nietzsche warned that if we stare too long into the abyss the abyss stares back at us. Perhaps, due in part to its profoundly disturbing nature, few psychologists have written for the lay reader on this topic. There are, naturally, forensic and abnormal psychology books on psychopathy. Even this genre of academic texts, however, is limited more to criminals than bankers. Novelists have engaged more with the topic than social scientists. It may take a more highly developed imagination than most social scientists possess to fully conceive the alternate universe of psychopaths' inner worlds. Works such as Patricia Highsmith's Mr. Ripley books (and the film), the Dexter novels (and the Showtime TV series), and John Sanford's extensive Prey series are all very popular today. Clearly we are very curious about psychopaths.

Though he was distinctly psychopathic in his behavior, depressive anxiety plagued the protagonist of the hit HBO television series *The Sopranos*. Tony Soprano's condition causes him to uncontrollably black out when his anxiety becomes unbearable. The display of weakness of any kind is a dangerous sign in a mob boss. Therefore, he is in a difficult place. He needs therapeutic help, but it is dangerous to his leadership position for anyone to learn that he is seeing a psychotherapist. Psychopaths rarely seek psychotherapy on their own. They are more often dragged in by spouses or sentenced to our care by the courts. They characteristically blame others for all their problems. Money, of course, figures as the raison d'être for most of Tony's criminal behaviors, so a virulent Midas Complex is clearly at work in his psyche. As my book *Knights without Armor,* explored, one of the more prominent features of heroic Western masculinity is the adoption of a "cool pose" as evidence of one's strength and likelihood for success in an adversarial economic system. When coolness degrades to coldness, psychopathy emerges.

For decades, film audiences have been fascinated with characters like those populating *The Sopranos.* Cold-blooded killers and heartless monsters are prominent in the cultural expressions of the American imagination. Why are we so fascinated with psychopaths and their exploits? From Nosferatu to Hannibal the Cannibal, the psychopath in film, literature, television, popular music, and video games is a recurring and increasingly more frequent theme. Moreover, "If it bleeds it leads" is the organizing principle of most twenty-first century news outlets that put significantly more resources into documenting psychopathic acts then they do the good deeds of heroes and responsible citizens.

In organized sports, psychopathy plays a role as well. Twenty percent of NFL athletes are felons. Hurting the other guy in football, boxing, hockey, car racing, and other sports is part of the spectator's expectations. The potential for injury is one rationale for the exorbitant fees such high-risk athletes command. "Extreme" cage fighting and other such combat sports are growing phenomena. They promise blood, fury, injury, and even the specter of death for their participants. The greater the degree of danger the more it drives up revenues. One characteristic most psychopaths share is an absence of fear of violence. They act out in ways that many of us fantasize, but our moral principles stop most of us from shooting someone for cutting us off on the freeway.

WHEN THOSE WE TRUST BETRAY

When a psychopath guts someone economically, the resulting experience can be quite physical. Victims may feel shaken, drained, confused, disoriented, hopeless, powerless, fatigued, nervous, or frightened and—most of all—betrayed. It is not the same for them as losing an investment in which they made a calculated risk. When we make a bad stock pick or that collectible plate we bought at a garage sale turns out to have little value on eBay, we may feel disappointed. Depending on the size of the loss, we may even suffer lifestyle changes as a result and feel troubled, even depressed by the reversal of fortune. However, when we trust someone with our assets and they destroy them, it represents another category of experience for most people.

When the real estate agent lies about hidden damage in the house we bought or a down-and-out friend spends the Money we gave him to buy groceries on drugs we feel taken advantage of and victimized. Losing Money to a psychopath is the monetary equivalent of date rape; someone we trust and are vulnerable around takes advantage of us. I know this, of course, from treating clients who have been lied to by trusted advisers. Moreover, I have learned this from direct experience.

I met Peter in my early twenties. I was working my way through college as a real estate agent. In Northern California during the early 1970s, many people were leaving large cities and looking for a more rural lifestyle. People called it the "back-to-the-land movement." I thought that in addition to securing my own little place in the woods I could help others trying to touchdown on a decent piece of land. This appealed to my sense of community service and it paid better than hanging sheetrock. It also worked well with my class schedule. I took some courses, got a state license to sell real estate, and started working for a small brokerage, which Peter had started. He struck me as a very kind and intelligent man.

Because of my full-time studies at the university and my proclivity for working with clients at the lower ends of the economic spectrum, I never earned large commissions. Nevertheless, Peter seemed happy to have me around. He taught me a lot about the real estate business and I always experienced him as someone who seemed honest in his dealings with people. Over the years, I came to trust him as much as I would a member of my own family. In fact, considering that my own father had operated on the shady side of the horse racing industry for many years, I trusted Peter more.

As my academic career progressed from BA to MA and eventually a PhD, my real estate career paid the way. In fact, it helped my romantic partner and other family members get through school as well. What I did not spend on my addiction to higher education I saved. I bought up old houses that had serious problems that scared most people away. I learned many of the building trades, tore down other old buildings to salvage recyclable materials, and fixed up the properties I acquired. All along, Peter smiled, looking over my shoulder approvingly as I worked my family out of poverty and into a comfortable middle-class existence. I kept buying bigger and more substantial houses along the way until I finally acquired a beautiful foreclosed house in the hills behind Santa Barbara. It was my dream house, really. It was spacious, full of light, had a generous use of wood, glass, and tile, and commanded a stunning view of the distant California coastline. The lot had many fruit trees and gardens. Thanks to all I had learned from Peter and my experiences in helping other clients, I got a terrific deal on the place.

I put every cent I had saved over twenty years of hard work and simple living into this house and was thrilled to have a home there. I had stayed in so many funky places over the years— crumbling basements, stuffy attics, sheds, shacks, chicken coops, water towers, and other such structures on the properties I rehabilitated. I was no longer selling real estate, now making my living as an educator. Having published my first book, I was finding myself in demand as a speaker and workshop leader around the country. Then one day, after not having seen him for several years, Peter came to the house. He said, "You know, Aaron, this is a beautiful place but I think California real estate is headed for a fall and I would hate to see you lose all you have accomplished over these years. You're busy with your new career now, why don't you let me help you out with your financial planning? I know you're going to want to retire some day and dedicate your life to good works. I want to support your future and have a wonderful opportunity for you."

Peter had been buying up foreclosed properties in Denver for a fraction of what income properties cost in California. And because of his superior knowledge in business I thought he must know better than I what was going to happen. Having never had any reason to mistrust his financial wisdom and goodwill for me, I sold the house and gave him the proceeds, my entire life savings, to invest for my retirement. He created a partnership with a Colorado millionaire whom I had not yet met, but whom he assured me had high integrity and a real knack for making Money.

I downsized to a small condominium and focused on my writing and teaching, thinking we had now assured a comfortable future for my family. The rental checks came in regularly and I spoke to Peter a few times a year to stay in touch. After a few years, I began to feel uneasy about the deal. They were selling off holdings and then purchasing new properties, frequently generating lots of commissions for themselves. When I expressed concern that the equities were eroding, Peter told me not to worry, that it was all part of a larger plan and that he guaranteed the capital with his considerable personal wealth. Had any other investor told me this I would have gotten out immediately. But Peter had my confidence. This is the key word—*confidence*. In fact, when he told me the business would be greatly facilitated if I would give him power of attorney so that he did not have to wait so long for escrow papers to be mailed back and forth from California to Colorado, I agreed—something I have never done with anyone else. It was the way he said it. It seemed so reasonable and I did not want to seem distrustful or make problems for the busy businessmen who were going out of their way to make a lot of Money for me.

More years went by and the rental checks kept coming, but the equities got so complicated that my accountant could no longer follow what was going on. He urged me to get out. I expressed concern again, and again received the same, albeit somewhat condescending, reassurances that I had nothing to worry about. It was just big business, beyond my level of sophistication, and I was the beneficiary of tagging along with millionaires as they grew their own wealth. On paper the equities were growing. Then the tax bills started arriving. Several hundred thousand dollars in capital gains that were never delivered to me but promised as profit at the end of the partnership.

As I wrote increasingly larger checks to the government at tax time, Peter assured me that this was just some adjustment that needed to be made before the final gains could be liquidated and sent to me. I asked to get out, but Peter told me that would be too complicated and costly right now and that I should wait just a few more years. In reality, as the tax bills increased the equities in the properties kept shrinking. Then the rent checks stopped. Again he assured me that this was just temporary. The downturn of 2008 had caused cash flows to slowdown, but the capital was secure, he said. When I turned sixty-two in 2010, the initial capital was scheduled to return to me along with all the profits so that I could retire somewhat earlier than most people could. Just like Bernie Madoff's clients, I was possessed by my own greedy fantasy that I was getting a better deal than most people because I luckily knew such powerful and wealthy men. Nevertheless, as you, my dear reader, have likely already guessed, it was gone. I had to learn it from his secretary, since he never bothered to even call me to tell me what had happened.

The last time I spoke with Peter, he did not even apologize but instead took most of the hour telling me about the many uncomfortable ways he was going to have to adjust his lifestyle as he started over again. He clearly wanted sympathy from me, his old friend. He laughed and told me it was fortunate I had not yet retired from my full-time job at Pacifica Graduate Institute since it looked like I was now going to have to work for many more years to come. He suggested I concentrate on building up my psychotherapy practice as a way to make up for the lost funds. When I told him I felt betrayed and that my family was devastated, he told me to "stop whining" and to remember that he had lost much more than I. Wealth, it seems, does not always rub off like dust off a golden coin. In fact, when a Midas Complex possesses them, the wealth and power of others can just as easily act more like a powerful magnet, drawing our wealth out of its protected savings and into their pockets.

Not all con games are a simple matter of a man approaching you on this street and telling you he has lost his wallet and needs twenty dollars for cab fare home. Some are elaborate, involving confederates and seemingly legitimate instruments. They can stretch out over time. An attorney called what happened to me "the long con." It happened to dozens of other investors who lost their savings in these Denver apartment buildings as well. The notes, once examined, turned out to be worthless. The properties, once reviewed, had nothing but debt. The contracts, drawn up between friends, I thought, were too casual to be enforceable. Where did all the Money go? I will never know.

My attorney thought it could cost more than I lost to pursue a suit and frankly, I simply did not have the heart to sue my friend of thirty-five years. Then I learned that I was also on the hook for hundreds of thousands of dollars in capital gains tax liability that the partnership reported to the government as my responsibility. I was terribly naive throughout this entire process and failed to act when I could have, even though a part of me knew something was wrong for years. The loss of this long friendship was as painful as the monetary loss itself. It also shook my confidence in my ability to detect falsehood in others. Me, the son of a con man! I share all this in the hope of ameliorating similar feelings in readers who may carry self- recriminations about their own financial errors.

Losing most of my life savings was very distressing. The Money serenity my wife possesses has thankfully been very helpful as counterpoint to my own neurosis. I was fortunate to have such a good partner to help aid me in weathering such a fierce financial storm. During the first year or so after the loss, however, I also had to remember almost daily that

1) I am not my Money; it is merely a resource that I have lost.
2) This loss has no bearing on my self-worth or my sense of self; it is an external element.
3) This loss contains valuable information from which I will learn and grow.
4) I am still the same person I was before the loss.
5) I still have all the health, love, shelter, employment, friends, talents, and most of the same opportunities that I had before the loss.
6) Because my friend betrayed me, it does not mean I am bad person, foolish, or have bad luck.

7) I have the courage and ability to try new things, to make more Money, and to adapt to a lower standard of living with the same or greater joy and appreciation of life.

I have been working with these affirmations since the loss and finding them to be true. While my balance sheet is still tattered, my life remains whole. As a footnote to this story, Peter's partner, whom I only met briefly and with whom I remained civil and understanding, has begun to send me small, monthly checks. He is under no legal obligation to do so. He, like Peter, made a personal promise to repay me half of the Money and he is trying his best to do it as a matter of personal integrity. I could write another book about the morality and generosity of strangers. Not everyone who takes from us is hard hearted. Some try their best and fail and it is as important for us to recognize their humanity as it is for us to avoid others who lack it.

MEETING THE INNER TERRORIST: THE PSYCHOPATHIC PSYCHE

Highly adapted psychopaths may amass great power or influence, but the cost is inevitably great to everyone around them. Power does not corrupt psychopaths; it simply never occurs to them to use power for anything but selfish aims in the first place. Those who hope to reap rewards through enabling psychopaths often succumb to the inevitable outcome of any psychopathic relationship—total destruction. They may be the last to go, and in many cases, are left holding the bag after the psychopaths have vanished like vampires into the night.

We can better understand, learn how to identify, and develop strategies to deal with people who care nothing for humanity, who even *intentionally* work against the common good. This book has indicated a number of social trends that appear to support the view that American culture is growing more psychopathic. There also exist achievable steps most morally sane persons can take to reduce the degree of psychopathy in the world around them.

What prevents sanity from reigning in any society at any particular historical moment? It has much to do with the degree to which moral citizens allow persons with psychopathic traits to influence the course of any nation. Periodically, social conditions fan the sparks of psychopathy, incipient in any group, into a conflagration. Then, inevitably, a holocaust of some kind ensues—step 7 on the list that opened this chapter. One thing often fueling such fires is a smoldering but silent citizenry.

In reading the foreign press, one can see that much of the world views American culture through a different lens from that of most domestic reporters. Increasingly, former friends are uneasy, even afraid of us. Many of the words describing us sound similar to psychopathic characteristics in individuals: *dishonest, manipulative, secretive, spying, self-serving, arrogant, dominating, greedy, exploitive, controlling, untrustworthy...dangerous.* This does not make it so, of course, but it is information. And there is a great deal of other data, which appears to point toward our drift down the seven-step, cultural psychopathy scale.

I write this as a psychologist who cares very deeply for America and the core ideals of freedom and inclusion that lie at our constitutional foundations. Just as we might speak of a nation's fiscal health, we can image our democratic traditions as a base line of the nation's mental health. Given that measure, if America were my patient, I would be concerned right now. I would seriously have to consider including it in my "unstable and dangerous patient" category. America's Midas Complex has entered a critical stage. All of us in the field know that psychopaths are the most difficult category of client to treat. Many feel that most are virtually untreatable, that their condition is so deeply etched that it will not respond to ordinary psychotherapy.

Psychopathy may be responsive to radical treatments requiring forced regressions, deconstruction of the rigid personality, and then the rebuilding of the person though human bonding. This is psychology-speak for something similar to a radical remodeling project, which requires that a contractor gut an entire house before he can redesign and rebuild it. Such a project is often more expensive than simply destroying the entire structure and starting over. Such therapy is beyond the skill and resources of most psychotherapists, which is one of the reasons most criminal psychopaths wind up in jail. However, as Charles Ferguson notes in chapter 6, other than Bernie Madoff and his crew, none of the perpetrators in the upper 1 percent who hijacked our economy have had to pay for their crimes against the nation with their freedom.

The elites protect their own, which in itself is a psychopathic trait that mimics organized crime's code of conduct to protect its own members from legal consequences for their acts. Similarly, one feature of many aristocratic societies is that royals maintain immunity from many of the laws that regulate the common people. We imagine, however, that we are a democracy in which the laws apply to all. In 2013, however, US attorney general Eric Holder confessed to the US Senate, "I am concerned that the size of some of these institutions becomes so large that it does become difficult for us to prosecute them."

In an interview with Bill Moyers, columnist Matt Taibbi discussed the dangers he sees from the government's fear of another economic calamity, causing it to turn a blind eye to unethical management decisions. He said, "The rule of law isn't really the rule of law if it doesn't apply equally to everybody.... you can't let higher ranking HSBC officials off for laundering $800 million for the worst drug dealers in the entire world. Eventually, it eats away at the very fabric of society when some people go to jail and some people don't."

If, as I believe, psychopathic traits are growing throughout American culture as symptoms of our Midas Complex, it is imperative to our society that we become much more knowledgeable about psychopathy—particularly its presence in the upper socioeconomic sector. We are called now to deepen our understanding about highly adapted psychopaths and the serious ways they can affect anyone's life. Many people may think that psychopaths are rare. It seems more likely, however, that psychopathy is actually rising to epidemic concentrations in our culture, but because so many of our culture mavens depict psychopathic behavior as normal, many remain hidden. Perhaps this one reason the myth of Midas has survived two millennia. It is a cautionary tale to remind each generation about the perils of unmitigated greed.

HOMOPSYCHOPATHUS: A VARIANT SPECIES?

Are psychopaths a variant species? Do people who are seemingly incapable of developing a moral conscience represent a specific strain or somewhat different variety of human being? It is possibly so. They certainly seem like visitors from another planet at times. Various theorists estimate that as much as 1 percent of the population displays psychopathic traits. Psychopaths' behavioral characteristics, brain functioning, information, sensory and emotional processing, "feeding" habits, and moral playbooks are different from the rest of ours. They inhabit human society as naturally as sharks dwell in the sea. Moreover, they are just as dangerous. Most will not change their antisocial behavior unless capable people firmly confront, expose, and, as is often needed, contain the range of their actions.

Although we all have psychopathic impulses, most of us are not likely to act on them. Morally sane people are not defined by their worst impulses—psychopaths are. I may momentarily wish that a particularly irritating colleague would drop dead, but I do not follow through and actually attempt to cause that to happen. What stops me is one of the things that keeps human culture whole. Sigmund Freud called it eros, the capacity to love. Those who are not stopped act out the worst of themselves. They suffer from a very peculiar malady. Whether by birth or life experience, it is as if people lacking eros exist without a soul. The roots of this inhuman condition are complex, but its symptoms are quite clear and understandable.

To really understand the Midas Complex, we need to better understand the psychopathy that can lie at the core of the complex. For over a century, psychology has wrestled with the dark side of the human soul and come to a variety of conclusions. Most of us in the human sciences remain quite limited in our understanding. The creepy feeling that some people have in the presence of psychopaths affects the field as well. Many therapists fear psychopaths for showing us the real limits to our understanding of the human psyche. Like most disorders, in its early childhood stages, psychopathy may be somewhat more treatable. Once the condition is fully developed, however, few psychopaths ever recover their capacity for humane behavior.

Most psychologists are confused about childhood psychopathy. The etiologies are complex. One theory is that some children are simply "bad to the bone." That is, they suffer from biological and genetic predilections that make them susceptible to acting out against society—so-called bad seeds. Social theories range widely concerning the question of whether psychopaths are born or made. We remain unsure if it is biological and genetic or caused by developmental traumas in early childhood. In many cases, it is likely a combination. Uncaring children are more likely to suffer more abuse—they are intrinsically less lovable. There are often a number of common traits in psychopathic histories. Children with psychopathic parents have a statistically greater likelihood of becoming psychopaths themselves. This does not, however, solve the biologically versus socially constructed (born versus made) debate.

Most incarcerated psychopaths have a history of child physical and sexual abuse and neglect, yet others come from seemingly good homes and have no documented history of abuse. In either case, children prone to psychopathy often exhibit symptoms of attention deficit disorders and oppositional defiance disorder, which can then develop into conduct disorder and eventually antisocial personality disorder—a linguistically diffused term for psychopathy. Increasingly, theorists speculate that early failure to meaningfully attach to an adult caregiver can result in the detachment and disassociation we see in many psychopaths. When children who display a lack of relationality and empathy for others are sent away to private schools by frustrated, socially advantaged parents, it can become the worst possible decision they will ever make. If a child does not learn how to love and care for others and only focuses on success and achievement, he or she may show up in the boardrooms of America as a pure predator on our national economy.

CAUTION: PSYCHOPATHS AT WORK

People whose lives are turned inside out by a psychopathic lover, mate, friend, investment counselor, or close acquaintance are often shocked when they realize the full extent of the damage that has occurred. A person whom they felt to be trustworthy, often someone who was party to their most intimate selves, has betrayed them. Victims of psychopaths are not simply naive. The best clinically trained professionals are often taken in. Most psychopaths are facile liars. Notably, of all trained professionals, only Secret Service agents are particularly adept at accurately detecting when people are lying.

Just as psychopathic personalities are more highly concentrated in incarcerated criminal populations, they also more frequently occur in certain professions. Psychopathy affects people in all races and cultures and across the spectrum of economic and social status. Soulless, predatory people blend into all aspects of society. Some arenas of American life attract financial predators and psychopaths to places and positions where prey are more abundant. As we saw in chapter 6, this often causes devastating impacts to the institutions and the people around them. Highly adapted psychopaths can thrive in today's more predatory economic climate. In certain professions, such as litigation, the stock market, politics, corrections, combat sports, politics, or warfare, psychopaths can be more highly rewarded. They can thus become more highly concentrated in those spheres.

In noncriminal organizations, some psychopaths become adept at hiding in plain view. They use various skills of adaptation, camouflage, misdirection, and ruthless action to create economic success and social status for themselves and whomever they see as essential to their progress. Some organizational setups actually reward psychopathic behavior. Working for such institutions can be extremely stressful for the vast majority of people who are not predators themselves. In such institutions, people advance in accord with their willingness to sacrifice their own and others' health, personal development, and familial relations to benefit the organization's productivity.

Stockholders often see executives with no remorse about firing entire departments, gutting entire companies, ravaging nature, or even destroying entire communities dependent on the organization as courageous. As such, they may be highly compensated for their ruthless management, noted only for their Midas touch, not the lifelessness that persists in their wake. A review of filmmaker Michael Moore's documentaries shows a line of inquiry from *Roger and Me* and *Bowling for Columbine* to *Capitalism: A Love Story*. We can understand his works as one artist's attempt to comprehend the incomprehensible. Psychopaths are simply confounding to most of us.

How, then, can employers assess managers, executives, and other high-stakes employees to better ensure that they do not negatively influence organizations? Robert Hare, who wrote one of the more definitive books on psychopathy, *Without Conscience*, also developed a psychological inventory called Hare's Psychopathy Checklist to help employers try and assess just that question. In America, this concern is particularly acute because corporations enjoy the legal status of personhood. Mitt Romney, when running for the 2012 presidential election, made a point of underscoring this reality to the consternation of many who feel businesses should not be protected with such human rights, particularly in being allowed to contribute to political campaigns without limits.

Wendell Berry writes in *Citizenship Papers* that

> the limitless destructiveness of this economy comes about precisely because a corporation is not a person. A corporation, essentially, is a pile of money to which a number of persons have sold their moral allegiance .... a corporation does not age. It does not arrive ... at a realization of the shortness and smallness of human lives ... It can experience no personal hope or remorse, no change of heart. It cannot humble itself. It goes about its business as if it were immortal, with the single purpose of becoming a bigger pile of money.

The Corporation, a documentary film, demonstrates that when one does imagine major corporations as persons, and then applies Hare's inventory to their values and practices, many tend to score extremely high on the psychopathic scale. In other words, if the corporation were in fact a person, he or she would be psychopathic. Even though many corporations do score this way, chapter 8 discusses corporations that are concerned with values beyond shareholder profits at any cost. They demonstrate corporate responsibility to create positive contributions to the culture and the environment. In other words, if they are persons, in this case they are caring, responsible, and contributing persons, not merely profit generators regardless of the cost to others. These are the sorts antipsychopathy corporations informed citizens should support with their patronage. Socially conscious organizations have the power to change the world for the better while making more Money for their shareholders at the same time.

For those of us engaged in give-and-take relationships it can be hard to conceive of individuals or organizations with the status of persons who, at their core, are only concerned about their own advantage regardless of the toll it takes on others around them. This tendency toward denial can make us somewhat naive in our dealings with psychopaths. A part of us just cannot believe that someone could take advantage of us without the slightest care for the ways in which their behavior impacts us and others. Survivors of psychopathic relationships wind up in my consulting room looking dazed and wondering, "What just happened?" My primary advice to people who find themselves in any sort of a relationship with a psychopath is simple—get away. It might be helpful to look at a phenomenon in nature to help better understand the influence of the psychopathic psyche on the interconnected and interrelated web of human culture.

BLACK HOLES AND THE EMPTY SELF

Most of us have heard about black holes, a phenomenon described by astrophysicists to explain the anomalous nature and behavior of certain stars. They commonly call ultradense gravitational fields, which are invisible to the eye and instrumentation, *black holes* or *collapsed stars*. Astronomers think that when a previously luminous star begins to burn out and collapse upon itself, as the star becomes smaller and denser and the gravitational field in its core becomes stronger, it creates a black hole. This more powerful field in turn pulls more of the star's gaseous material to it, creating irreversible cascade of collapse. The star loses its luminosity. Its light turns brown and then darker and darker still until astronomers can no longer see it at all.

Once the star fully collapses, the remaining matter is so compact and its gravitational field so powerful that not even light can escape its grip. One of the ways astronomers try to describe this phenomenon is by calling this sort of astral body a *gravity well*. What they mean is that a black hole acts as if it were a deep fissure in space. All light and matter traveling through the cosmos into the vicinity of the black hole appear to vanish at some point as if it were going down an infinitely deep well. Where they go nobody knows. Speculations about parallel universes and other such theories go beyond the useful metaphor for understanding something about the psychodynamics of the psychopathic psyche. What is relevant to our understanding, however, is the way in which astronomers allude to the existence of something that they cannot see or measure.

At a certain point of proximity, where light and matter disappear, is a line (actually a surrounding sphere) of demarcation called the *event horizon*. Beyond the event horizon, only empty space appears. That "space," however, exerts an extraordinarily powerful influence on all manifest phenomena around it.

We can understand psychopathic individuals as the collapsed stars of humanity. It is as if their very souls—the life-giving, life-sustaining nature of their deep emotional bodies—have gone dark. Their true nature becomes invisible to the human senses and yet continues to exert a powerful influence on everyone around them. One of the common interrogatories thrown at psychopaths is, "What is the matter with you, don't you have a heart?" The real answer is, "No, not really." Not in the way most of us understand what it means to have a heart. Having a heart implies we possess the capacity for empathy and compassion toward the struggles and suffering of other human beings. When King Midas lost his heart, his beloved daughter turned into a golden statue and he finally woke up to the shadow of his gift. He begged the gods to rid him of his psychopathic greed and was returned to his senses and his capacity to love life as it is.

Despite whatever pleasure psychopaths may feel in their capacity to take whatever they want from others without suffering guilt or shame, they also struggle with a profound psychological and existential challenge. Like black holes, they have no luminosity within. Even though we all feel empty at times, psychopaths have a profound lacuna in the center of their psyche. This hole is so enormous and dark that many of them feel like the walking dead.

It is not very pleasant to feel dead inside. In fact, the experience of pervasive inner emptiness and deadness is unbearable for most psychopaths. In a manner that recapitulates the black hole's drawing into itself all the vibratory forces surrounding it, psychopaths attempt to suck up all the life and resources that surround them. Some may try to assuage their pain of emptiness through various kinds of consumption: alcohol, drugs, sex, acquiring things, high-risk excitement, and ultimately Money. They want your Money—all of it, if they can get it.

I cannot say for sure if Bernie Madoff is a psychopath. We try not to diagnose at a distance. His cautionary tale, however, does exemplify many of the common features of psychopaths. Typically, everyone in his or her field of influence eventually becomes infected and ultimately ruined by encounters with people who possess no conscience. People either run for their lives once they discover they are in a relationship with such a person or risk being sucked into the unimaginable density of that person's gravity well. Once the psychopath's infinite vacuum has drained their psyches and then discarded them, their lives are often ruined. As the Bible cautioned humanity for centuries, "By their acts ye shall know them." The best way to tell if you are working for or in a relationship with a psychopath is to notice if everyone around him or her appears to be suffering but he or she seems fine. The psychopath will be the one who points to everyone else as "the problem" while never being willing to look at him- or herself. Psychopaths actually lack the capacity for self-reflection.

As discussed earlier, Money is like a drug for many people, a substitute for real intimate relationships, and a symbol of substantial reality. As chapter 2 noted, many of us have a fantasy regarding Money that there is a certain amount that will convey to us a feeling of "enoughness." Money-sane individuals who have recovered from their Midas Complex or were never even infected by one know this is a fantasy. They try other methods to create wholeness in their lives. Psychopaths, however, chase that fantasy to their ultimate destruction and/or the destruction of everyone around them. For the empty self there is no such thing as fullness, completeness, or wholeness. There is never enough—the ultimate Midas Complex. There is instead infinite, bottomless hunger. Moreover, through their futile attempts to assuage that hunger they will attempt to consume everything of worth in their environment. Evangelical preachers tell us that the devil's greatest trick is in getting us to believe he does not exist. The same trick applies to the psychopath's charm, getting us to believe that our Money is safe with him or her when in fact we have just hired the fox to watch our henhouse.

Another way to understand psychopathic hunger is through the pervasive myth of the vampire. Profound inner lifelessness characterizes vampires. They are the walking dead. Having no real life within themselves, they must transfer life from others through sucking out their life's blood. Like psychopaths, vampires can be extremely charming, exerting a seemingly hypnotic power over others, and this can cause people to set aside their common sense and willingly become victims. Vampires do not appear in the mirror. Like psychopaths, whom psychotherapists generally consider as poor candidates for psychotherapy, they have no capacity to reflect upon their behavior and their inner lives. I believe it is no coincidence that television shows, movies, and best-selling novels about vampires are proliferating in American culture today; these stories represent some attempt by the collective to understand the proliferation of psychopathy in our contemporary culture. In fact, one of the more recent terms used by critics to describe the sorts of predators that inhabit the "vulture" capitalism depicted in chapter 6 is *vampire squid*.

PSYCHOPATHIC SAVIORS: THE MIDAS COMPLEX IN SHEEP'S CLOTHING

Something that has troubled me in recent years is how many of my clients and students report that people who held a position of intimate trust in their lives had violated them. These perpetrators are often professionals such as clergy, teachers, therapists, coaches, or other personal advisers. One of my graduate students wrote her dissertation on therapists in training whose previous therapists had had sex with them. She easily found no shortage of trainees with this past to study.

In Freud's era, families largely kept the true prevalence of incest hidden. Victorian cultural standards inhibited the airing of family secrets, particularly among the privileged classes, until Freud began to validate women for having had such experiences. Ironically, as these disclosures began to negatively affect his practice, bringing him to near poverty, he changed his theory. He began to regard such events as more likely evidence of neurosis and fantasy than true memories of actual parental deviance. A generation of feminist therapists took him and his revised theory to task for this. We might also blame his Midas Complex, since his change in theory also brought a change in fortune as he then became more palatable to upper-class Viennese patriarchs who paid the bills.

In a manner similar to Freud's upper-class incestual fathers in nineteenth-century Europe, pedophilic priests became a national symptom in late twentieth century American culture. Yet the church and other powerful organizations allied to protect it over victims' best interests have often suppressed reports of abuse by people whom society holds to high moral standards. Coaches, too, are not immune to abusing their power over boys who idolize them, as the widely publicized Penn State University scandal evidenced in 2011. There, football coach Jerry Sandusky reportedly sexually assaulted numerous underage boys over a period of many years. Just as many church officials protected their priests from prosecution, various university officials allegedly covered up this abuse, too, in an attempt to protect the school and its football program from scandal. Cover-ups often involve "hush Money." This is cash paid to buy silence from victims or their guardians. Money can move or mute us depending on how it is applied.

Psychopaths can embed themselves in large institutions that can enable them. "Spiritual" psychopaths, who attempt to personally profit from the meaning business, are just as likely to take our Money as business and financial service-oriented ones. Spiritual psychopaths prey on the very sheep they purportedly protect. I regarded my friend Peter as a very spiritual person. He was a devoted naturalist and seemingly charitable to various organizations. My belief in his innate goodness blinded me to his dark side—a cavalier relationship to the Money with which I entrusted him just as many nonprofit organizations gave their funds to Bernie Madoff, trusting him to protect and further their good works.

Several teachers of Eastern spirituality who came to Europe and America in the later decades of the 20th century accumulated considerable wealth at the expense of their Western devotees even though lives of simplicity and chastity were traditional elements of most of their teachings. I have worked with several clients and students who handed over their entire estates to charismatic gurus and were left shaken by what they had done later in life. Wealthy donors were often elevated to coveted inner circles but then exiled when their Money ran out. Many students felt betrayed as they began to realize that those at the top of some of these organizations were living in luxury while those on the front lines who volunteered labor, sacrificed careers, and handed over personal wealth lived humbly, following the tradition they had been taught. As one example, followers of Bhagwan Shree Rajneesh purchased 93 Rolls-Royces for his sole use, the largest number controlled by one individual in the world at that time. Prior to his death in 1990, his followers had intended to raise that number to 365, so he could ride in a different Rolls-Royce every day of the year.

The Vatican lends evidence that the Catholic Church has struggled with similar economic dichotomies as have many other religious institutions. My clients who left the Scientology organization tell me similar tales to those of other charismatic leaders who promise some sort of awakening and wind up funneling the assets of their followers into an aristocratic lifestyle for themselves and their inner circle. The psychology of many cult leaders—from the more sinister Charles Manson and Jim Jones to quirky scammers like televangelists Jim and Tammy Bakker—usually reflects extreme grandiosity. Their shameless narcissism encourages their followers to give them their Money, time, work, freedom, sexuality, or even their lives to support a greater cause. Characteristically, such "leaders" inevitably fail to live up to the very doctrines they attempt to inculcate in their students. Many are eventually caught in moral transgressions that violate their own promoted moral charters.

We see similar paradoxes from some of the most vocal promoters of the so-called moral majority, from Bill Bennett's extraordinary gambling to preacher Jimmy Swaggart's prostitution scandal and the past narcotics addiction of Rush Limbaugh to name a few. One of the tenets of depth psychology is, that which we fail to bring into consciousness tends to possess us. That is, if we have some tendency that is not in accord with our idealized self-image, we may repress it into our unconscious. There it provokes us to act out in ways completely contrary to our imagined sense of self. Better, we psychologists believe, to live an examined life in which we try to integrate the repressed, darker impulses we may possess. When a Midas Complex takes hold of us, we must face the drive to gain more at any cost before it consumes us.

The biblical story of Simon Magus is one of the roots for widespread concerns about the juxtaposition of Money and spirituality in Western culture. He was a Samaritan sorcerer who at the time of Jesus attempted to purchase spiritual powers from the disciples Peter and John. He offered them Money to grant him the spiritual power to lay hands on others in order to transfer the power of the Holy Sprit to them. In the Middle Ages, as financial corruption became widespread in the church, the practice of selling all things spiritual began to be called the sin of Simony.

A way to tell the difference between a spiritual predator and a real healer is to ask ourselves if we are really improving or just being stroked for improving the life of our teacher, priest, or therapist. This means reclaiming our power through taking personal responsibility for our mental and spiritual health and not naively turning it over to those who claim to know the way but will only help us if we sacrifice our wealth or personal treasures to them. Should healing be free? Many people think so. It is problematic in this age. In tribal times, the shaman would help people in emotional or spiritual distress. Those who felt helped would then give him or her a chicken, a blanket, or other needed supplies. Today, most of us have to exchange Money. I am not sure what my office suite mates would do if a client brought a live chicken to a therapy session with me.

Some therapists engage in trade, yet, curiously, our ethical guidelines actually caution us against doing so. Psychologist James Hillman remarks in *Soul and Money* that a survey of psychoanalysts showed they believed that lending Money to a client was less ethical and more damaging to the therapeutic alliance between client and therapist than the harm that could arise from swearing, hitting, kissing, getting naked, and even having sex with them. Clearly my profession still has a long way to go to overcome its own Midas Complex.

GLOBAL BANKRUPTCY

Various studies indicate Americans from all walks of life are worried about the collective effects of the Midas Complex: 90 percent are concerned about the pervasiveness of greed and selfishness, 86 percent about environmental deterioration, 83 percent about increasing stress, 72 percent about the gap between rich and poor, and 73 percent about our focus on material wealth.

The Midas Complex, at its most extreme, is psychopathic just as a collapsing star is a black hole at the conclusion of its inward compression. Midas turned all life into a glittering assemblage that was wondrous to behold yet dead as a petrified forest. A wide range of positive, prosocial, antipsychopathy, post-Money trends exist in our national culture today. Many people focus on hope and underscore the opposite end of the psychopathic spectrum, which we could call extreme altruism.

Many Americans today are resisting despair and fear. They are enacting powerful and creative initiatives to counter the influence of others who are destroying the natural environment, unraveling the social fabric, undercutting the national economy, and eroding our political trust. Some visionary leaders are making significant contributions to our national health by creating more human-scaled, antipsychopathic economies. Such movements, which chapter 8 will discuss, can help us to better understand how all citizens can feel more empowered to improve the conditions of their individual, familial, and community lives. Just like mushrooms, a nation's psychopathy grows in the dark. The quest for a reimagining of our collective relationships to Money is calling us like an angel's trumpet.

As the United States entered the First World War, our national debt increased from approximately $1 billion in 1917 to $25 billion by 1920. On the eve of World War II, our debt rose to $40 billion. By that war's end, it was $258 billion, increasing tenfold in a quarter of a century. Much like our human population explosion, it began increasing exponentially. In 1982, our debt crossed the trillion-dollar mark. It doubled to over $2 trillion by 1986, doubled again to $4 trillion in 1992, doubled again in 2006 to $8 trillion, and was over $16 trillion in 2013.

A trillion is somewhat difficult number for most of us to conceive. A trillion dollars is a million, million dollars: $1,000,000,000,000—twelve zeros. In his book *Innumeracy*, mathematician John Allen Paulos writes, "There is a sense that when numbers are too big...the brain just shuts off." Let us try, anyway. A trillion dollar bills laid end to end would reach the sun. A trillion dollars could repurchase every US home foreclosed in 2007–8. If you spent a million dollars a day, it would take you three thousand years to spend a trillion. A million seconds is roughly eleven and a half days. A billion seconds is about thirty-two years. A trillion seconds equals 32,000 years.

A stack of one trillion one-dollar bills would be roughly 68,000 miles tall; about a third of the way to the moon. By some estimates, the total debt in the world today, including all forms of government debt as well as the debt of financial institutions, nonfinancial businesses, asset-backed securities, derivatives, and households, is approaching $200 trillion. While difficult to precisely measure, our historically unprecedented stack of debt clearly now goes far into outer space.

We have collectively accumulated a debt that is likely too large for the next generations to ever pay down. In other words, most nations of the world today essentially have negative worth; they are effectively bankrupt. It is difficult to see indebting of entire future generations to satisfy this genera-tion's greed as anything but psychopathic. The spirit of King Midas has finally possessed the entire planet. Not only have the national treasuries been gutted, the energy and vitality of the earth itself is getting used up at a nonsustainable rate. We are leaving future generations with an environ-mental, energy and carbon debt of historically unprecedented proportions.

My old friend, the poet Robert Bly, used to jokingly call me: The Keeper of Ugly Facts. But that title should now pass to former vice-president Al Gore, who is a prominent keeper of staggering environmental evidence about what is happening to our global environment. I refer you to him for the latest unnerving statistics. In brief, global warming is no longer a theory about some future threat. By 2012, climate science had clearly demonstrated that we had already passed the tipping point. No longer a future prediction, it has already happened and is well under way to get-ting worse.

Just as global warming calls for radical new energy solutions to drastically reduce our carbon emissions in order to regain a more stable climate, we are just as challenged to reduce our economic debt in order for a more equali-tarian prosperity to reign. Will reconciliation of our debt come through some sort of global bankruptcy, debt forgiveness, or the creation of a new economic system? Only a few million elites are prospering in the current system. In that no amount of wealth can securely protect families from the onslaughts of climate change, even their prosperity is an illusion. This situ-ation is the direct outcome of an unrestrained national and global Midas Complex. This is a radical problem. Any real solutions will likely have to be radical as well.

At this time, many nations are teetering on the brink of economic failure. In our own nation, increasing numbers of cities and even entire states are virtually bankrupt. Most solutions—predominantly just printing more unsecured currency—are mere Band-Aids on gaping economic wounds. Sadly, too few political leaders have any significant training in finance. So how do we stop the Midas takeover? It does not seem, given the unprecedentedly enormous size of the debt, that any new prosperity alone will save nations drowning in it. Something altogether new may need to happen, as chapter 8 will explore.

CHAPTER 8

BEYOND THE MIDAS COMPLEX: TOWARD A SANER SOCIETY

The deadliest form of violence is poverty.
—Mohandas K. Gandhi

Midas Myth #8: *Without Money, we are lost.*
Reality: *People invented Money. We can change it, too.*

RADICAL GIVING

In 1876, the Canadian government passed a new law called the Canadian Indian Act. This regulation banned a widely practiced Indian ritual called the potlatch. The natives of Canada had a radically different idea about how one gained prestige through the accumulation of wealth. In colonial societies, for the most part, the amount of a person's personal wealth conveyed status upon him or her. This often happened regardless of the manner in

241

which wealth had been acquired. These native people, however, conveyed status more by how much a person gave away than though how big a hogan they owned. Those who accumulated the largest pile of fine furs, blankets, and other valued goods would then hold a big party—a potlatch—in which they gave it all away. Thus, a man was notable by the substance of his generosity to his clan and neighbors, not by how much wealth he kept and controlled for himself. Their economy was the opposite of one driven by a Midas Complex.

In 1927, the Canadian ban on potlatches went even further. Feeling that the 1876 law was ineffective, legislators strengthened it by setting prison sentences for disobeying the ban. In 1951, they finally repealed the law but by this time the ritual aspect of native Canadian culture had virtually ceased to exist. This one cultural history shows just how much resistance there can be in a capitalist society against monetary systems that are based more on mutual aid and community support than the pursuit of wealth for a few at the expense of the many.

In many Native American cultures, gift giving was also a key feature. White settlers, who encountered Indians as they colonized the West, were often puzzled by a certain behavior. An Indian would give a settler a gift. However, after some time passed, he would show up and demand that the finally woven basket now gathering dust on the settler's fireplace mantle be returned. This bred mistrust in the settlers toward Native American gift givers. Their resentment gave rise to the derogatory term "Indian giver" to describe a despicable person who gave a gift but then later took it back. The Native Americans, however, were just as mystified by the colonist's behavior. In a society where there were few finely made artifacts, their understanding was that objects of beauty were meant to circulate through the community. They were thus either loans, like books from a library, or trades that could be reversed when the original trade good was returned, not gifts. They viewed the settlers' habit of keeping and collecting such objects as vulgar and against the spirit of the "gift," which was meant to be shared repeatedly with others.

Altruism is deeply encoded in our genetic heritage. Without the impulse to be generous, to selflessly help others, it is doubtful our species would have thrived. If the impulse toward selfishness ever completely won out, not many people would have survived various psychopaths' repeated attempts to rule the world. What then, is the antidote to what may be psychopathy in many of the economic leaders of our era? Just as revolutions and wars have been fought to throw off tyrants who attempt to seize nations for the benefit of a few, a strong counterforce must now mobilize to meet the rampant greed at the top of our economy if the nation as a whole is ever going to thrive.

The shadow of Money is very dark and profoundly dense. Roughly 400 US families now control more wealth than is owned by 60 million other US families combined, about 60 percent of our population. Most phenomena, however, have a polar opposite. Money is no different from other phenomenon in this respect. Although great harm and selfishness happens in the name of Money, there is also a great deal of generosity and positive transformation brought into the world through the conscious use of the power of Money to create beneficial change. If armed robbery and corporate piracy are at one end of the Money acquisition spectrum, then ultra-altruism and spectacular generosity lays at the other.

A number of very wealthy people like Bill and Melinda Gates, Warren Buffet, George Soros, Intel cofounder Gordon Moore and his wife Betty, AOL co-founder Steve Case and his wife, Face book co-founders Mark Zuckerberg and Dustin Moskovitz, financier Carl Icahn and investor George Kaiser reject the ideal of endless accumulation of capital for its own sake and are practicing radical altruism—a sort of global, twenty-first century potlatch. They and others like them are mounting a counterrevolution to some of the have-mores' philosophy of increasing gains for their class regardless of the cost to the rest of society.

A number of businesses are also beginning to assess something greater than their quarterly profit as the prime indicator of their success. "Triple bottom line" organizations add two more P's to their mission orientation. The first, as in all business, is *profit*. Triple bottom line companies, however, include *people*

243

(social capital) and *planet* (environmental capital) in their accounting. The measures of their worth thus expand beyond Money as the primary indicator to also assess their impact or contribution to the social realm and to the environment. Such organizations are as concerned about stakeholders as they are stockholders. They hold themselves accountable to all who are influenced by their enterprise. In addition to many nonprofit organizations and some governmental ones, large corporations like General Electric, Unilever, Proctor & Gamble, 3M, and Cascade Engineering are adopting forms of this new ethos.

The core of this philosophy is that organizations can make a profit and be altruistically concerned about the welfare of all at the same time. Destroying the environment or the welfare of others to make a short-term monetary gain is a Midas Complex–driven approach. King Midas's gold came at the cost to all life around him until he realized it put his own life at stake too. Then he changed. Ultimately, we are all interconnected on the same planet. Now that we understand that, we simply can no longer afford to allow some to garner great monetary wealth at the expense of the lives of many. Some states are now offering tax breaks to induce companies to become "B" (benefit) corporations who adhere to these new principles of corporate responsibility.

Radical altruism is the opposite of psychopathy. It is both the antithesis of and cure for the Midas Complex. Radical altruists do not seem to hold the fantasy that their wealth somehow makes them superior to others. As W. C. Fields used to say, "A rich man is nothing but a poor man with money." The reverse is just as true.

One of the darlings of extremist conservatism, author Ayn Rand, wrote, "If any civilization is to survive, it is the morality of altruism that men have to reject." Social Darwinists, who believe that only the most advantaged (i.e., the strongest) should survive, create a great deal of the wealth-before-health politics driving the world into environmental chaos and class divisions today.

Mitt Romney made what he thought was a candid comment to his have-more donors during the 2012 campaign, which one attendee secretly recorded. He said that "47 percent of the people...who are dependent upon government, who believe that they are victims, who believe that government has a responsibility to care for them, who believe that they are entitled to health care, to food, to housing...pay no income tax." Mr. Romney then added that his role was "not to worry about those people. I'll never convince them they should take personal responsibility and care for their lives." Ironically, only 47 percent of Americans voted for him as this peek behind the curtains of his campaign, largely by and for the elites, likely brought an end to his presidential aspirations and with it, I imagine, an ongoing abhorrence for the number 47.

At the time, many noted that over sixteen million elderly Americans pay no federal income taxes only because of existing tax policy and millions more pay no federal income taxes because they do not earn enough after deductions. This group includes many millionaires. The facts simply did not bear out Mr. Romney's analysis of almost half the nation as parasitic. The comment, however, resonated with a cadre of have-mores who seem to believe that others without wealth somehow possess an inferior character and are thus undeserving of assistance when needed. We can understand this as a symptom of a severe, collective Midas Complex.

The altruistic billionaires mentioned above, however—and at least 60 others like them in the US—intend to give away the majority or even all of their wealth before their deaths. They believe that they can use their wealth to improve the conditions of others around them who have not been as fortunate. They understand that, to some degree, some of their wealth accumulation happened by chance or as a result of others developing their innovations in profitable ways they had never imagined. In addition to working hard, like most people, their success came also through being in the right place at the right time, inheriting, knowing the right people, stumbling on the right formula, using the infrastructure that others built and insider access. As discussed above, few become wealthy because they simply worked a lot harder, were significantly brighter or more talented, or lived more frugally than the poor.

Most of us, however, are not billionaires or millionaires. Nevertheless, anyone can be a philanthropist. As my experiences in central India will reveal below, we can all give in meaningful ways, from our own capacity.

We can also support companies that embrace triple bottom line economics. Moreover, those of us who lack massive assets as leverage against the entropy of our era can help create new economic institutions that are more inclusive and empowering than those of the current system.

One percent of the global population now owns forty percent of the world's wealth. According a 2013 report by the international relief agency Oxfam, one hundred of the world's highest earners could eliminate poverty for all of the poorest people in the world, while still remaining dramatically wealthy after such an act. Nevertheless, the charitable giving of the global economic aristocracy accounts only for about 5 percent of all monies received by charitable organizations. The rest comes from people with lesser incomes. We can no longer afford to be like children who attempt to rely on vast wealth holders, corporations or governments to solve the global problems of our era. Particularly where the Midas Complex has taken hold of powerful people and organizations, grassroots philanthropy, innovation, and cooperation offer great hope for change.

NEW MONEY FOR A NEW WORLD

Today, largely in response to the great downturn of recent years, there are a wide range of informal economic activities emerging such as local skill–based and professional service trade groups, free stores, day labor exchanges, electronic flea markets, farmer's markets, purchasing cooperatives, and cohousing. Many like-minded groups are also creating their own currencies and economic systems independent of the US dollar. This is an act as forbidden by our government today as it was by King George of England for the American colonies. Nevertheless, some people are finding creative ways to work around the prohibition against creating alternative currencies. Creative attempts to legally work within the constraints of the government-controlled currency system are empowering people normally disenfranchised from participation in American financial markets. They are spawning a new ethos of socially and environmentally conscious investing.

As distinct from universally recognized national or federal currencies, like the US dollar or the Indian rupee, only a specific community or locale recognizes local currencies. In the early twentieth century there were a number of local currencies. Thousands of alternative currencies were in use during the Great Depression. However, these "scrips," often as simple as a credit for a company store in lieu of wages when cash was short, fell out of favor over time. Now, they are showing up again in various places with a renewed vitality and increased sophistication.

During the late seventeenth and early eighteenth centuries in Britain, a significant shortage of copper and silver coins occurred. Thus, the use of foreign coins and privately made tokens became common. In North Carolina during the early seventeenth century, there were seventeen different forms of legal tender in use. This occurred because North Carolina, like all the other British colonies in North America, had a huge shortage of official British coins. In the beginning of the eighteenth century the State of Ohio issued its own paper warrants as legal currency for the same reason that the Chinese invented paper Money a millennium before—a coin shortage.

Today local currencies support an affiliation of local businesses that agree to accept them, which in turn gain an increased capacity to create a mutually supportive economic community. Some years ago, when foreign competition began to take a serious toll on some American business, most notably car companies, a nationwide, patriotic slogan began to circulate widely: Buy American. Local currencies today say, Buy Local. Support your friends, local labor, local businesses, and neighbors over sending your Money to some corporate headquarters perhaps not even located in your nation, much less your neighborhood or state.

Local product and business start-ups can benefit from the word of mouth along with associations and catalogs that list local currency participants. Local currency gives people a choice to be more knowledgeable about and to participate in the formation and stimulus of local commerce. For hundreds of thousands of years humans cooperated toward the mutual support of those in their immediate sphere of relationship in addition to trading outside for goods and services that the locality could not provide. In many ways, the invention of Money gradually replaced the robust kinship based systems of mutual support and reciprocity that existed in the millenniums before Money.

People who choose to use local currency make a commitment to buy local as much as possible, and to try to keep a dedicated portion of their wealth circulating in their immediate community. They in effect reverse the flow from the siphon-up economics of large multinational corporations, some of which exploit the local resources of the many for the benefit of a distant few. Local currencies can support alternative, interdependent, cooperative economic futures for their communities, which circulate wealth for the benefit of all, not just a minority of stockholders. As national currencies serve nations—or even a cooperative group of nations as with the Euro—local currencies serve local economies by enhancing trade within a specific region. They do not replace national currency. Remember what happened when Ben Franklin asked King George if the US could print Continental dollars? War. People exchange local currencies for national or federal currency at a fixed rate and printed in denominations similar to their national currency.

There are currently at least seventy-five local currency groups in the United States, and many are starting up in other parts of the world as well. In the United States, local currencies began to reappear in 1991, starting in Ithaca, New York. The Ithaca Hour is equal to US$10, or one hour of work. It is divided into six denominations: the Hour, two Hours, the half Hour, the quarter Hour, the eighth Hour, and the tenth Hour. More than $100,000 worth of Hours are in circulation and have facilitated several millions of dollars in transactions.

Unlike our US currency, which mostly has pictures of deceased presidents on it, this colorful new currency features pictures of children, animals, a waterfall, and a steamboat. Many local currencies display the work of local artists and celebrate the natural beauty and intrinsic wealth of the surrounding regions. They depict local history and monuments, which represent symbols of shared local values. The Ithaca Hours system is currently one of the longest serving and largest local currency systems. Following Ithaca, the Madison Hours Cooperative in Wisconsin issued its own Hour.

The Burlington Currency Project in Burlington, Vermont, is issuing Burlington Bread, a currency similar to Hours.

BerkShares is a local currency for the Berkshire region of Massachusetts. The *New York Times* called the invention and implementation of this new currency, which started in 2006, a "great economic experiment." Over two million shares have been circulated to date and over four hundred businesses have agreed to use the currency. One hundred BerkShares can be exchanged for US$95. However, participating businesses accept them at face value. A customer can pay for a $20 dollar meal at a participating restaurant with twenty BerkShares even though they only cost $19 to purchase. Everyone who agrees to accept the currency has thus built in a 5 percent discount to the benefit of his or her customers. The regional businesses that take BerkShares enjoy increased sales and stronger, more loyal local support from their cooperating currency community's base. The program has issued over two million BerkShares since it began.

Pennsylvanians started Equal Dollars in 1996, which is one of the few alternative currencies to incorporate checking as part of the program. Many other complementary currencies hope to create checking and other financial services with their currencies, including loan programs. In North Carolina, the Piedmont Local EcoNomy Tender (PLENTY) began circulating in 2002. In 2003, in Humboldt, California, locals started Humboldt Community Currency. In 2005, the Traverse Area Community Currency Corporation in Michigan created Bay Bucks. In 2009 in Detroit, Cheers were launched. New Yorkers are organizing the Brooklyn Torch.

Oregon has Cascadia Hours, Corvallis HOURs, and RiverHOURS created by the Gorge Local Currency Cooperative. They state that they "seek to create and sustain a local currency system in order to build community, promote regional economic independence, support local business and trade, encourage entrepreneurship, honor diversity and enhance the local minimum wage."

Canada also has a few local currency groups. Calgary Dollars started in 2002 and Salt Spring Island Issued Dollars, or $$, began in 2001. In 2006, in addition to the bills already in circulation, Salt Springers minted one thousand pure silver coins. All major businesses and over 95 percent of all local small businesses are currently accepting the Salt Spring Dollars. Their larger bills use the highest levels of anticounterfeiting technology available anywhere in the world today. The Toronto Dollar began in 1998. Time traders use Tamworth Hours in rural eastern Ontario, and Unity Dollars serve various towns and villages in the Madawaska Valley.

There are also local currency groups in Mexico. Sistema TLALOC issued the Dinamo, which is being used in the region southwest of Mexico City. In Dolores Hidalgo, in Guanajuato, a network of low-income producers has created the Mezquite to enhance the economic life of peasants, artisans, and commodity producers in that region.

Europe is also experimenting with local currencies. BonNetzBon (BNB) is the alternative currency of the Social Economy Network Cooperative in Basel, Switzerland. It is distinct as the only transnational, regional currency. BNBs, backed by Swiss Francs, can also be exchanged against local currencies in neighboring areas of France and Germany. In Bayern, southern Germany, the Chiemgauer trades at par with the Deutsche Mark. In Brixton, England, the Brixton Pound (B£) began in 2009. The Lewes Pound is popular in Lewes, East Sussex, and Totnes Pounds are active in Totnes, Devon, England.

Some local currency groups are working to get their local governments to accept the currency for taxes or other services. Others are trying to use their currency to contribute funding for local projects while various nonprofit groups raise funds through participating in the currency. For any readers interested in starting or participating in a local currency program, a multitude of resources are available at the E. F. Schumacher Society's website, www.smallisbeautiful.org/local_currencies.html.

It will take real work, profound cooperation, creativity and daring for us all, in our own regions and communities, to create fresh approaches to and relationships with Money. Complementary currencies, by virtue of being based on cooperation instead of competition provide virtually immunity to a Midas Complex infecting them as it has much of the federal currency systems. Because they are fundamentally based on people's time in a specific locale, they are not subject to international market forces that drive the values of federal currencies up and down every second of the trading day.

Clearly, much of our current fantasy of Money is not working for the majority of people. Like many challenges of the twenty-first century—such as the pressing need for sustainable and nonpolluting energy systems—new monetary systems must be created that can better foster sustainable economies. We require more equitable distributions of and access to the basic means of life along with ecologically responsible production and transportation of raw materials and products. We need an economic system for both producers and providers of goods and services and their consumers that breeds cooperation, mutual support, and community while creating more lateralization of wealth, equal opportunity, and personal empowerment. Local currency is one of several tools with the potential to help bring about such change.

MICROCREDIT FOR ALL

Most of the discussion in this book has concerned American culture. It is important to note, however, that the Midas Complex also affects global issues. Two percent of the world's population now owns more than half the monetary wealth of the planet. According to the United Nations, if you have over $60,000 in assets you are in the upper 10 percent of global wealth holders. Those with half a million in assets are all "one-percenters" by global standards. Conversely, more than half the seven billion people in the world today are living on less than two dollars per day. The following discusses some poverty eradication work I experienced with families in India who live on less than one dollar per day. I think they have something to teach us all about how we might recover from our own Midas Complex as well as the capacity most of us have to enhance our life experience and feelings of self-worth through practicing philanthropy in some way.

251

Several years ago, I had the opportunity to produce an award-winning documentary with *Rikshaw Films* titled, *Awakening: The Social and Economic Liberation of Outcast Women in the Third World*. This film explored the burgeoning economic success of Untouchable women in India and post-Taliban women in Afghanistan through microcredit lending initiatives. Similar programs appear to be working well with similarly marginalized populations in the United States. For example, one group of people I interviewed for the film and this book are residents of the Ogallala Sioux reservation in South Dakota. This region contains the two poorest counties in the United States. Their per capita income is approximately $3,500 per year. Can you imagine living on $300 a month in the United States?

Karlene Hunter, director of the Lakota Fund there says, "Individuals have to realize that they can take control of their futures, of their destiny, that they don't have to settle for less than. And for so many years in economically depressed areas, we were expected to settle for less than, and you know, [we are] really finding out that we don't have to settle for that, and we will not settle for that, and my children won't be susceptible to any of that type of mentality." Through this fund, the Sioux are using microlending to bring back the buffalo, once the foundation of their economy, as a vital, renewed economic component in their current communities. We visited a herd on a traditional range, thriving over a century since they had seemingly disappeared from Indian lands forever as the consequence of a Midas Complex that infected white hunters in that region.

In the shadow of today's global economy, over two billion people still lack access to any form of credit. Imagine your life without loans to equip a small business, purchase a home, buy a car, or even acquire an education. Although many see their poverty as inescapable, some of the world's poor are awakening to other possibilities. Through microloans and education that challenges their oppression, many are liberating themselves from generations of economic apartheid. Microcredit is an instrument of development for resolving problems of inequality, exclusion, and poverty.

One of the main informants for my film is a Catholic nun who organizes women's empowerment groups in the poorest region of Bihar, which is the

252

most impoverished state in India. Women who join Sister Mary Lobo's organization, called Nari Jagran Manch, learn to save small sums and then invest their capital as a group. As they gain financial literacy, access to microloans and small grants help further their initiatives. She asks, "How do we reach out in simple, concrete ways to take advantage of globalization and help the poorest societies get a better deal and have fair resources in some way?"

Sister Mary says,

> What I really wanted to do all along is be of service to the poor, and be really radically committed to creating a better world along with other people around the world and finding ways of service to relevant to the times. Work like this, microcredit and women's organizations from the grassroots as we have here, have a new dimension to bring into the whole picture and contribute very much to changing or transforming rural society. With economic globalization on a wide level and these local, grassroots initiatives there can be a dialogue in the coming together toward more hopeful change.

Bina, a local Untouchable woman who is a coordinator of the whole program, says,

> The main thing is that Nari Jagran is a success. Whatever it takes, we will work hard and make this program successful. For many generations we have been stuck in a bad place. How can we better ourselves if we've never even had an opportunity for education? This is why we do trainings that we receive here. I believe that if we can get one person to move up, then we can get the whole village to move up too. We give people training to help solve the issues of our community. Every community has the same issue. How can we rise up? How can we better our lives? How can I get a job? How can I make a living? What is a woman's life? We work all day and still in the evening the men ask, what have you done?"

In rural India today, Untouchable women suffer the nation's highest rates of indentured servitude, child marriage, rape, and murder. Sister Mary explains,

The Manji caste is aboriginal to of this area. They were subdued by the invading Aryans and kept on the outskirts. The Aryan invaders took over the land, took over the forests, took over all the resources, and drove the aborigines into the mountains. Some went off into the jungle, the forests a little south of this place, and some remain here on the outskirts of the villages and were from the beginning treated as the lowest in the outcasts, lowest in the caste ladder. [They are called] unclean, impure, rat eaters. They're known as the *Manjis*, sometimes the other word for them is *Buyas*. Buyas are people of the soil.

They are the menial workers of the upper castes and all along they've been very marginalized, discriminated against, treated unfairly, kept in subservience, uneducated, kept far out of everything that goes on in society. This is still the mentality. It really hasn't changed much in these parts of the country and still discrimination is there. The whole idea of keeping these outcasts where they are, that still continues. And really, once again, they are the same, marginalized, despite the legislation [outlawing discrimination toward the Untouchables]. Social pressures are far too great. Legislation has not been that effective. These are people from survival levels, as you say, so as individuals, life is a struggle. For that reason I find this group approach, as we do it, microcredit, women's groups, self help groups, that is good, you know, because then, we don't make the decisions, it's the community.

Nari Jagran's groups are radically democratic. The women decide among themselves which member's projects to fund, and plan together on how to best assure her repayment. One Nari Jagran member told me, "There are a lot of advantages in belonging to the group. It's a very helpful thing. If we need one thousand or two thousand rupees [US$40], we can take it from the group. If I have an emergency, I can take a loan and buy a goat. We'll raise the goat and it will have babies, which we can sell and make some money. And little by little we can start to earn a living."

Harish Swathi Ma commented, "My young boys are going to school now. I am getting them educated and now they have food and clothes. Compared with the old days before we had these groups, There's much more hope."

With their savings secure in banks, no one outside the women's group has access to the funds.

Sister Mary Lobo explains,

> Each woman saves 20 rupees a month [US40¢], sometimes 30 rupees a month, and in some places, even 50 rupees. And so, if every member of the group saves 20, the group of ten will have 200 rupees at the end of the month. And then when they function like this for some time, they go to the bank and open their accounts and, that's again a sort of a more stable and more legal kind of a reality. So, the capital grows a little. So, with that, they have enough. And then we have our loan programs, this is the money, which comes in through donations. So this is sort of growing, and it's becoming a resource fund for these microloans.
>
> As I went along, of course there were different things to be done; there was education. I was reflecting on the whole phenomena of globalization in the last five or six years and the new and great policies that were being promoted in all these developing countries. So then we said, "Now, what can be done at our level? How do we reach out?" Very concrete, simple, direct ways taking advantages of globalization and giving the have-nots, poorer societies a better deal or helping them to claim their place under the sun, claim their rights and have a share of the resources in some way.

I accompanied Sister Mary to a small farm where a previously impoverished family was prospering. There she told us, "The initial capital that they had, they used a good bit of it for the mill [to grind grain]." She gestured around the farm, saying, "Then came this gardening and these animals and the cow. Organic farm, vegetables, it has come, developed over the years. Initially there was nothing much. She took money from the group, spent it for the mill, income from that they went on and on, sometimes from the group, sometimes from the profits of all this. They keep on doing new things; they are very busy."

After six years in Nari Jagran Manch, the women of one village bought their land back from the landowners that their families had served for generations. Many who previously lived in ramshackle huts now had solid buildings to house their families and new businesses. Despite a 98 percent illiteracy rate and centuries of cultural restrictions against speaking out without permission or leaving the confines of their homes, many women are finding their voices through this program. The pride and stature of these women and the health and vitality of their children stood out to me in visible contrast to the rest of their class in this harshly impoverished area of India. They seemed happy and looked well.

Sister Mary thought about this, saying, "Here you have a group, a community, caring for each other, and yet it's a mixture, the individual too is important. I often thought of it, that this is, I don't know, I wouldn't call it third way or the middle way; an alternative way, it combines both the community as well as individual initiatives, you know."

Bina told us, "After receiving the training Sister Mary encouraged me to speak in the community. Get in front of the village and speak out. Mary said to me, 'Although you are poor, you're from a good family, so you should come forward and have courage to speak out and get ahead.' Now it's my job to speak up. And from her encouragement, I kept on moving forward. Today, I am at the place where I have respect. I am moving forward. Now there's no looking back!"

Kesorie, another member of the group, said,

> I saved everything I could to start my store and help my family. With our group savings and my first loan, I began organic farming behind my house. When we need money, we borrow from the group. When we have money, we give it back. In the beginning, men would laugh at us working women. They would ask, "Are you going to learn how to beat us up?" We know that by doing this work, we are able to improve the quality of our lives, and we women are together in this effort. Many women in the group are borrowing money. They are starting different businesses like buying livestock or opening shops. As an individual with only twenty rupees, the banks won't open an account for me. As a group, we go to banks with five hundred rupees and it changes

everything. I've tried to do many things alone without the strength of the group, not much has succeeded. In my life, I have learned that women can become like the trees and rivers. I give shade and life to my community.

During the course of our filming we met a young woman who was living with her children in a rickety stick hut covered with empty, plastic cement bags. When it rained the entire dwelling leaked and the floor became a pool of mud. When it was dry and temperatures reached 120 degrees Fahrenheit, there was no escape from the heat. Even the extremely impoverished people we were interviewing regarded her conditions as unbearable. I asked how much it would cost to build her a solid mud-brick home. Three hundred dollars was the reply. So, the director, my godson Dominic Howes, his partner Joel Weber, the cinema photographer, and I put in a hundred dollars each. In six weeks she and her children had a new, clean, weather-tight home. No need for expensive governmental permits stalled the process, which would have taken more than a year in the United States.

At another site, one of the remarkable schools for Untouchable children built by US citizens Bob Chartoff and his wife Jennifer, I noticed that the children were not studying in the concrete schoolhouse he had built them. This was the only structure in the entire village not built of mud, but they were studying in the hot sun at the opposite end of the village. When I asked why, one of the teachers pointed to the well near the schoolhouse saying, "It does not work anymore and the only other water source is at the other end of the village." Therefore, the children had abandoned their tidy little schoolhouse, which was cool inside, and were baking in the summer heat, in order to be close to water. How much to fix the well? One hundred dollars. This was little for us, but three months' salary for a schoolteacher there.

A week later, the schoolhouse was in full swing again. It is extraordinary how much so little can do in an impoverished region. Consequently, microloans of fifty or a hundred dollars can go a long way to changing the lives of people on the margins. I learned that even a middle-class professor could practice philanthropy and make a real difference in people's lives. Microcredit clients around the world average payback rates above 95

257

percent, far higher than the rates in first world economies. It seems that their "social collateral," women's felt sense of obligation to their community group, is a more powerful guarantee of loan repayment than physical collateral in form of goods or homes that banks can repossess.

TAKING A STAND IN AFGHANISTAN

Our research also took us to flourishing micro-credit groups in South America and Afghanistan. Before the Taliban forbid them, women played major roles in the Afghan economy. They were doctors, lawyers, educators, farmers, and businesspeople. After the Taliban's fall in 2001, a microfinance cooperative called Parwaz began helping women regain their vital place in the nation's economy.

An Afghani man who served as a driver for our film crew there, discussed local economics and microcredit lending saying, "In my country, Afghanistan, the history is a very dangerous one. At the beginning of the Russian Invasions when the Mujahadeen began fighting life was still good here. But later when the Russians were defeated, the Mujahadeen began to fight among each other. The county was destroyed. Family economics were terrible. This program Parwaz is very good for the poor and working people of Afghanistan. They receive loans from Parwaz. They use this for the improvements of their families and to feed themselves."

Katrin Fakiri, the director of Parwaz, an Afghani microcredit group, says,

> For people who are not familiar with microfinance, it's basically a bank for poor people. We operate just like a bank does, but our methodology is different, and our target group is different. Life went from one extreme for people under the Mujahadeen era into this completely different extreme under the Taliban era. So, people haven't had a normal life in Afghanistan for a good decade, if not more. Credit bureaus, nothing like that exists in Afghanistan, or other developing countries, so microfinances have to use social pressure as a collateral. They have

nothing. We're working with people who barely make a dollar a day. They live in mud homes. They don't have land. They don't have anything that we can use as collateral. So by forming groups, of women primarily, we ask them to guarantee one another.

One Parwaz member we interviewed said,

> During the time of the Taliban, the people were suffering, but now this time has past. In the past, it didn't matter whether we were hungry or full. My children were sick and I had to work for eight Afghanis a day [US16¢] and I would spend all of it just to feed them. My husband was a worker. I was working also, but they sent us home. The Taliban were beating people, mainly women. If we went outside without a man, we would be thrown in jail. It happened to hundreds of women. They forced our husbands to divorce us.

Another Parwaz member informed us, "When the Taliban came, my daughter was in second grade. They threw her out of school. So we fled to Iran. My two daughters and my son couldn't go to school for the past seven years. Now the children are asking us to send then to English, math, and other classes in addition to their regular schooling because they are so far behind."

The per-capita income of Afghan women is one-third that of men. Less than 2 percent of women own land, 86 percent are illiterate, and the majority live in absolute poverty. Women needing Money for any reason typically must turn to male relatives, which often places them in a subservient relationship with them.

As Debra Boyer, a microfinance specialist in Afghanistan, explains,

> The group is responsible for those loans to get repaid. Often times, that is also combined with savings. It's like a collateral substitution. If a group member can save money each week, then that's evidence that they're going to be able to repay a loan each week. And with that and the group guarantee, it leads to a credit product of very small amounts, usually one hundred dollars; one hundred fifty dollars is enough in an

environment like this to make the difference between a business that's not going anywhere to a business that actually is producing family income on a monthly basis.

Patrick Fine, the director of USAID Afghanistan, says,

> So we look at what's necessary to facilitate people starting business and growing the businesses that they have, what's necessary to encourage entrepreneurs to be entrepreneurial. One of the constraints that people run into here is lack of access to capital. They may have an idea, they may have something to produce, they may know where they want to sell it, but they can't get the start-up capital to put that business idea into motion. And, often times, it's not a large amount that's needed. Very often these are community-based activities, it's serving a group of neighbors or maybe a neighboring community.

Lila Jahn is a Parwaz group leader. She told us, "When I find a group of eight to twelve people, I sit with them and explain the content of the program. We determine how much of a loan they are asking for. Our loans are from two thousand to five thousand Afghanis [US$40–$100]."

A Parwaz member chimed in, saying, "We don't have many options for loans. If you go to other lenders, or your own family often they don't help you or they say we don't have any money. Other lenders pressure you to pay it back all at once."

Most microlending initiatives attempt to create economic solutions that empower poor people in ways that support the needs of their community. When Lila Jahn asked a group of Parwaz members, "What work are you doing? What are you going to use the loan for?" One by one, going around the room, they told us.

One answered, "I am taking a loan to help my son's business. He has a small cart that he pushes in the streets."

Another woman said, "It is for my tailoring work. My daughters and I are working together."

260

Another said, "It's for my husband's shop."

Shanoos told us, "This loan is also for buying cows."

Others also shared they were taking loans for animal husbandry or making domestic utensils like wooden spoons.

As Patrick Fine notes, "Microfinance is a very good instrument, that has proven itself around the world. There's a good methodology that is transferable and scalable. It appears to work across cultures and at different levels of magnitude. It can work with 10 people, 100 people or 10,000 people."

Today, lenders make about thirty million microloans each year. Tiny, right-sized investments in individual lives create lasting benefits for entire communities.

Shakila is a middle-aged Afghani woman who displays significant scars on her face and all other exposed parts of her body. She told her poignant and triumphant story to us:

> My name is Shakila. I think I am thirty-seven years old but I don't remember which year I was born. We are in the Pashtun tribal area. Before I got married, I had a very good childhood. Then, during my childhood my family engaged me with my cousin. I have been married since fourteen years ago. It worsened my life. My life was miserable. We didn't even have one piece of bread. So, after three months of marriage I started tailoring and my husband was out working as a laborer. Sometimes he works with carts, carrying goods in the bazaar from one shop to another. He brings home some money and I bring home some money. It's just enough to get by, but not for all the things that I wish for. It was not my wish to marry, but because of my parents' wishes, it was necessary. His name is Shabudin. We try to make a good life.

Shakila sighed and then showed us two pictures of her as a lovely, younger woman. It was a shocking contrast to the somewhat disfigured woman before us. She pointed to one saying,

This picture is two months before my marriage. And the second is of my wedding day. We then became refugees and fled to Pakistan. From that time, our life became much worse. I thought I could work and do tailoring and sell my goods in the markets there. But I didn't speak their language in the bazaar. So, after three months we came home to Afghanistan. My child became very sick and my husband was without work. I told him to take our son to the doctor. But, we didn't have any money. My life became even more miserable. This was the time that I lit myself on fire. Because of all the pain, worries, and suffering, I thought it was better to leave, to go from this world. I spent six months in the Red Cross hospital.

For the next six months I never saw my face, but then I realized that I was burned over my whole body. Shabudin would come to the hospital and ask what I needed. I would tell him I don't need anything and to just feed the children, who were living with my mother. Shabudin used to walk by foot to the hospital many miles from our home to the hospital and back home again.

Shakila then reported on her success with her microloan from Pawaz after coming back home:

I took the clothes [I made] to several stores because I needed some contracts to sell my products. At the first two or three shops I gave them samples of my own designs to see if they would buy some. They said, 'Yes, please bring some for us to buy from you.' Then I took the second loan and bought sewing machines. Parwaz then gave me a gift of three hundred dollars and I bought a generator. Thanks to God, I am doing well now. My business is still growing. I could use more sewing machines for all my apprentices.

Patrick Fine responded to this account of economic survival saying, "When you talk to people and see what they've gone through and then their hope and willingness to work and sacrifice for the future, the Afghan people are extremely hardworking people. As infrastructure rebuilds, I think we'll see more foreign investment coming in, but the key here is going to continue to be domestic investment, people here building businesses and developing the economies of their communities." Perhaps this is also a hopeful message to those of us in the United States who lost homes, businesses, and savings in recent years. Across the globe, investment into the well-being of workers and the middle classes supports the national economy much more than tax breaks for those who already possess extreme wealth.

Sister Mary Lobo's overarching view on where this global initiative might be heading is, "A new ethos is being born. A new world is being born with some alternative values like sharing, mutuality, collaboration, a lot of concern, and closeness to nature. These are the values precisely which economic globalization and the corporate world need to be challenged with." She is articulating a potential cure for the global Midas Complex now possessing most of our planet.

She asked Bina, "What are your dreams?"

Bina replied, "We dream of true quality of life for our families. We don't need to be rich, but we don't want to remain poor. We want to live like human beings. At least this is what we dream about. All we really want is a decent life and a decent house. We don't dare dream much more than that!"

Sister Mary Lobo then inquired, "Do you see some problems with being rich?"

Bina laughed aloud and replied, "Those who are rich are only thinking of how to become more rich. Look at the rich people who have many buildings already. Now they want more and more buildings!"

"Do you have a message? Sister Mary asked.

Bina replied, "My message is people who have four cars, give one to the poor! If you have a five-floor building give one floor to the poor Sister! What can I say? Something should be done!"

Sister Mary then commented,

People should be able to have control over the resources, should be able to manage, and there's something called the threshold limit. If you put too many resources into any group or any person's hands, it'll be beyond their control and mismanaged. So, people have to be trained, gradually, how to manage a little, and then go on with more amounts if needed. The whole thing is to invest it in productive activity, not just speculative activity where you generate more interest or you just generate more profit in the abstract, because money is an abstraction, you know. Ultimately, it comes down to hard realities of food, clothing, housing, education, and health. These are the grassroots needs of the poorest. The poor really have strength. Going through all these hardships and hand-to-mouth existence and big family, but still there's that joy and that determination to face...you know...to overcome. That's amazing, that's a value which helps me a lot, and I learn a lot from that, too.

The individual feels responsible and accountable to the group, of course. Responsible for what she's taken, of a common pool or whatever resources there are, she feels she should make the most of it, make it productive. And then her own personality or her own leadership or whatever, her own human spirit develops with that. She can fall back on the group and say, 'OK, I belong to this group. On my own I would not have managed anything, or just remained at that poverty level that has always been there, but now it's both.' It's tricky, but it's working.

When we got back to her village Bina exclaimed, "Now we can do anything! Once the community moves ahead, there's no looking back. We can show the world what we have accomplished. And, if we don't finish it then our daughters will take over and do it! We will do what we can and make our daughters strong so they'll move ahead! I am like a tree providing shade for my community. I want my daughters to help people and become an even bigger tree giving more shade to the village."

While several men from the landlord class at the edge of the group stood listening in with astonishment written on their faces, another village woman said, "We have come to realize that women are also strong. In the past, men would not allow women to go outside. Now we can go here and there, outside the community. We can go to the meetings. We have to come to the realization that our people are no longer weak."

Sister Mary Lobo reflected on this further, saying,

> Finance is a means to attain this quality of life. So, if the finance can be geared toward making life more complete and holistic, it will achieve its aim. It will serve as a very valuable means, but it's not an end in itself, money is not an end in itself. We can become very rich if we want, all of us can have beautiful big houses and vehicles, but is that going to improve the quality of our life? Or, do we go along, gradually, and get better facilities for our families, education for our children? Perhaps they'll be able to cope more? And while we're watching what goes on in societies that have so much—consumer societies, consumer values—what is the outcome of this, ultimately, in terms of quality of human life? This is microeconomics that we're talking about.

Several hundred million people, in nearly every country, could benefit from expansion of these programs. One dismaying postscript to this story is that some large banks have recently jumped on the micro-credit bandwagon, realizing that there is Money to be made in a large volume of small loans. Some have exploited poor microfinance borrowers with high interest rates, which continue to subjugate rather than liberate and cause higher failure rates. Once profit motive enters the picture, the altruistic component of this technology for global poverty eradication can be lost in the shadow of the large lender's Midas Complex. The good news is that as long as microcredit initiatives remain in the hands of the poor and are built from the ground up, there is a real hope for the eradication of the most severe forms of poverty in the world. Until this new financial instrument emerged, most people believed that this lowest level of poverty in the world was intractable. But, the Midas Complex has many holes in it. And we can remember that King Midas himself was forgiven for his error and relieved of his problem once he woke up to the true meaning of wealth and humbled himself.

AWAKENING FROM THE SPELL OF THE MIDAS COMPLEX

In a world of limited resources, the fantasy of unlimited growth, which once fueled the westward expansion and other colonial efforts and currently undergirds global capitalism, now appears as pathological as King Midas's lust for gold. The vision of endless expansion is colliding head on with the growing knowledge that our planet has finite resources. The opposing philosophies of sustainability for the maximum human benefit of the many versus exploitation to create maximum short-term profits and luxury for the few are increasingly unable to coexist. Yet we all want prosperous lives. Most people do not want to surrender whatever comforts they have gained, and many long for increased economic prosperity.

So, where do we go from here? We seem inextricably linked to a system that has inherent flaws and is even antithetical, in ways, to healthy living. Like a drug, Money has addictive properties, requiring ever-larger doses to satisfy cravings and stave off symptoms of withdrawal.

When most addicts face the prospect of kicking their drug of choice, it is hard for them to imagine life without it. Life without cocaine or bourbon seems colorless, flat, and missing an element of excitement. Many think about life without increasing amounts of Money the same way. In early recovery from addictions, however, because their lives have become so much better, most former addicts have a moment when they cannot imagine why they allowed themselves to suffer for so long before seeking help.

The Midas Complex depletes real capital and undercuts real prosperity. In a sort of Gresham's Law redux (bad Money such as debased coins drives good Money, like precious metal coins, out of the market), when fake Money abounds, people hoard real wealth. Real capital is that which can help create and sustain human-scale economies and a genuinely prosperous life for all.

The future viability of American and global economic systems is uncertain. We can understand many of the current models of Money as pure abstractions, theoretical concepts, unexamined fantasies, illusions based on distortions of thought, and confidence games based on the misapplication of trust. King Midas awoke to the error of his Money quest, which turned all that was vibrant into dead material. I hope that before we turn all that is precious in the world—our fertile land, clean water, pure air, vibrant forests, pristine oceans, wild animals, and other natural things of nourishment and beauty—into electronically etched numbers on silicon discs, we will move toward a vision of a less Money-centered society. In such a world, I imagine individuals and families can apply more local, ecological, and human-scaled values to their own circumstances and financial planning.

David Korten articulates some powerful ideas toward a positive future. He notes,

> Democracy is based on the principle of one person, one vote. The market functions on the principle of one dollar, one vote. Consequently, under conditions of unequal economic power, a society ruled by the market is a society ruled by those who have the most money—the antithesis of democracy.... Real wealth is in food, fertile land, buildings, or other things that sustain us.... To navigate a transition to a New Economy we will need to create the frameworks and tools of a new economics that begins not with the study of money, markets and pricing, but rather with the study and deep understanding of the living systems structure and the dynamics of Earth's biosphere.

It is highly ironic that American currency is mostly green in appearance. Even though a little extra color has been added to our bills recently, *greenback* persists as one of the many slang words for our currency. Despite our widespread, notable generosity to other nations in distress, America's economy has also done more harm to the global environment than have the economies of most other nations.

I have heard it said that in capitalism one group oppresses another and that in communism it is just the opposite. As this sardonic comment indicates, each of the major economic systems in play today has a considerable shadow. People suffer differently in each, but just as widely. I doubt that one form of monetary policy is ultimately superior to another in this regard. Both economic forms lay heavy siege to the natural world in their quest for monetary wealth, and both create minorities of privileged elites and huge cohorts of people who suffer poverty and disenfranchisement.

THE REAL GREENBACKS

In the nineteenth century, many people made their own clothing and tools, built their own homes, produced their own energy (firewood, mostly), grew their own food, and raised animals. Before the industrial revolution, around 80 percent of the population lived off the land. Our impact on the environment was much less dramatic than it is today. The work was hard, but people enjoyed a fierce independence. There was not a great need for Money. Most transactions happened through trade.

In the twenty-first century, a range of new tools and technologies replace the backbreaking labor of previous centuries. They also, in many ways, replace the need for society to foster a large labor force of unskilled and uneducated laborers. During the Great Recession, millions of Mexicans returned to their villages since they could no longer make Money in the United States. They returned to the land, which had supported their families for centuries.

Until the early 1970s, the people in the remote Himalayan region of Ladakh had no internal sense of poverty. They lived in accord with centuries of tradition, working close to nature and creating most of what they needed from their local environment. By many reports, they were a happy people. After a new road opened and a decade of increased contact with Western visitors and Money followed, many young people began regarding themselves as poor for the first time. They lacked cash to purchase the new Western goods introduced to their markets. Many conflicts ensued, which were previously unknown in their culture including environmental degradation. After twenty-five centuries of conquering the Moneyless cultures of the world, Midas finally found his way to the farthest reaches of the planet.

Most of us have no ancestral lands or communities to which we can return. This is of no real consequence, however, since when innovation fails, human evolution seldom returns to its root traditions. We develop new ways of being. Culture evolves. Nevertheless, there are aspects of traditional subsistence cultures, which may have something important to offer us today about living within our means and in harmony with our environments. Perhaps ancient cultural wisdoms combined with new technologies can help us find our way to a more sustainable life in balance with nature that still affords us the leisure and comfort previously less evident in subsistence cultures. Significant change is coming whether we call for it or not; so some preparation could be prudent now.

I do not think the revolution we need today is a political one. Politics largely dedicates itself to serving the interests of those already advantaged by existing accords. Programs for the disenfranchised are often merely attempts to keep social unrest at bay. Even though some notable elites have genuine concern for the less advantaged, the best interests of those already in power motivate more legislators than does any real compassion for the poor. Regardless, politics of confrontation have a long, repetitious history of failure to provide lasting solutions, so I do not think that is the direction to which we need to look.

What we may need today is a collaborative grassroots effort of proportions never previously seen in the modern age. What would happen if we, one by one, just stopped participating in the petrodollar economy? What if we voted with one of the most powerful tools for social change available to all—our pocketbooks? Some of the discussions in this book have pointed toward the need for us for to create and sustain more community watering holes, more caring subcultures within uncaring governments and Money-centric institutions for whom growing Money is the primary mission.

Through the creation of alternative currencies, we may be able to opt out, in part or whole, of a tax system that often uses our Money to oppress others and entitle the few over the many. We could also opt out of a carbon-based monetary system that is destroying the planetary ecology in our lifetime. Many people, even in the industrialized nations, are now living fully off the power grid. Much more is possible. When we think about homeland security, if the whole planet is our homeland, then caring for the global environment should be at the foremost of every nation's security agenda. This might call for a new additional pledge of allegiance to the planet, which parallels our pledges to our individual nations. If we begin to imagine ourselves as holding dual citizenship, global and local, it will shift the way we do business.

Then we begin to think about our carbon footprint and other impacts our local lives have on the rest of the world. We might begin to calculate just how much carbon dioxide each one of us is contributing to the atmosphere, which every sensible scientist today now admits has a real effect on the global environment. There are some such calculators on the web. For most of us living in the United States it can be pretty eye opening to visit such a site. With less than 5 percent of the planet's population, we consume over 25 percent of the world's energy and release roughly a fifth of the world's human-activity produced carbon dioxide. Only China exceeds our national total, but with 1.4 billion people, it has considerably smaller amounts per person then we who consume twenty-five tons of raw materials each year per person and drive one-third of all the gas-powered vehicles on the planet.

REAL WEALTH AND FISCAL HEALTH IN A POST-MONEY ECONOMY

What is real wealth? What if we suddenly no longer believed in US dollars as real currency? What if our currency became so devalued that no one would recognize it, like North Korea's won, the Zimbabwean dollar, and the Somaliland shilling today or the continental and Confederate dollars of our past? What would wealth mean?

Land would still have value. That is why we call land *real estate*; it is real. You can live on land, grow food on it, create energy, build shelter, raise a family, start a church, lie down and dream on it, and even house some chickens. If you do not own secure land with good water and vital soil, your store of wealth is dubious.

270

Clean air is real wealth. We can only live about three minutes without air. I lived for several years in my youth with absolutely no Money. We can breathe oxygen, but not carbon dioxide. Therefore, rising CO_2 levels should concern us all. No air = no life.

Clean water is real wealth. We need clean water to survive. We can only survive for about seven days without water. I am sure, however, that many readers have gone more than a week, at some time, without Money. Close to one billion people no longer have access to something as fundamental to life as clean water. We should be concerned about dwindling reserves of fossil water, the clean water stored beneath the land's surface. Some American farmlands are already facing drought from below. Coal, gas, and other mining practices along with intensive corporate agriculture and high-density building in water-scarce environments are rapidly depleting this priceless resource at a nonrenewable rate. Water tables are dropping below ground as freshwater ice on the surface is melting into the sea. Massive quantities of surface water and growing areas of ground water are also contaminated. The rate of desertification is increasing at thirty to thirty-five times the historical rate, imperiling about one-third of all land now. We must preserve our water wealth or we will perish.

Family and community are also a form of wealth. We are not islands. Even monks in caves need locals to bring some rice once in while. We are social animals, and we need to feel a spirit of cooperation with one another. In third world marketplaces, people often take the time to speak and interact with one another during the course of shopping and conducting other sorts of business. This activity builds local community and strengthens social connection. As chapter 2 underscored, social connection is an element that universally fosters happiness and well-being. Big-box stores, online transactions, and digital payment through waving a card at a computer require no social interaction. These trends, convenient as they may be, are also having a corrosive effect on our social ecology.

If you have not been to a local farmer's market, I suggest you go. If you do not have a cooperative of farmers in your area, you could try to foster one. It feels quite different from the rush through the artificial environmentally controlled space of a supermarket with its visual assault of packaging lures and advertising. At least, we can get our fresh produce this way and support our local food producers. They then will not need to ship their goods all over the country, using up gas and oil, and having their food lose some of its essential vitality and nutrition during its long commute to market.

Even though we remain very dependent upon oil, the search for alternatives is widespread. In various parts of the United States and around the world, a new breed of entrepreneurs is arising. These people are trying to liberate us from dependence on the petroleum-based economy by embracing renewable nonpolluting energy. Some promising alternatives to oil are emerging in response to that quest. Fuel from algae and other biomass seems on the horizon, as do economically viable solar power, wind power, and other low carbon-producing energy sources like tidal power, which could harness the near infinite energy of the ever-moving sea.

Life-supporting weather is also a form of wealth. If our pursuit of Money at any cost eventually causes the low-lying land to be submerged through the melting of glacial ice and much of what remains is unbearably hot or plagued with superstorms, then we will have converted our earthly paradise to a living hell for most of humanity. It is actually possible that, like the dinosaurs, we will suffer a massive die-off. The earth will abide, however, and life will continue. We humans just might not be part of the next geological epoch if these climate trend lines continue unabated.

I have worked on this book for several years and certainly do not have all the answers. Perhaps I have only an invitation for the reader to dwell on this question about Money with me so I do not feel so alone with it. I do know, however, that the time of Money as we know it has passed, just as the time of oil has passed—even though most people do not realize it yet.

Money allowed us to make some extraordinary concentrations of wealth that facilitated remarkable events like walking on the moon. Nevertheless, Money has also allowed the worst in the human psyche to become stronger and in greater control of everyone's lives. The love of Money, the addiction to Money, Money as a drug, a weapon, a substitute for love, a fake god, a mirage of true liberation, or a means to fulfillment in life are all false promises. If Money, in addition to being just a form of energy, a tool, or a useful medium of exchange, is also a con game, a pyramid scheme, a psychological complex, an illusion, an abstract tool understood by a few to the subjugation of the many, then how do we break the spell and wake up from the dream?

We can work and live more locally. We can reach out to and share with neighbors. Start local currencies. Grow some food. Under suburban lawns, there is often good soil. Start local energy and water companies owned and operated by the communities who use the local resources and sources of power. That is, through community-building we can take back our essential resources from multinational corporations that are now trying to control every aspect of the means to our existence, from the seeds we plant to the food we eat. Many people are trying to figure out ways to kick their dependency on Money with trade and barter. Cohousing concepts allow neighbors to share certain features such as laundry rooms, garages, and gardens, which each private home need not replicate. We can live more simply, with less clutter and more free time. We can make cooperation with one another a more prominent value than competition. I look forward to hearing your own ideas.

CONCLUSION

Psychologists often try to name psychological phenomena in an attempt to make the infinite complexities of the human psyche seem more comprehensible. The truth is, however, that the condition discussed in this book is very difficult to label. No single title can really do justice to the depth, breadth, density, intensity, and complexity of what I have referred to as the Midas Complex. One reason the name of God traditionally could not be written out in the Old Testament or spoken aloud is because the very attempt to name God was deemed disrespectful to the numinous mystery of creation. Old Testament scholars called it the "ineffable" or "unutterable" name. It is hubris to think we can fully grasp the meaning of the creative intelligence that sustains the universe.

Money is not God, of course, but—as discussed throughout this book—it does act like a god in the minds of many, and even trumps God's importance to some people.

The uniquely human desire some people possess to accumulate more than is needed for survival, comfort, and even luxury is putting life on this planet at risk. So if it is a god, it is currently a more destructive than creative one. Many great wealth holders use their economic leverage for the common good—they are the culture guardians of our era. But those who accumulate solely for their own sense of power and control are dangerously unrestrained in our current economic system. By whatever name we call the complex that drives them, it is very powerful. And the very same complex drives many of us who suffer in our individual, personal relationships with Money.

The only way someone can escape from the powerful influence of an unconscious complex is to turn and face it. Those who have recovered from an addiction, obsession, or depression know that it takes courage and perseverance to consciously engage with their complexes, come to understand them, and liberate themselves from their negative influences. The Midas Complex is the bull in our china shop and the canary in our gold mine. It is both a pull toward destruction—a force—and a red flag, a warning sign on the field of human society.

Is the Midas Complex powerful enough to pull us over democracy's cliff into a cultural abyss more like the European aristocracy our ancestors fought to found this nation? Will the Midas Complex destroy our natural environment through our consumption of more energy than we can ever replenish and the release of more carbon than the planet can reabsorb in our lifetimes? If so, then only a widespread, collective response may be powerful enough to resist or change its direction—a second American revolution. But this is not a call to arms; it is, rather, a call to sanity and cultural awakening.

We could pay closer attention to the tendency of some people to unquestioningly embrace their greed at the expense of all others. Instead of admiring such characters, we could begin to openly question their sanity, just as we would any other person who engaged in destructive behavior. We are clearly concerned about nations that accumulate weapons of mass destruction. We use armies, intelligence agencies, economic sanctions, coalitions of nations, and corps of diplomats to confront national leaders who misuse their martial powers. But there is very little in our collective arsenal to confront people who wield Money as a weapon.

As the chapters in this book have discussed, during the Great Recession most oversight agencies appeared asleep at the wheel or simply too afraid to rock the boat of massive companies and banks designated "too big to fail." Many in positions of policing our economy, including our nation's top law enforcer, felt it better to look the other way and ignore the bad acts of some economic leaders rather than risk further destabilization of the economy by holding them accountable. This is how tyrants have gotten away with heinous behaviors for ages. They either make people too afraid of the consequences that could ensue were anyone to hold them responsible for their bad acts, or they cleverly frame their behaviors as necessary evils in support of the common good. The creation of a small group of elites beyond the law is an aristocratic ideal, not a democratic one. So regardless of our politics (right, left, or center) or our economic standing (wealthy, middle-class, or poor) we should all be more concerned about this small but immensely powerful new class. Some of the worst actors in the Great Recession are still in business.

The situation many Americans find themselves in today reminds me of the pattern many therapists witness in abused spouses who come to accept some periodic battering as normal. These victims make excuses for their abusers—they just needed to blow off steam, they were having a bad day, they were drunk, or they didn't really mean it. "He's really a good man, he's just going through a rough time," one might say. Many even blame themselves, saying they should not have said or done something that angered the spouse. They are reluctant to confront their abusers, fearing that, should they make them angrier, there might be more serious injury next time. The small corps of Money manipulators who rock the world with market maneuvers that cause national currencies, entire industries, life-sustaining commodities, and housing markets to rise or fall for their personal profits are interesting, even admirable, to many people. As noted above, many people also find mob bosses and serial killers fascinating. We are drawn toward power and those who wield it. But good citizens are also required to contain the violence of those who abuse their power and not to remain numb or silent on the sidelines as others commit atrocities.

We all want to be too important to fail. Every one of us should carry that status. If we felt that everyone was too big to fail, the way most of us feel about our own children, then we would vigorously apply more resources to assure their success: education, health care, job skills training, and real economic opportunity. We would enact more supportive and fair tax policies that rewarded middle-class people for working hard instead of creating headwinds that push them backward. Our politicians would also be more concerned about empowering the poor to contribute their gifts to society and become taxpayers instead of gutting government services while trying to create more tax breaks for billionaires. In 2012, over 600,000 US citizens were homeless. Any one of our top earners could have provided housing for every one of them, for the entire year, out of his or her annual income alone. But no one did so.

Perhaps there is no way to reach the more-is-always-better crew. That wealth-equals-worth ideology is deeply rooted in some who even conflate it with democracy itself—the freedom to profit by any means. But democracy was not imagined to empower a small group of elites against the interests of the whole. Rather, it was envisioned as the antidote to an oppressive aristocracy and as a force for equality through which human worth was based more on a person's character than his or her stock portfolio. The average corporate head makes a historically unprecedented $5,000 per hour, compared to the $7.25 per hour that millions of minimum-wage earners receive. So what can be done to make both these extremes of our Money-centric culture feel their needs and rights are protected while still serving those at the other pole? How can we encourage people to innovate and take risks, knowing they might enjoy privileges as a result, without also relegating tens of millions to abject poverty as a side effect?

We collectively possess great wealth and spectacular poverty. The wealth comes, in many ways, from the abundance of the land we occupy and the democratic principles we embrace. The poverty comes largely as a side effect of our collective Midas Complex—a psychology of all for me and none for them. As world leaders we are more compelled to find solutions to the ways in which Money divides us and to model moral principles, which empower all people to maintain a good quality of life. This means we must move beyond the prevalent understanding of Money as a zero-sum game.

We can educate the next generation differently. Teachers in particular could begin to hold some kind of Midas Complex seminar in their history, social studies, psychology, theology, civics, economics, or other courses. Religious leaders could speak out more on behalf of the disenfranchised. Graduate schools of business and law could emphasize ethics in more equal measure to profit production. They could inculcate more triple-bottom-line ideals for corporations while still continuing to equip their mostly already advantaged students to grab bigger shares of the pie. As someone who enjoys the privilege of being a graduate school professor, I believe we carry an obligation to the entire culture, not just the economic welfare of the students in our classrooms. Increasingly, many of my colleagues feel similarly today.

As human worth increasingly gets mixed up with concepts of material worth, the Midas Complex subsumes many of the more troubling biases of our age. As chapter 5 discussed, many concepts of inferiority and superiority in our culture are influenced by a person's monetary worth. Racism, sexism, and classism are all exacerbated by the misapplication of Money as a measure of human value. How can we sustain a society that on one hand prizes equality as a fundament yet on the other enables a privileged class with businesses too big to fail, who are taxed at lower rates, and for whom even the application of criminal justice is applied differently because they are often deemed more important than others? These radically differing principles cannot comfortably inhabit the same national culture forever.

Through the efforts of this book and many other publications, our collective shadow is out of the closet. Our virtual worship of materialism and sanctioning of the greatest wealth inequality in the world is now fully visible to the entire planet. According to an extensive 2012 study on global wealth by Credit Suisse, of over 140 nations only Lebanon, the Ukraine, and Russia have greater gaps between their have-mores and their have-nots. But none of those nations are noted for their dedication to democracy and equality. Historically, dramatic economic gaps like these tend to foment revolutions if left unremediated for too long.

In addition to the social action required to provoke external shifts in government, business, and our culture, recovery from the Midas Complex requires psychological action to provoke internal shifts in each one of us. How do we know when a Midas Complex possesses us? When we find ourselves valuing Money more than our personal relationships, happiness, and mental or physical health. When we notice that we are valuing stuff more than free time and pleasure, or exploiting rather than empowering those around us, it may point to an unconscious pull away from the good life and into the complex of greed. Of course, most of us need to make some sacrifices to survive economically, but those choices are conscious, not driven by this complex.

When we don't understand why Money is not bringing more happiness, we can recall the cautionary tale of King Midas and return to sanity. We can recover from the unconscious pull of hidden longings and fears to remember what real wealth is all about. Most of all we must consciously break the spell of Midas, who constantly whispers in the background that we do not have enough and will never be happy until we do. In parting, please consider taking an important inventory. It might surprise you. Here is how it goes:

Who am I without my Money?

I am a man, a husband and father, a brother and son, a cousin, an uncle, a writer, a lover, a friend, a citizen, a poet, a singer and dancer, a dreamer, a teacher and healer, an advocate, a gardener, a sailor, a philosopher, a nature lover, a child of the great mystery that some would call God, and a silent witness to existence. Money does not determine any of these roles or identities. If I lost all my Money, I would still be all these.

Who would you be?

ABOUT THE AUTHOR

Dr. Aaron Kipnis is a licensed clinical psychologist with a private practice in Santa Monica, California. He has worked with a broad spectrum of clients—from individuals and families in the upper 1 percent of the economy to those living on a dollar a day in the poorest regions of India. Since 1997, he has been a full-time psychology professor at Pacifica Graduate Institute in Santa Barbara County. His classes include a popular course on the deep psychology of Money. Dr. Kipnis has written five books, numerous book chapters and articles, a produced play, and is the writer/producer of an award winning documentary film. He has been an expert witness in court proceedings and a consultant to educational, mental health, corporate, and governmental organizations. Aaron is often featured on national news media, as a keynote speaker for professional conferences, and periodically offers Midas Complex workshops around the country. He lives in Topanga Canyon, California with his wife and two children.

For more information or contact with the author please visit:
http://www.aaronkipnis.com

www.ingramcontent.com/pod-product-compliance
Lightning Source LLC
Chambersburg PA
CBHW061003280326
41935CB00009B/813